NEW ESSAYS ON CANADIAN THEATRE
VOLUME TWO

NEW CANADIAN REALISMS

ALSO IN THIS SERIES:

ASIAN CANADIAN THEATRE
EDITED BY NINA LEE AQUINO AND RIC KNOWLES

ALSO BY THE EDITORS:

NEW CANADIAN REALISMS: EIGHT PLAYS

NEW ESSAYS ON CANADIAN THEATRE
VOLUME TWO

NEW CANADIAN REALISMS
EDITED BY ROBERTA BARKER AND KIM SOLGA

PLAYWRIGHTS CANADA PRESS
TORONTO

PLAYWRIGHTS CANADA PRESS
The Canadian Drama Publisher
215 Spadina Ave., Suite 230, Toronto, ON, Canada M5T 2C7
phone 416.703.0013 fax 416.408.3402
info@playwrightscanada.com • www.playwrightscanada.com

Playwrights Canada Press acknowledges the financial support of the Government of Canada through the Canada Book Fund and the Canada Council for the Arts, and of the Province of Ontario through the Ontario Arts Council and the Ontario Media Development Corporation, for our publishing activities.

Cover photo of Cindy Mochizuki by Shannon Mendes, provided courtesy of Theatre Replacement
Cover design by Leon Aureus
Book design by Blake Sproule

LIBRARY AND ARCHIVES CANADA CATALOGUING IN PUBLICATION
    New Canadian realisms / Roberta Barker and Kim Solga, editors.

(New essays in Canadian theatre ; 2)
Includes bibliographical references and index.
ISBN 978-1-77091-072-0

    1. Canadian drama (English)--21st century--History and criticism.
2. Realism in literature. I. Barker, Roberta II. Solga, Kim, 1974-
III. Series: New essays in Canadian theatre ; 2

PS8169.R42N49 2012   C812'.60912   C2012-902127-X

First edition: May 2012
Printed and bound in Canada by Marquis Imprimeur, Montreal

For all the realist innovators—artists, colleagues, friends.

CONTENTS

GENERAL EDITOR'S PREFACE

RIC KNOWLES

New Essays in Canadian Theatre (NECT) is a book series designed to complement and replace the series Critical Perspectives on Canadian Theatre in English (CPCTE), which published its last three of twenty-one volumes in 2011. CPCTE was primarily a reprint series, with each volume designed to represent the critical history since the 1970s of a particular topic within the broader field of Canadian theatre studies. Most volumes, however, also included essays specially commissioned to fill gaps in the coverage of their respective topics and to bring the books up to the moment. These new essays, some of them scholarly prize winners, were often among the volumes' most powerful, approaching the field and the discipline from important new perspectives, regularly from those of minoritized and other under-represented communities.

NECT consists entirely of newly commissioned essays, and the volumes themselves are designed to fill what I perceive to be gaps in the critical record, often, once again, taking new approaches, often, again, from minoritized and under-represented perspectives, and always introducing topics that have never before received book-length coverage. NECT volume topics may range as broadly as did those of CPCTE, from the work of an individual playwright to that of a whole community, however defined, and they are designed at once to follow, lead, and instantiate new and emerging developments in the field. Volume editors and their contributors are scholars, artists, and artist-scholars who are doing some of the most exciting and innovative work in Canadian theatre and Canadian theatre studies.

Like those published in CPCTE but more systematically, NECT volumes complement the catalogues of Canada's major drama publishers: each volume serves as a companion piece either to an already existing anthology or to one published contemporaneously with it, often by the editors of the NECT volumes themselves. As a package, NECT and their companion volumes serve as ideal introductions to a field, or indeed as ready-made reading lists for Canadian theatre courses in these topic areas.

But generating new materials and entirely new fields of study takes time, and while CPCTE published at the heady pace of three volumes per year, the production of NECT is more leisurely with, initially at least, only one volume launched each spring, beginning in 2011. The first of these was *Asian Canadian Theatre*, edited by Nina Lee Aquino and myself and designed to ride the tide of a flurry of activity in the first decade of the twenty-first century among Asian Canadian theatre artists. It complements Nina Lee Aquino's two-volume anthology *Love + Relasianships*, published by Playwrights Canada Press in 2009. The second, third, and fourth volumes are concerned with new Canadian realisms (edited by Roberta Barker and Kim Solga), Latina/o Canadian Theatre (edited by Natalie Alvarez), and affect in Canadian performance (edited by Erin Hurley), and each of these are or will be accompanied by companion anthologies.

It has been exciting for me to see the development of Canadian theatre criticism since its inception as an academic discipline in the mid 1970s, when the first academic courses on the subject were offered, and the first journals were founded, together with the then Association for Canadian Theatre History (now the Canadian Association for Theatre Research)—the first and only scholarly association to specialize in Canadian theatre. It was also very satisfying to serve as founder and general editor for the CPCTE series that tracked that development and made some of its key writings widely available and key critical histories and genealogies visible. In embarking on this new series, I am equally excited by the opportunity to contribute to the further development of the field by opening up new areas of study, introducing fresh new voices, and making innovative new work readily available to scholars, teachers, students, and the interested general public.

ACKNOWLEDGEMENTS

Like its sibling, *New Canadian Realisms: Eight Plays*, this book originated as a commission from Ric Knowles and Annie Gibson at Playwrights Canada Press (PLCN). Enduring thanks to them for their faith in and support for both projects. Enormous thanks to Blake Sproule of PLCN for his thoughtful engagement with all aspects of both books, and for his profound patience. Thanks as well to the Social Sciences and Humanities Research Council of Canada (SSHRC), without the financial support of which these books could not exist.

In January 2011 we held a SSHRC-funded symposium at Dalhousie University to act as a launch pad for this collection: we invited five hosts whose work we admired and asked those hosts to bring a clutch of panellists to Halifax in order to engage—sometimes as fellow-travellers, sometimes as contrarians, always as passionate thinkers and makers—with the ideas and the practices of contemporary realism. We acknowledge and celebrate the crucial intellectual and imaginative labour of everyone who participated in that event: Natalie Alvarez, Bruce Barton, Candace Brunette, Jill Carter, Catherine Cyr, Claire Gallant, Mimi Gellman, Nelson Gray, Ric Knowles, Susan Leblanc-Crawford, Louis Patrick Leroux, Stewart Legere, Parie Leung, Edward Little, Alex McLean, Anna Migliarisi, Monique Mojica, Stéphanie Nutting, Kirsten Pullen, Sheila Rabillard, Ramón H. Rivera-Servera, Nisha Sajnani, Julie Salverson, Ben Stone, Sophie Tamas, Heidi Taylor, Evan Webber, and Harvey Young. Sincere thanks to those at Dalhousie and Western University who supported this event: the offices of the Dean of Arts and Social Sciences and of the Vice-President Academic, Dalhousie University; the office of the Dean of Arts and Humanities at Western; and Research Western. Thanks as well to our generous support workers and volunteers at Dalhousie: Gini Cornell, Luciana Fernandes, Elaine Laberge, Bryn Robins McLeod, Nicole O'Connor, and Lauren Walsh-Greene. Kristin Slaney offered particularly expert help at many vital moments.

Elan Paulson has worked alongside us every step of the way, and has graduated (both figuratively and literally) from assistant to colleague over the course of our shared efforts. This book is also her achievement.

FROM ROBERTA BARKER

This book was completed at the end of my term as Chair of the Theatre Department at Dalhousie University; the two projects could not have coincided without the tremendous support and patience of both my collaborators on the volume and my colleagues in the university. I should like especially to thank Jure Gantar, Susan Stackhouse, Robert Summerby-Murray, and Sylvia Nielsen for all the times when their aid was more vital than they knew.

Special thanks to my admired friends, the artists of Halifax's Zuppa Theatre, who gave our "New Canadian Realisms" symposium the gift of their theatrical engagement with the nineteenth century, *Penny Dreadful*.

Love to all my family, and especially to Shannon Brownlee, Diane Murray Barker, and David Nicol, without whom there would be nothing.

It has been my privilege to work with Kim Solga, an extraordinary collaborator and a true friend, on these volumes.

FROM KIM SOLGA

For me, to revalue realism has meant necessarily to resist (or at least to rearrange) some of the most important freight in my intellectual luggage. Yet the teachings that comprise that freight have formed me, and without the whip-smart women behind them I could do little. My profound gratitude, then, to those icons of feminist performance scholarship who helped me find my path: Elaine Aston, Susan Bennett, Sue-Ellen Case, Gay Gibson Cima, Elin Diamond, Jill Dolan, Teresa de Lauretis, and Janelle Reinelt, among many others.

Love to B.M., partner in hedonism, and to Jarret, partner in life.

Finally, a glass raised to Roberta: brilliant, supportive, generous, and kind.

INTRODUCTION: RECLAIMING CANADIAN REALISMS, PART TWO

ROBERTA BARKER AND KIM SOLGA

New Canadian Realisms: New Essays in Canadian Theatre, Volume 2 continues where its companion collection, *New Canadian Realisms: Eight Plays*,
ends. As in the latter book, our goal here is to think critically about what
realism*s*, plural, have done and continue to do in and for Canadian theatre
and performance. We approach our work optimistically: it is our belief as
scholars and arts workers that stage realism is much more than the sum of
its twentieth-century critique, and that its political potential, so crucial to its
nineteenth-century European development, has much to offer artists working
in a variety of live art and theatre genres today. The essays we have collected
here attest to this potential, but they also revisit, usefully and cautiously, the
most intractable problems associated with realism's various modes in Europe
and North America over the past century. This is a book that celebrates realism's contrarian powers and seeks to return it, seriously, to debates about
contemporary Canadian performance, but it is not a book that places the
genre on a pedestal. In these essays, we and our contributors are most interested in the ways in which realism, in its many forms, has come to influence
and even shape some of the most powerful *non*-realist work in Canadian
theatre practice.

   In our introduction to *New Canadian Realisms: Eight Plays*, we outlined
the emergence of realism and naturalism in *fin de siècle* Europe, considered
briefly the powerful critique of stage realism levelled by (especially) American
performance studies in the later twentieth century, and then offered a brief
history of stage realism in Canada. Rather than repeat this work here, we will
augment it. First, we will discuss the critique of realism in significant depth,

providing a firm theoretical and critical basis for the essays that follow. Next, we will discuss the historical complexity of realism in Canadian theatre, where reliance on European models and implicit critique of those models have often gone hand in hand. Finally, we will advance an argument for contemporary Canadian realism as "unsafe": that is, not as "Realism" (fixed, conservative, and linear in outlook) but as "realisms": plural, adaptable, attentive to difference, alive to paradox and uncertainty, and thus politically formidable.

AGAINST REALISM

"Realism" is often understood in British and North American theatre studies through a conflation of genre (the dramatic realism of such modern playwrights as Ibsen and Chekhov, for example) and performance technique ("psychological realist" acting and directing styles, buttressed by fourth-wall naturalism in stage and lighting design). While these two things—genre and technique—developed together, each evolving to support the demands of the other, they should not simply be equated. In strictest terms, "realism" refers to the development in late nineteenth-century Europe of a genre of theatre dedicated to the direct mirroring of everyday life. Early realist drama is often characterized by the more specialized term "naturalism." Kirk Williams writes: "Naturalist theatre [took] a stand against subjective interpretation; leaving very little to the imagination, it [seemed] to reject metaphor utterly, embracing in its stead the metonymic 'truth' that seems to reside in detail." This focus on detail brought together "material existence and psychic life as never before" (97), leading in the early twentieth century to the development of psychophysical acting techniques that could best capture the reality of such a stage world.

The system of psychophysical practices that have come to be known as "psychological realism" was pioneered by influential Russian theatre director Constantin Stanislavsky, and because much of Stanislavsky's work developed around the staging of social realist dramas, many scholars understand his system to be designed to "fit" such work. And yet, as a number of researchers have recently demonstrated, this "fit" is by no means a given (Beck; Carnicke; Gross; Lutterbie; Vanden Heuvel; T. Wiles). In North America, Stanislavsky's "System" was adapted by Lee Strasberg as "The Method"; while the distinct differences between these two practices remain a matter of debate, scholars tend to agree that Strasberg de-emphasized Stanislavsky's interest in the playtext and physical action and focused instead on actors' intensive psychological work on themselves, resulting in a closed world in which any potential for change must reside within an actor's existing psychological makeup. And yet, again, recent reassessments of the Method suggest many of these assumptions are inaccurate (Marla Carlson; Krasner, "I Hate Strasberg"; Margolin; McConachie; Stroppel; D. Wiles). At its inception, realist performance may have been defined less by a univocal world view—the most consistently damning, and consistently repeated, argument against realist theory and practice—than by a series of fundamental paradoxes that created deliberate tension between page, stage, and world and provoked both audience discomfort and public debate. This attention to, and entanglement in, the paradoxes of the "real" is what Kirk Williams calls early realism's ethics, and what we pinpoint as the heart of its political potential: "It confronts the question of subjectivity and ethical action, and . . . leaves the question open" (108).

Over the last thirty years realism has come primarily to be defined by political failure, especially in its representations of gender and of queer and minority subjectivities. Michael Vanden Heuvel notes the "negative consensus" that had by the early 1990s converged on the form, most notably in work by prominent feminist theorists.[1] He sums up the critical anxiety: "Realism simply replicates existing—and therefore arguably bourgeois, patriarchal,

---

1   A complete discussion of the feminist critique of realism—which became the de facto argument against realism in performance studies in the 1970s and 1980s—is beyond our scope here, but we invite readers to dig in on their own. Excellent work includes: Belsey, "Constructing the Subject"; Butler, "Performative Acts and Gender Constitution"; Case; De Lauretis; Diamond, "Brechtian Theory/Feminist Theory," "Mimesis, Mimicry, and the 'True-Real,'" and "Realism's Hysteria"; Dolan, "'Lesbian' Subjectivity in Realism" and *The Feminist Spectator as Critic*; Forte; Mulvey; and Reinelt. For broader post-structuralist arguments about realism's politics, see Auslander; Derrida; and Worthen.

racist, oppressive, and oedipal—discourses, and functions as a mode of con-ciliation, assimilation, adaptation, and resignation to those discourses" (48). In a famous 1988 essay on feminist theatre's turn to Brecht, Elin Diamond, perhaps the most influential of the prominent theorists to whom Vanden Heuvel refers, suggests that realism's largest problem for women lies in the way realist technique (she uses the term "conventional iconicity") "lami-nates" acting body to character body, turning one seamlessly into the other and leaving no room for a critical look at either identity in its historical dif-ference from the other (or from audience identities) ("Brechtian Theory/ Feminist Theory" 89 and passim).

As the demands of realist text and technique clashed with the nuances of late twentieth-century identity politics, the theories of Bertolt Brecht waxed and those of Stanislavsky waned. Brecht was early modern Europe's *other* powerhouse director-theorist, and his experimental performance practic-es encouraged dialogic engagements among character, actor, and audience member. Actors were to "show" their characters rather than inhabit their roles, and audience members were encouraged to contemplate the juxta-positions this technique created between a character's politics and those of the production as a whole. Brecht famously damned naturalist performance for the hypnotic effect it supposedly had on audiences; he termed this ef-fect "empathy," and insisted that it was the enemy of political engagement at the theatre. As David Krasner has recently demonstrated, however, Brecht's definition of empathy was not only scientifically unsound, it has hampered those who came after him from coming to terms with the potential that em-pathy, and other affective responses, may hold for a more embodied—and therefore more cognitively comprehensive—form of theatrical witnessing ("Empathy and Theater" 261).

Recent work on stage realism has also shown that ontological distinctions between Brecht's working practice and Stanislavsky's have been exaggerated. Scholars have begun to recognize that Stanislavsky's psychophysical tech-niques were designed around a constitutive dualism, also characteristic of Brecht's practice, that promoted "an active creative negotiation between self and role" in actors both in rehearsal and on stage (Beck 268; see also Marla

Carlson; Carnicke; Gainor; and Krasner, "I Hate Strasberg").[2] Perhaps most significantly, this new work has been accompanied by fresh interest among performance scholars in the role emotions may play in audiences' experiences of a theatre event and in their ability to parse that event critically. In light of theatre studies' "affective turn," realism's landscape of feeling must be understood as far more than a simple, cathartic empathy that asks us to identify with the protagonist, weep for him or her, and leave the theatre redeyed but satisfied.

Brecht's critique of what he dubbed "dramatic" theatre also tended to collapse historical and social difference in a manner made immediately apparent by the other term he used for mimetic realism: "Aristotelian" theatre. This title brackets together works from Sophocles's ancient *Oedipus the King* to Ibsen's modern *A Doll's House* on the grounds of shared linear causal structures and demands on spectatorial empathy, both of which Brecht related directly to the arguments about tragic form in Aristotle's *Poetics*. Such an equation, however, risks negating the vast differences in time, space, and ideological context that separate these (and similar) works. Brecht's critique of "dramatic" or "Aristotelian" theatre thus contradicts his own fierce emphasis on the specificity and contingency of notions of the "real" in different eras and places. Post-Brechtian critics have sometimes been guilty of the same simplifications when accusing all realisms of reifying the assumptions associated with "white, middle-class, male privilege" (Dolan, *Feminist Spectator* 85). Realist dramaturgy and acting have very often been used by marginalized

---

2   A moment from Stanislavsky's "Perspective of the Actor and the Role," recently given new life in Jean Benedetti's fresh translation, captures nicely the parallels between Brecht and his apparent ideological opponent. Tortsov, the text's narrator (and stand-in for Stanislavsky), tells his students: "When he is performing, an actor is divided in two. Salvini said, 'When I am acting, I live a double life, I laugh and weep and at the same time analyse my laughter and tears' . . . As you can see, a double life doesn't stop you being inspired. On the contrary! One helps the other. We are also split in two in the real world. But that doesn't stop us living or feeling deeply" (456). Tortsov goes on to frame this "double life" on stage as "two perspectives, running parallel": "One of them has to do with the role. The other with the actor, his life onstage, his psychotechnique as a performer" (456).

artists and communities who fall outside the boundaries of that privilege in order to express lived experiences and to fight for socio-political goals. To dismiss completely the political potential of Lorraine Hansberry's *A Raisin in the Sun* (1959), for example, due to its realist form would be to deny that form's crucial role in Hansberry's powerful critique of racial oppression for both white and black audiences.

Rather than relying on blanket dicta, an effective consideration of the limitations and possibilities of *particular* theatrical realisms must pay close attention to their relationships to the contexts from which they emerge. And, rather than squeezing into a one-size-fits-all mimetic model or commanding preordained emotional results, the best contemporary realisms are alive to the extraordinary variation in options, outcomes, and reactions at stake whenever one works on or in the realm of the "real." Instead of travelling linear trajectories—be they narrative or character "arcs"—this work, which we elsewhere call "unsafe" realism, mobilizes what Elin Diamond terms a "double optic" ("Modern Drama" 11): expectation alongside its failure, empathetic connection alongside uncertain allegiance, and degrees of spectatorial pleasure alongside visceral discomfort as audiences work to figure out exactly how they ought to feel, what they ought to think. Imagining realism as a genre driven by, rather than terrified of, paradox and inconsistency will, we suggest, allow for the development of a fresh theory and practice of stage realism that, first, accounts more completely for the complexities and contradictions inherent in viewing a stage world that purports to be "real" but of course can never be, and, second, attempts to harness the discomfort that may arise in realism's watching, using that discomfort for politically productive ends.

CANADIAN THEATRE AND THE POLITICS OF REALISMS

The history of Canadian theatre offers an excellent example of realism's complexities in action. As we argued in the introduction to *New Canadian Realisms: Eight Plays*, a realism shaped by *fin de siècle* European models played a crucial role in the emergence of a Canadian drama that intervened in the lived realities of its own time and place. Gratien Gélinas's well-made Ibsen-esque plays *Tit-Coq* (1948) and *Bousille et les justes* (1959) offered excoriating mimetic reflections of the hypocrisy, cruelty, and narrow-mindedness of the mid-twentieth-century Québécois middle classes under Duplessis, prefig-uring both the dramatic innovations of Michel Tremblay and the political advent of the Quiet Revolution. John Herbert's prison drama *Fortune and Men's Eyes* (1967) used Strindbergian naturalism to expose the brutality of ju-venile incarceration in Canada and to foreground queer sexualities at a time when they remained deeply taboo. David Freeman's *Creeps* (1971) embraced a Zola-esque naturalism that found human dignity and suffering in the toi-lets of a group home for disabled adults.

Strikingly, however, each of these dramas contained elements that foregrounded the theatricality behind their realist illusions. *Bousille et les justes* featured a number of broadly satirized characters among its more conventionally naturalistic figures, but it invited audiences to find the natural even in these apparent caricatures (see Hare). Herbert placed a drag performance by the transgendered Queenie at the very heart of *Fortune and Men's Eyes* and chose as Queenie's drag icon the epitome of feminine masquerade, Mae West, troubling the very notion of a "real" gender identity. In *Creeps*,

> Three times the remembered outside world breaks into the men's lav-atory with circus clowns, hot dogs, Shriners, and pretty girls. They treat the men like children and like freaks (or creeps) in their circus show, but it is really they, in their silly costumes and phony benevo-lence, who are the creeps. (Messenger 102)

By such tactics, even these apparently conventional examples of Canadian realism defied the cliché that the genre seeks to hide its own operations. Instead, they reminded spectators that the "real" they viewed onstage was itself a construct—and that the lines between the real and the constructed were not so easily drawn.

In the years since these plays entered the canon, realism has established itself as a dominant performance language across Canada, gaining particularly close associations with key regional traditions. To take just one example, from David French's Mercer plays onwards, kitchen sink dramas featuring troubled east-coast families staring out at the sea (or expatriated Maritimers longing for it) have become virtually synonymous with the theatre of the Atlantic provinces. Yet many of the most popular of recent Maritime realist plays have emphasized the paradoxes and breaking points of realism, rather than relying on its apparently smooth and linear surfaces. For example, Wendy Lill's adaptation of Sheldon Currie's novel *The Glace Bay Miners' Museum* (1996) features a laundry list of the clichés of Cape Breton naturalism. Lill takes from Currie a fractured and impoverished mining family, a grandfather dying of "black lung," a bereaved and embittered mother whose traumas have infected her children's lives, a neurotic but feisty heroine in search of emotional and erotic fulfillment, a handsome and hard-drinking newcomer to town (complete with bagpipes), a strike "down the pit," and the fatal shriek of the mine whistle sounding its voice of doom—all of it washed down with innumerable cups of tea around the kitchen table. Yet the playwright also inherits from Currie's novel the challenge of Margaret MacNeil's decision to memorialize her lost loved ones by preserving their most characteristic body parts in large jars of formaldehyde. These grotesque "pickles" parody key aspects of theatrical naturalism: its scientific and domestic impulses; its emphasis on the physical over the spiritual; its urge to preserve traces of ordinary lives; and its tendency to culminate in titillating scenes of suffering, death, and resignation. Strikingly, Lill chooses not to represent these artifacts physically, but rather to evoke them only through Margaret's retrospective narrative, offered to the audience in a direct address that breaks the realist "fourth wall." The notebooks in which she records—and from which she reads—her memories stand in metaphorically for her macabre preserves. Lill's realism not only admits its own limits, figuring the theatrical *un*representability of the shattered human body, but asserts in the process the power of the female voice and of female memory. Unlike the naturalistic plays traduced by second-wave feminist critics as "lethal" to women (Dolan, "Feminist Performance" 437), *The Glace*

Bay Miners' Museum complicates its own realist dramaturgy in order to stage a woman's survival.

Such qualified realism is a recurrent feature of drama by Canada's leading women playwrights. In *Blood Relations* (1980), for instance, Sharon Pollock represents the key days in the life of the notorious Lizzie Borden as a series of realist set pieces. To tell the story of one of the nineteenth century's most infamous murder cases, Pollock makes appropriate use of the tropes of nineteenth-century realism: the cluttered and stifling bourgeois household ruled over by a forbidding patriarch, the near-hysterical daughter longing to escape, the perceptive servant, the flirtatious visiting doctor, the simmering threat of violence. All this appears to lead, as in the best well-made plays, toward the revelation of a long-concealed secret—in this case, Lizzie's guilt or innocence in the murders of her father and stepmother. Yet Pollock disrupts the "reality effect" of these scenes by placing them within a metatheatrical frame in which the older Lizzie, formally acquitted of the murders, deliberately plays out the scenarios of her own past along with an actress who may or may not be her lover. Lizzie distances herself from her own experience, enacting the role of the maid, Bridget, opposite the actress's version of Lizzie Borden. The realism of the "dream scenario" in which the two women dramatize the Borden murders is exposed as one possible fantasy among many, with less claim to the exposure of scientific truth than to the fulfillment of the spectator's desire for closure. The troubled and trespassing woman both exists within and defies the strictures of the realist vocabulary that serves as a tool for her carefully managed self-disclosure.

Negotiation between critique and appropriation of European realist models is also one of the striking features of Indigenous theatre in Canada. As Monique Mojica argues in this volume, the very notion of "Canadian realisms" depends on the prior assumption of a unified "Canadian real" that risks reifying colonial boundaries and rendering alternate understandings of and engagements with reality invisible. The vital work of First Nations artists such as Mojica, Floyd Favel, Erika Iserhoff, and Jill Carter, among many others, has eschewed European realist models, choosing instead to perform Indigenous realities in a manner that "returns Aboriginal people to the sources of Aboriginal knowledge" (Brunette ii). In *Chocolate Woman Dreams the Milky Way* (2011), for example, Mojica weaves storytelling, traditional Kuna textiles, and physical theatre methodologies into a unity that expresses the lived experience of Kuna women in whose lives ancient spiritual truths inform contemporary political struggles. In plays such as Drew Hayden Taylor's *Someday* trilogy (1993–2005), Tara Beagan's *Dreary and Izzy* (2005), and Yvette Nolan's *Annie Mae's Movement* (2006), meanwhile, European realist dramaturgy is used as one of a varied compendium of tools for the telling of Native stories to a wide audience. Kevin Loring's *Where the Blood Mixes*, which won a Governor General's Literary Award for English Language Drama in 2009, depicts the playwright's hometown of Lytton, British Columbia (called "Kumsheen" or "the place inside the heart where the blood mixes" in the Ntlaka'pamux language). Realist scenes set in barrooms and kitchens represent both the witty vitality of the community and its struggle with the emotional and psychological legacies of the residential school system, manifested visibly in violence, gambling, alcohol and drug abuse. At the same time, dream sequences, ghostly apparitions, and constant reminders of the presence of the town's two rivers and of the ancient sturgeon who lies in their depths link the everyday world of the living to the spiritual world of the ancestors. The two realities, expressed by complementary dramatic vocabularies, interpenetrate. In their inextricability, which attests to the survival of ancient Indigenous truths in the face of cultural genocide, Loring locates hope for his people's future.

A similar dialectic is at work in Tomson Highway's widely produced plays *The Rez Sisters* (1986) and *Dry Lips Oughta Move to Kapuskasing* (1988). Here, naturalistic settings, highly psychologized characters, and plots that appear causally driven by the quests of individual characters (the women's drive to get to the Biggest Bingo in the World; Zachariah's need to find his shorts, save his marriage, and start a business) coexist with the presence of the Trickster, Nanabush, a spiritual force whose reality within Ojibway culture cannot be contained by positivist European conceptions of the "real." By each play's end, it becomes clear that it is as much Nanabush's trickery as the characters' choices and desires that drives the action. The mimetic principles of European realism exist in tension with, and are finally folded into, a "grander, larger 'design'" born of Native mythology as Highway stages the struggles of a group of men and women surviving (and sometimes thriving) on the fraught border between two versions of the "real" (Highway, "On Native" 31).

In 2011, a new production of *The Rez Sisters* at Toronto's Factory Theatre telescoped the enduring value of Highway's interventions into the politics of the real on the Canadian stage. Director Ken Gass, with Highway's blessing, cast a mixture of First Nations, black, Asian, and white actors in the roles of Highway's Native women. The choice raised difficult questions. Was it proof of forward momentum for actors of colour in mainstream Canadian theatre? Of the inherent inclusiveness of contemporary Canadian realities? Or was it further evidence of the ongoing marginalization of First Nations experiences? Would a stricter, more traditionally realist "lamination" of actor to role have served more or less effectively the play's politics of decolonization? Such questions attest to realism's ongoing power—both as text and in performance—to provoke, to challenge, and to discomfort Canadian audiences and practitioners as it travels across traditions and weaves into contemporary debates. To do some measure of justice to this journey is a core goal of this volume.

EXPLORING CANADIAN REALISMS

New Canadian Realisms begins with three complementary examinations of the ways in which realist paradigms deriving from dominant European models have shaped, and been reshaped in their turn, by specific Canadian institutions, personalities, and social contexts. Anna Migliarisi opens the book with an historical prologue to the papers on more contemporary work that follow. "The Hidden History of Stanislavsky in Canada" chronicles the multiple paths by which Stanislavskian praxis entered the mainstream of Canadian actor training despite the politically influenced cancellation of the Moscow Art Theatre's proposed 1923 visits to Toronto and Montreal. It further invites scholars to take a new look at the dissemination of System- and Method-based acting in Canada and to consider "the degree to which Stanislavskian praxis has been naturalized by Canadian actors."

Kirsten Pullen takes up the latter challenge and brings the volume firmly into the contemporary in "Real Canadian: Performance, Celebrity, and National Identity." Pullen argues that the identification between actor and character—so vital for Stanislavsky and his American follower, Strasberg— has affected not only performers but also their audiences in North America to such an extent that it has shaped our very markers of nationhood. Reading the careers and public reputations of Canadian actresses Rachel McAdams and Sandra Oh, Pullen shows how "the realist paradigm" inflects their performances before going on to consider how their "Canadian" personalities have been identified (sometimes productively, and sometimes reductively) with those performances in popular media. As Harvey Young suggests in "Plaitform Concerns," however, such totalizing constructions of the "Canadian" inevitably mask the experiences of marginalized communities and the voices of artists who do not fit the dominant mould. One such artist is Trey Anthony, whose experience of exclusion within the mainstream Canadian theatre was one of the determining forces in her creation of the phenomenally successful 'da Kink in my hair. Young unpacks the show's origins, not only within Anthony's biography and career, but also within the realist tradition's core emphases on affect, empathy, identification, and the everyday concerns of "ordinary people." Where many have criticized such traditional realism's conception of the "ordinary" as founded on a norm of white, middle-class, male subjectivity, Young sees 'da Kink's realism as promoting "an understanding of the intersectional experiences of black Canadian women who endure societal racism, sexism, homophobia, ageism, and xenophobia." In the process, it revises the limited parameters of the "Canadian" identity Pullen finds in mainstream film culture.

The next four essays consider the revisionary engagements with European realist models offered by contemporary experimental theatres. In "After the Apple," Jenn Stephenson reads Garden//Suburbia, a site-specific walking tour of Toronto's Lawrence Park neighbourhood created by Melanie Bennett in collaboration with Hartley Jafine and Aaron Collier. Such a performance, taking place in a "real" setting and built around the autobiographical experiences of its creators, seems at first glance the apotheosis of a realism that aims faithfully to reproduce the contours of everyday experience. Stephenson finds in it instead an example of "post-lapsarian realism": an encounter with the real that is sharply aware of, and indeed built around, the paradoxes and limitations of the enterprise of staging the "truth." Autobiography returns in our next two papers, both focused on Québécois performance. Catherine Cyr's "The Workings of the 'Real': Système Kangourou's Performative Theatre" explores a young Québec company's efforts to create moments of encounter between performers and audiences, and discovers a "permanent blurring . . . of the borders between past and present, between the 'real' and the invented" in this work. Often site-specific and mixing the aleatory with the planned, Kangourou's work discards realism's careful mimetic strategies in favour of moments of chance and play that may allow for "irruptions" of a different kind of "real." Similar irruptions permeate Louis Patrick Leroux's "From *Langue* to Body: The Quest for the 'Real' in Québécois Theatre," as Leroux traces the twentieth-century shift in Québec theatre from a realism centred on linguistic verisimilitude to a "corpo-real" and "existential" realism focused on artists' often very personal narratives told on and through bodies under pressure. Such embodied pressures also fascinate scholar-practitioners Bruce Barton, Alex McLean, and Evan Webber as they discuss the possible relationships among various forms of realism and the processes of theatrical devising in "Devising Realisms (An Exchange)." While devised work has often been viewed as realism's ideological and methodological opposite, Barton, McLean, and Webber suggest that even as devising rejects the claims made by what they term capital R "Realism," it seeks "practical strategies for approaching the real without attempting to contain it." If "Realism" is no longer a viable option for these artists, "realisms, plural" seem very much a part of their creative and political arsenal.

This sense of the political potential of realisms, their strategic utility as well as their intractable limitations, marks the third group of essays. In "Realisms of Redress," Natalie Alvarez brings a sophisticated critical eye to the endlessly recurring question of "non-traditional" casting. Using the representation of Latina/o characters in Carmen Aguirre's *The Refugee Hotel* as her case study,

Alvarez teases out the paradoxes inherent in the iconic logic of realist acting's lamination of actor onto character: it may serve to create opportunities
for ethnic minority actors who (under this logic) *must* play characters of their
ethnicity, but in the process it threatens both to eliminate opportunities for
those actors elsewhere and to ghettoize them. Not despairing, Alvarez theorizes
within this conundrum, arguing finally for the possibility of an "indexical realism" in which the "'failure' to live up to the notional might serve as the ground
upon which realism's politics of visibility are revised." Parie Leung similarly
suggests that the tidiness and linearity of traditional European realist structures may be inadequate to explore the lived experience of Chinese and Hapa
Canadians whose lives and families have been disrupted by the repercussions of
discrimination. In two recent works on the federal government's redress for the
historical wrong of the Chinese Canadian Head Tax, David Yee's *lady in the red
dress* (2010) and Alan Bau and Kathy Leung's *Red Letters* (2010), Leung finds
instead what she calls "operative realisms": instances when elements that reflect
the dominant Euro-American realist tradition are juxtaposed with or disrupted
by anti-naturalistic techniques. These moments slice surgically into the body
of the realist text, pointing to the wounds historically experienced by the represented community and claiming for that community the right (against the
complaints of critics who often prefer a more "correct" realism) to represent its
lived realities on its own terms. Like the artists discussed by Alvarez and Leung,
the women practitioners both past and present considered by Susan Bennett
and Kim Solga must make difficult choices about their strategic uses both of
realist approaches and of the term "feminist." Bennett and Solga offer important correctives to the orthodoxies of feminist theatre scholarship in the 1980s
and 1990s, showing how canny uses of realism can pay off for women artists
by creating spaces for feminist goals within the mainstream. Recognizing the
risks as well as the benefits of such artistic and political choices, they remind
us of the importance of fully understanding the "material power" embedded
in the often contentious labels "realism" and "feminism," as well as in the frequently troubled relationship between the two.

Our last two contributors take us outside the walls of the theatre to consider some of the implications of new definitions of realism for our shared

futures. In "Scripting Reality in the Subjunctive Mood," Susanne Shawyer considers the competing scripts at work in the mass protests at the 2010 Toronto G20 Summit and particularly in the police's "kettling" of demonstrators. She shows how protestors' and commentators' uses both of protest gatherings and of social media worked to create scripts that, like the conventions of nineteenth-century realism had done in their day, organized and aestheticized lived experience in order to achieve particular political goals. Further, as archived social and mainstream media keep performing today the everyday life performance of the Toronto G20, the scripts thus offer ongoing access to the summit's "new realisms": new and plural representations of day-to-day existence that grant their actors and audiences the ability to choose between multiple potential futures.

Monique Mojica's "In Plain Sight" closes the volume with a poetic, moving, and deeply political meditation on a mode of Indigenous performance founded upon the enduring presence of material and spiritual Indigenous realities. Mojica begins by acknowledging her troubled relationship as an Indigenous artist to Eurocentric "definitions of realism (and what is perceived and presumed to be real) [that] depend on my continued erasure." She then generously invites the reader to join her on a journey of embodied research into the effigy mounds and earthworks created by her ancestors, which will serve as the dramaturgical framework for a new play. Her explorations render visible and tangible the unbroken presence of First Nations cultural expression in the Americas, and look towards a positive and transformative future. "The effort required to connect my body to the inscriptions made on the land through the extraordinary knowledge of my ancestors," writes Mojica, "is my 'realism.'" That "realism" may not be the realism of William Greaves or Trey Anthony, of David Yee or Système Kangourou, but it coexists with all of them, attesting to the ongoing vitality, complexity, and importance of contemporary Canadian theatre's engagements with the real.

THE HIDDEN HISTORY OF STANISLAVSKY IN CANADA

ANNA MIGLIARISI

No one working in the professional realms of theatre or film today, especially in Europe and North America, can refute a monumental debt to Constantin Stanislavsky and his teachings, represented in their totality as the System and re-imagined by Lee Strasberg, Harold Clurman, Elia Kazan, and others as the Method in North America. The word *system*, however, does not adequately capture the extent of Stanislavsky's insights into the actor's creative process. While Stanislavsky believed that art should be on good terms with science, he had no pretensions of being scientific (qtd. in Benedetti, Translator's Foreword xxiv, xxvii). System implies theory, "a theory with precise rules of what to do exactly at each moment" (Strasberg 41). Stanislavsky's system is not theory—or philosophy, or religion—but a path, a practical course of action. "In a word," writes Stanislavsky in his original draft preface to *An Actor's Work: A Student's Diary*, "whatever scientists may wish to make of my book, and whichever way they proceed, its import is purely practical" (xxv).

Well-meaning "admirers" of the System, simplistic teachers, clever directors, and above all "'unintelligible' disciples" who "take refuge in fine-sounding phrases, essays [and] learned words which have no meaning," Stanislavsky writes, "are harmful to our professional practice and fill the heads of actors and audiences alike with irrelevancies" (qtd. in Benedetti, Translator's Foreword xxv). In committing the System to paper, Stanislavsky was "haunted" (xvi) by the possibility that his exercises and techniques—derived from in-depth study of great actors, rooted in "nature's creative laws," and verified in extended trial and error—would be superficially understood and simplistically applied. His fears were well-grounded, as proven by what Jean Benedetti calls the subsequent "accidents of history" (Translator's Foreword xvi)—from copyright and censorship problems to discrepancies in translations.

Stanislavsky has become a myth, and his so-called System continues to be the subject of fiery contest and confusion. Dissonant voices from diverse schools of thought—from realist to naturalist to expressionist—claim to understand the "truth" of what Stanislavsky meant, in spite of the fact that, like that of all great artists, Stanislavsky's thinking was not only constantly evolving but often contradictory. Debate over the Americanization of the System is unremitting.[1] Books and articles on discrete elements of the System, on its legacy in modern performance, on the heirs of Stanislavsky, and on the great master teachers of the American Method are turned out year after year. Prominent among recent examples are well-known Stanislavsky scholar Jean Benedetti's translations of *An Actor's Work: A Student's Diary* (2008), an amalgam of *An Actor Prepares* and *Building a Character*, and *An Actor's Work on a Role* (2009), previously *Creating a Role*. In 2010, *The Lee Strasberg Notes* were published: an articulate representation of Lee Strasberg's "method," which in Strasberg's own words is a complementary synthesis of the ideas of Stanislavsky, Yevgeny Vakhtangov, Vsevolod Meyerhold, and the Group Theatre. Also published in 2010 was *Acting: The First Six Lessons: Documents from the American Laboratory Theatre*, which presents important source materials pertaining to Richard Boleslavsky, who ahead of any other individual was responsible for the first enunciation of Stanislavsky's teachings in the United States. It is hard to overvalue the influence of Constantin Stanislavsky on world theatre and film, particularly in the United States.

The place of Stanislavsky's teachings in Canadian practice, however, has been scarcely acknowledged. No in-depth study has emerged that recognizes and documents the presence and absorption of Stanislavsky's ideas in Canadian approaches to acting and directing. My own recent book chapter,

---

1 Throughout this paper, I discuss the Stanislavsky System and the American Method together, as the two have coexisted and intermingled with one another throughout most of the history of Stanislavskian influence in Canada. For more on differences between the System and the Method, see Carnicke, *Stanislavsky*, and Krasner, *Method Acting*.

"Stanislavsky in Canada: A Critical Chronology," published in 2008, is simply that—a chronology. It provides an outline of facts: basic information that aims to bring to light the extraordinary—and, until that time, unrecorded— history of the subject.

Laurin Mann's 1999 article, "'Stanislavski' in Toronto," based on her doctoral dissertation, offered a groundbreaking investigation into the influence of modern acting theories on the training methods of a select group of Toronto-based master teachers working in the 1990s in conservatory-style settings. While this study is not exhaustive, Mann's findings are to the point: almost ninety percent of the teachers surveyed recognized their theoretical debt to Stanislavsky and strongly advocated his internal techniques, as they understood them, in acting classes (212). Hands-on transmission of these "inside, out" ways of working was predominantly by way of American mentors, from Strasberg to Sanford Meisner to Stella Adler to succeeding third, fourth, and fifth generations of Stanislavsky followers. Texts on acting—including the English-language translations of Stanislavsky's books (particularly *An Actor Prepares*) and books by and about Stanislavsky's followers (e.g., *Strasberg at the Actors Studio* in 1965)—also played a significant part in the passing down of information. Mann observed that the subject of actor training was a little-explored area of research in Canadian theatre studies, especially in English-language theatre. We have no definitive account of Canadian performance practices and, unlike our American and European counterparts, no compilations of actors and their methods nor analyses of the techniques and ideas of contemporary Canadian acting teachers (207–08). It follows that we also lack studies on the ideas of Stanislavsky and their place in Canadian training of actors and directors. The situation has not changed significantly since Mann completed her work.

As a result of this lacuna in the Canadian theatre literature, theatre scholars have taken almost no notice of the fact that the 1923–1924 inaugural tours of the Moscow Art Theatre (MAT) in America—tours that revolutionized performance practices in America and the English-speaking world—initially included scheduled appearances at both His Majesty's Theatre in Montreal and the Royal Alexandra Theatre in Toronto. These appearances were cancelled abruptly at the eleventh hour. The particulars of these events are important, as they establish recurring patterns that help explain Stanislavsky's "hidden" place in Canadian theatre history.

The MAT first arrived in New York City in January 1923, where they were greeted by Richard Boleslavsky, a former member of the MAT and First Studio who had immigrated to America the year before. They launched their American program with Tolstoy's *Tsar Fyodor* on January 8 at Jolson's 59th Street Theatre, and played in Chicago, Philadelphia, and Boston. While the idea of adding an appearance in Canada at the end of the American run was discussed at this time, it was ultimately abandoned because of the time limit placed on the actors by the Russian government ("Planning to Bring"). However, in September 1923, when a return engagement in America of the MAT was formally announced by Russian-born American producer Morris Gest, it was decided that in mid-December Montreal and Toronto would round off the company's limited eight-city North American tour ("Planning to Bring").

The Canadian newspapers immediately made public the news that the Moscow Art Theatre would visit Montreal and Toronto. The repertoire would include the Art Theatre's now legendary productions of *Tsar Fyodor*, Maxim Gorky's *The Lower Depths*, and Anton Chekhov's *The Cherry Orchard*, as well as Carlo Goldoni's *The Mistress of the Inn*. The Toronto *Globe and Mail* described the reputed skill and versatility of the Russian actors in character delineation and "the stark realism in stagecraft and attention to minute detail in ensemble, which constitutes the basis of their art" ("Famous Russian Players"). The Montreal *Gazette* listed the sixty-odd actors that made up the ensemble, including Olga Knipper-Chekhov, Ivan Moskvin, and, of course, Constantin Stanislavsky. It touched upon the unfortunate crisis faced by the MAT in the wake of the political climate of Bolshevik Russia, and the difficulties overcome by Stanislavsky and Vladimir Nemirovich-Danchenko, in partnership with Gest, in setting up the North American tour ("Montreal to See Russian Players").

The *Gazette* commented on the historical magnitude of the approaching appearance of the Russian players in Canada. The Art Theatre was "the fountain head" of modern Russian theatre. The distinctive quality of their productions had "seldom been seen in this country." The reception of the work in Europe and the United States had been consistently powerful and influential ("Montreal to See Russian Players"). Gest appointed English impresario Percy Burton as his representative in Canada and manager of the engagements in Toronto and Montreal ("Famous Russian Players"). Burton was established as a theatre manager and publicity expert of repute; he had previously organized both European and North American tours of the greatest actors of the day, from Henry Irving to Sir Forbes-Robertson. Following the formal announcements of the Canadian engagements, Burton travelled to Canada to make the necessary arrangements. He formed the Committee of Canadian Patrons, chaired by a Mrs. R.J. Christie from Toronto, whose duties were to welcome the Russians to Canada and to provide accommodation, translation, and other support during their Canadian stopover. Through November, while the Russians performed to great praise in the United States, the Canadian newspapers continued their intensive advertising campaign. The anticipation was palpable.

Nonetheless, between the November 19 opening in New York City and November 25, Mrs. Christie caught wind of disturbing "rumours" in Toronto of a "strong undercurrent of criticism" toward the Russian players ("Says Russ Dramatists"). She immediately contacted Percy Burton. The following morning the *Evening Telegram* reported "a misconception in some circles in Toronto" ("No Bolshevist Taint In It"), but the Toronto *Daily Star* and the *Globe and Mail* singled out the University of Toronto as the hub of the rumour:

> It seems that in University of Toronto circles a sentiment has developed against an extension of local influential patronage to the noted Russian organization on the ground that it has a political and financial understanding with the Soviet Government, and that its profits, or a proportion thereof, go to the Bolshevik treasury. ("Russian Players Meeting Opposition")

Burton stated clearly to reporters that the allegations were "ridiculous" ("Says Russ Dramatists"). He promptly wired the news to Morris Gest in New York and, in an attempt to quell the rumours, requested an official letter of denial from the Art Theatre directors, who were disturbed by the reports from Toronto. Gest wired back immediately and expressed with "not a little resentment" his dismay at the increasingly tense situation:

> The whole thing is ridiculous. France investigated the Moscow Art Theatre before and invited them as guests of the country. America did the same. I personally investigated it thoroughly. Positively no foundation for it . . . the grounds of the objections were purely political. ("Says Russ Dramatists")

The allegations reported in Toronto fuelled renewed antagonism from the American Defense Society, which the season before had initiated a scurrilous print campaign against the Russians. This campaign, reissued in December 1922 by the *Globe and Mail*, accused the players of acting as "spies" on behalf of the Russian government ("Russian Artists Pledged"). The chair of the American Committee of Patrons of the MAT stepped in to help resolve the situation, but the growing opposition toward the Russians in Toronto had its effect. Within hours, the *Evening Telegram* reported that the Art Theatre would not perform in Toronto after all ("Russian Plays Off").

Meanwhile, the *Montreal Gazette* reported that in spite of the situation in Toronto, the performances at His Majesty's Theatre would go ahead but at a later date ("Moscow Players' Routing"); word was that the Russian players could expect "an enthusiastic welcome" from that city ("Moscow Players Will Be Seen Here").[2] The plan was to redirect the Art Theatre to Montreal either before or following the scheduled performances in Boston in January. As it turned out, this change in the schedule proved impossible for transportation reasons, and the performances in Montreal were also cancelled.

Stanislavsky, who was performing in Philadelphia, was distraught and wrote to Nemirovich-Danchenko:

---

2   This response already points to the marked cultural difference in the makeup of these two cities and to the competition that existed between them as they vied for dominance in Canada's developing cultural, economic, and political landscape in this period.

Moscow accuses us of disloyalty. But we get even blacker looks
abroad. . . . We only managed to get a favourable result [in France]
by circumventing French law. In Paris a considerable number of people, both French and Russian, boycotted us because we came from
the Soviet Union and therefore were communists. Now they won't let
us into Canada, officially declaring us Bolsheviks, and all our plans
have collapsed. (qtd. in Benedetti, *Moscow* 319)

The *Evening Telegram* published an obvious justification of the Toronto cancellation, in which Lawrence Solman, manager of the Royal Alexandra Theatre,
stated that the Art Theatre's performances were cancelled on account of the
gloomy subject matter of the plays in the repertory, which were "not of a character that would be acceptable" during the Christmas season. The fact that
the plays were to be performed in Russian, moreover, made them "impracti-
cable" from a business point of view (qtd. in "Russian Plays Off").

In an interview a couple of months later, James Mavor, professor of political economy at the University of Toronto and father of Canadian theatre
icon Dora Mavor Moore, claimed that the Moscow Art Theatre "would have
failed in Toronto" for lack of an audience. In his opinion, the population
of Toronto, "unlike New York, with its many wealthy Russians and Russian
Jews," is "poor and not a theatre going class"; and to English-speaking people, the performances would have been nothing more than pantomime (qtd.
in "Russian's Fault"). In this article, Mavor seemed to oppose previous allegations against the Russian actors as Bolshevik spies by suggesting that one
had to be wealthy and émigré European—and possibly Semitic—to enjoy the
MAT performances. However, he quickly contradicted himself by conclud-
ing that the Russian actors' "exact responsibility" to the Bolsheviks had never
been clarified, implying that the protests in Toronto might have been justified.

Not all Torontonians shared Mavor's views. A few days after the cancellation, an individual by the name of B.L. Bilniok, resident of Euclid Avenue,
wrote a letter to the *Globe and Mail* that was published in the "Voice of the
People" section. In the letter, Bilniok harshly criticized the "deplorable" conservatism that led to the cancellation, and expressed "severe disappointment"

on behalf of the many who were looking forward to the Art Theatre's performances: "A great opportunity will be missed if those who are in a position
to take action fail to uphold the [performance] agreement" ("The Moscow
Art Theatre").

It may be helpful to understand the "conservatism" to which this arts
patron alludes against the backdrop of emerging Canadian cultural pro-
tectionism. In his well-known 1911 essay, "The Annexation of Our Stage,"
for instance, Montreal theatre critic B.K. Sandwell railed against the highly
profitable control of Canadian professional stages by American syndicates.
Historian J.E. Middleton, on the other hand, claimed a few years later that
Canada had "always been indebted either directly or indirectly to the United
States for her drama." This should not be cause for complaint, he suggested;
rather, it was a "natural condition" (654). In 1923, American-born Canadian
critic Merrill Denison expressed the view that "Canadian culture" was a mis-
nomer: English-speaking Canada, which had always flourished under the
shadow of Britain and the United States, had no distinct culture to speak of.
Toronto was deemed the "centre" of things only because it was the seat of the
country's largest university ("Nationalism" 53). The University of Toronto,
in Denison's opinion, was "not sufficiently distinguished for the warmth and
enthusiasm of its human atmosphere to have become even the foster mother of any creative undertaking" ("Hart House" 61)—a sentiment that clearly
reinforces a view of the university as the conservative source of the 1923 ob-
jections against the MAT.

In subsequent decades, disagreements on these questions of national
awareness and cultural identity intensified on all sides. They reached their
zenith in the 1967 celebration of the nation's centennial, which inspired
a burst of professional theatrical activity. In the push toward creative au-
tonomy, however, a counter-narrative of what Don Rubin calls cultural
"chauvinism" unfolded (11). This was particularly true in English Canada,
where the historical pull between the "genteel" traditions and aesthetics of
British colonial theatre and the perceived "vulgarity" of American cultural
production was deeply felt (Wagner 36). This cultural chauvinism may explain, at least in part, why the American Method was more often than not

rejected as "not for us" (Janine Manatis, qtd. in Migliarisi, "Stanislavsky" 290), or worse, was simply ignored, at least by cultural historians (as opposed to actors and directors, who, as Mann's study confirms, generally embraced it). Hence the cancellation of the Art Theatre's performances in Toronto in 1923 may be read as a prophetic symbol of this trend of rejection.

In the longer term, French-speaking Canada seems to have been more hospitable than its Anglophone counterpart to the arrival of the System. In Montreal, the influence of the System can be traced back to the 1930s Workers' Theatre movement. Stanislavsky's ensemble-based aesthetics were ideal in the making of theatre with socially transformative ambitions—a mission obviously shared by workers' theatres across the country, including the Toronto-based Theatre of Action (see Ryan 108–224). This movement is a crucial link in the fractured story of Stanislavsky's dissemination in Canada: without a professional home-grown theatre to draw on, these groups had little choice but to seek out New York City–based teacher-directors to provide actor training.

The arrival of David Pressman in Toronto in 1936, and later of Albert Lipton, Daniel Mann, and Paul Mann at Theatre of Action and Montreal's New Theatre Group, marked the first official "invasion" of American teacher-directors. These passed on to Canadian actors the "early" precepts of Stanislavsky's System and its American adaptation, the Method. A description of Pressman's methods may be found in a late 1970s dialogue in Toby Gordon Ryan's *Stage Left* with Johnny Wayne and Frank Shuster, who, in tandem, make a strong case against popular misrepresentations of the Method as an emotionally undisciplined "realistic" style of acting (122–26).

Naturally, Pressman, Lipton, and Daniel and Paul Mann passed down the Method as they themselves received it from Lee Strasberg, Stella Adler, Harold Clurman, and other prominent Group Theatre members such as Elia Kazan and Sanford Meisner. Direct experience of the Russian system of training in Canada, however, was passed on principally by Yiddish actress, singer, director, and teacher Chayele Grober in the 1940s in Montreal. As one of the original members of the Moscow Habima, Grober was trained first-hand by Stanislavsky and Vakhtangov. She left Russia in 1927 to perform in the Habima's first North American tour, and at its conclusion remained behind to pursue a professional career in New York City. She settled in Canada after the outbreak of the Second World War, and made her mark as a teacher-director of the System in the burgeoning Yiddish theatre of Montreal. Grober left an important book, a memoir of roughly two hundred pages, written in 1952 in Yiddish and translated into Hebrew in 1973.[3]

Of special interest is a chapter entitled "Stanislavsky and His Influence on the World Theatre," which, as the title suggests, examines Stanislavsky's contribution to world theatre as well as his creative process and the evolution of the System. She provides a fascinating account of the day-to-day exercise and application of Stanislavsky's concepts at the Habima by Stanislavsky and his protege Vakhtangov. This description is invaluable because it predates Raikin Ben-Ari's 1957 book, *Habima*, which is generally considered the definitive account of Stanislavsky's work at the Habima. However, other than the pages in my possession, no English-language translation or study of this important chapter or book exists. Except for *Le théâtre yiddish à Montréal/ Yiddish Theatre in Montreal* (1996) by Jean-Marc Larrue, no critical writing exists on Grober or on her understanding and instruction of Stanislavsky-based working methods.

Another surprising omission in Canadian theatre history research concerns Montreal's role in the 1950s as home to the Canadian Drama Studio, the first official satellite of New York City's legendary Actors Studio. Established by New York–born William Greaves, this satellite flourished for about a decade as a pre-eminent training ground for English- as well as French-speaking Canadian actors and directors. Trained through the Canadian Drama Studio, these actors matured into a veritable *Who's Who* of Québécois stage and screen: Marcel Sabourin, Monique Mercure, André Plamondon, and the late Luce Guilbeault (see Migliarisi, "Stanislavsky" 265–66, as well as footnotes 15, 20, 21, 23).

Although today Greaves is recognized by film scholars for his groundbreaking work in independent cinema and for his promotion of African

---

3   Grober's *Tsu der groyser yelt* (1952) was translated into Yiddish by Yosef Aḥa'i under the title *Mi-shene tside ha-masakh*. The English translation of Grober's chapter on Stanislavsky in my research files (unpublished) is by Sharon Levinas.

American artists, he was an original member of the Actors Studio, where he was mentored alongside the finest American actors of the day. Outraged at the "many falsehoods" (qtd. in Migliarisi, "Stanislavsky" 263) that were being perpetrated about African Americans in the United States and at the scarcity of non-demeaning roles available to black actors in film and theatre, Greaves moved to Ottawa in 1952 to apprentice at the National Film Board of Canada (NFB), determined to carve an independent path as a documentary filmmaker. As Greaves diligently worked his way up through the ranks, some of his colleagues, directors, and producers requested that he teach them Stanislavsky-based technique; before long, Greaves was conducting acting classes in one of the NFB's studios. Members of the professional acting community caught wind of what Greaves was doing, and eventually he was offering professional master classes in Montreal and later in Toronto and Ottawa. When the NFB relocated to Montreal in 1955, Greaves rented out the attic of the Monument-National to conduct his classes; this space became the official headquarters of the Canadian Drama Studio.

The classes at the Monument-National were held two or three times a week and were conducted in English. Language "politics" were simply not a subject of concern at the Studio; the membership was a veritable model of diversity. The instruction was firmly rooted in "Stanislavsky-Strasberg" technique and followed the protocol of the Actors Studio in New York: exercises in relaxation, concentration, sense and emotion memory, and improvisation were followed by moderated scene-study sessions. From time to time, Greaves invited members from the New York Actors Studio to the Monument-National to conduct master classes, including the late, well-known Method-acting teacher Peggy Feury and the legendary Lee Strasberg himself. A condensed but detailed account of Strasberg's master class in Montreal by Canadian Drama Studio member Shannon Baker may be found in my 2008 critical chronology (272–76).

Greaves was well aware that he was teaching in Canada at a time of widespread controversy over the school of Method acting, especially in the United States, where it was at its most intense through the mid-1960s. Disagreements revolved inevitably around Strasberg's applications of Stanislavsky's "inner techniques" (Garfield 185). For Greaves, the negative criticism arose out of a basic ignorance of what the Method was (Duff). Creating and sustaining a credible inner life of a role, revealing the fullness of subtext, was the mark of a forceful and effective actor. Greaves employed Strasberg's "inner techniques" liberally, including the controversial affective memory. In a 24 June 1961 interview for the *Toronto Star*, Greaves observed that

> Canadian actors do not know enough about acting. They speak clearly, are able to move and can project in large theatres such as Stratford. But they are unable to influence an audience so it takes part in the life of the play. Actors who cannot accomplish this are not actors. (qtd. in Duff)

Greaves admitted that his remarks were a "blanket generalization" about Canadian actors and that there were notable exceptions, but for him

> [t]he actor who cannot bring his audiences into the life of the play is like a musician who cannot elicit sound from his instrument. A fiddle player may have bow work that is fabulous and his finger work may be impeccable. But if no sound comes out, what the hell? (qtd. in Duff)

Method training was clearly the way for Canadian actors to achieve this sound, and Canadian Drama Studio actors embraced the work.

In line with its New York City counterpart, Greaves envisioned the Canadian Drama Studio as a permanent place where the actor could always return "to refurbish his [or her] talent. It is like the gymnasium to the boxer" (Greaves, qtd. in Duff). There was discussion at one point of establishing a Toronto-based branch of the Canadian Drama Studio with a producing theatre wing patterned after the Group Theatre (Duff). But the plans did not materialize after Greaves returned to the United States. In a documentary created for the Criterion Collection reissue of Greaves's film *Symbiopsychotaxiplasm: Two Takes*, St. Clair Bourne comments that by his own account Greaves felt very much at home in Canada, but that privately he yearned to return to his place of birth to be of service to the Civil Rights movement as an "acknowledged" documentary filmmaker (*Symbiopsychotaxiplasm: Two Takes*). Greaves finally left Montreal in 1963 to make films for United Nations Television in New York City, where he and his wife, French Canadian Louise Archambault—as well as several other Canadian Drama Studio members—reside today. This exodus to New York City, typical of the migration of Canadian actors from the 1930s on, speaks as much to the Drama Studio members' high regard for Greaves as to a prevailing "hunger"—as Drama Studio member Shannon Baker has described it (Migliarisi, "Stanislavsky" 275–76)—for a particular kind of actor training that persists to the present day.

In 1968 Greaves began work on a unique two-part film project called *Symbiopsychotaxiplasm: Two Takes*. While it was shot in New York City, this project features a number of Canadian Drama Studio members both in front of and behind the camera, and offers a rare glimpse of Greaves's methodology "in action." The story revolves around a series of screen auditions for a film-within-a-film that a Stanislavsky-Strasberg director—Greaves himself—is trying to make. Actors of every type play out a pre-scripted scene of a couple arguing as Greaves-the-director hovers tenderly over them; he nods approvingly, asks questions, makes suggestions, praises the actors, and provokes them, their frustration leading inevitably to powerful performances. As screen test after screen test is being recorded, a second assembled crew shoots the scene of the crew that is shooting the screen tests. A third crew shoots the larger picture of actors, director, and crew, as well as bystanders and everything else that is happening in and around the shooting in the park. The overall effect is quite remarkable. In the sequel, one of the actor-couples, featuring Canadian Drama Studio actor Shannon Baker, is brought back together to play the updated drama for which they tested years before.

While prominent film scholars such as Scott MacDonald and Amy Taubin have recognized *Symbiopsychotaxiplasm* as a landmark study of the creative process, it remains virtually unknown to theatre scholars, Canadian or otherwise. Yet the project stands out as a demonstration of Greaves's legacy in

Canadian practice. It also represents an untapped source for vital questions about the role and function of the Method director, power and control in ensemble work, and the complex workings of the actor's creative process.

Greaves's departure from Montreal in 1963 did not end the crossover of Method teachers from the Actors Studio to Canada. In the following year, Eli Rill—another protege of Lee Strasberg—settled in Toronto, beginning a career as a mentor to many performers working on stage and in film. The entire cast of Don Shebib's groundbreaking 1970 film, *Goin' Down the Road*, for example, emerged directly from Rill's studio. Rill had first arrived in Toronto in 1957 to teach a class to a group called the Actors' Lane Workshop ("Eli Rill Teaches"). Here was a group of people who were "hungry" enough to contact the Actors Studio in New York City to ask if anyone would be willing to travel to Toronto to teach (Migliarisi, "Stanislavsky" 280). As long as Greaves was teaching classes there from time to time, Montreal remained the epicentre of the Canadian Drama Studio; consistent Method training was unavailable in Toronto. Strasberg spoke to a couple of people at the Studio and one of these, Rill, accepted the challenge. Rill commuted between New York and Toronto for a time before finally taking up residence in the latter city in 1964; he remained until 1977 when he relocated to his present home in Los Angeles.

Virginia-born Janine Manatis also arrived in Toronto in the 1960s with impressive credentials. She was an award-winning New York actress trained by three of the great teachers of the Method: Strasberg, Adler, and Meisner. As one of the few women in the Actors Studio Directors Unit, she had worked with one of the world's greatest directors, Elia Kazan. She had been mentored as a writer first-hand by James Baldwin, and was later chosen by Edward Albee to succeed him as the moderator of the Actors Studio Playwrights Unit. There she introduced actors' exercises to the playwrights of the Unit. At first, Manatis split her time between working in the Studio in New York City and teaching some of Rill's acting classes in Toronto ("Janine Manatis Quits as Studio Playwright"). She also formulated with him the concept of a Toronto playwrights' studio, where actors, writers, and directors would come together to explore the creative process. This culminated in 1964 with the short-lived and—aside from Herbert Whittaker's coverage in the *Globe and Mail*—under-recognized Playwrights Studio. The

Studio was unprecedented in English-speaking Canada at a time when there was no "Can" dramatic literature to speak of. Over time, Manatis took up residence in Toronto, where she continued to be sought after as a teacher, writer, and critic of theatre and film. And when NFB producer and filmmaker Beryl Fox fatefully asked Manatis, "If you could do anything that you wanted here, what would that be?" Manatis responded,

> I would like to develop the equivalent of the Actors' Studio for writers, directors and actors and producers in Canada. I believe it is desperately needed and the absence of such a place is holding Canada back. It's not a lack of talent, or enterprise, but it is the absence of such cohesive training. (qtd. in Migliarisi 289)

In that moment the Ensemble Workshop (EW) was conceived.

Whereas the Actors Studio was organized into three autonomous units for actors, writers, and directors, Manatis united the training at the EW into an ensemble that met twice a week for two years, from 1974 to 1976. The group gathered during the first few months at Toronto's historic Enoch Turner Schoolhouse before moving to the top floor of the "old" NFB production offices at Church and Adelaide streets. Aside from NFB employees, everything at the EW, from space to equipment, was financed by the film board and the only salaried person was Manatis. Like the Actors Studio, the EW required no membership fees; acceptance was based strictly on talent. The EW produced some of the most recognized Canadian names, particularly in film and television, in virtually every capacity from writing to performing to cinematography.[4]

---

4   Manatis, who resides in Toronto, continues to evolve her Method practice in the context of current research in the cognitive sciences and is currently drafting a book called *Actors' Exercises for Everybody*. As Rhonda Blair notes, neuroscience is radically redefining accepted notions central to Method work, such as presence, will, psychology, embodiment, emotion, and sense memory in ways that are richer, deeper, and more complex than Stanislavsky and his direct heirs, Boleslavsky in particular, could have imagined (Blair xxiv). Manatis's methods in general, and deep grasp of sensory work in particular, are

The Method is, of course, not the only way to work or the only alternative for the Canadian actor and director. However, it remains an unacknowledged force in the history of English- and French-speaking performance practice, and it merits attention from critics and scholars. There is much work to be done: further recovery and study of the contributions of individual System- and Method-based practitioners and of landmark sites such as the Canadian Drama Studio, comparative analysis of System-Method training practices in French and English Canada, study of the influence of Stanislavsky in major Canadian training institutions such as the National Theatre School, and examination of the degree to which Stanislavskian praxis has been naturalized by Canadian actors. Historically, Canadian actors, as I've tried to make clear, have embraced System-Method practice more readily than scholars. If academic dismissal is ultimately of little import to practitioners—paraphrasing Harold Clurman, the historical "problem" with the Method has always been that it was made a subject of theoretical "conversation" by academics and critics (39)—some consideration of how this dismissal might affect theories of performance, especially in the context of "Canadian realism," is crucial. How can we move forward if we don't recognize and make sense of what happened in the past?

I favour the words of two great Canadians. Mavor Moore warned of the dangers of throwing out the proverbial baby with the bathwater, declaring that "we should use *all* skills that serve *our own ends*" (15). And playwright and thinker George Ryga responded to the suggestion that the Vietnam War was a turning point for Canadian artists because they realized they did not wish to be identified with the United States or its culturally discordant values by saying, "But to reject, we must understand what we reject, and replace the vacuum" with something of value and humanity (32). I suspect that in November 1923, our theatre patron B.L. Bilniok had a strong sense that what was being rejected in Toronto was something already filled with both.

---

important because they reflect the ongoing engagement with "scientific" research that continues to shape Method practice. For any system to grow, it must incorporate the newest discoveries: "Therein lies Stanislavsky's influence and legacy" (Manatis, qtd. in Migliarisi, "Stanislavsky" 291).

REAL CANADIAN: PERFORMANCE, CELEBRITY, AND NATIONAL IDENTITY

KIRSTEN PULLEN

Before I moved to Calgary from the United States in 2003 (I've since moved to Texas), I had spent less than seventy-two hours in Canada. But I knew all about Canadians: they are nice, beer-loving hockey players. Rather than the US "melting pot," Canadians created a "mosaic." I acquired this knowledge through hundreds of popular culture representations, enabling fictions that allow Canadians and non-Canadians alike to imagine a land called Canada. But these markers of distinct Canadian national identity elide two equally enabling national fictions. First, Canadian national identity is difficult to define but a "perennial preoccupation" for its poets, politicians, academics, and even its average citizens (Cameron and Berry 18); and, second, "[o]nly by aspiring to be different from Americans have Canadians been able to . . . identify themselves as Canadians" (Berland 155).

Thus, despite an international circulation of images of Canada, definitions of Canadianness are processual, contingent, and often framed in the negative. At the same time, Canadian pride and patriotism are linked to "uniquely Canadian characteristics, achievements, or actions" such as hockey prowess, the natural landscape, niceness, and multiculturalism (Cameron and Berry 29). In 2000, Molson Brewery launched a successful (and quite tongue-in-cheek) television ad starring "average" (white, male, English-speaking) Canadian Joe. Hesitant at first, Joe champions hockey, beavers, and bilingualism before yelling "Canada . . . is the best part of North America!" As the stunning popularity of "Joe's Rant" demonstrates,[1] popular culture

---

1   As of this writing, the commercial has been viewed over two million times on YouTube;

representations inform discourses of national identity, though (however tinged with irony) they are often simplistic and stereotyped. Further, Canada's culture industries have historically been linked to a program of nationalism.[2] For example, beginning in the late 1960s, the Canadian Film Development Corporation (CFDC) financially supported Canadian film that demonstrated and created "a Canadian cinematic 'identity'" (Manning par. 6). Whilst the links between popular culture and national identity are well established within cultural studies generally and Canadian studies in particular, the role that actors play in the production and distribution of fictions of national identity has been largely overlooked. At least since the 1950s, when Method acting was established as the dominant technique for both stage and screen actors, a realist paradigm has structured audience response to performers and their roles. In particular, the realist paradigm (by which I mean the synthesis of self and role that defines modern Western, commercial acting) collapses performer with character. In many ways, this collapse enables multivalent responses to character and narrative, especially within film. It also predisposes audiences to link celebrities with national identity, creating stars based on citizenship, a process that may generate limiting stereotypes but paradoxically may also make room for multiple points of identification.

Following from Prague School discussions of the semiotics of the actor, which suggest that performers are always already both a character and an actor,[3] I explore the interplay between personal and national identity as well as

---

it can be seen here: http://www.youtube.com/watch?v=BRI-A3vakVg. According to a 2001 national poll, "95% of Canadians identify with the ad" (Berland 144).

2   The 1949 Massey Commission developed the framework for future government oversight of the arts. For more, see http://www.collectionscanada.gc.ca/massey/index-e.html. For more on Canadian broadcasting policy and production, see Serra Tinic's excellent *On Location: Canada's Television Industry in a Global Market* and Marc Raboy's *Missed Opportunities: The Story of Canada's Broadcasting Policy*.

3   Prague Linguistic Circle member Otakar Zich "distinguishes between the figure of the actor 'who appears on the stage and the dramatic character that exists not on the stage

self and role through the careers of Sandra Oh and Rachel McAdams. Oh and McAdams are strategic choices. They are not, for example, Pamela Anderson or Jim Carrey. Instead, Oh and McAdams have generally appeared in "quality" productions in order to demonstrate their acting range and skill. Rather than capitalizing on their appearance (like Anderson), or talking through their butt cheeks (like Carrey), Oh and McAdams pursue subtle, nuanced characterizations. Further, their personae clearly demonstrate how the realist paradigm collapses performer and character as well as how this collapse may serve to enable fictions of national identity. The national-identity based components of their personae may interpellate audience members who privilege their extratextual knowledge of Oh or McAdams over their characters or the narratives they inhabit.

Sandra Oh and Rachel McAdams may be understood as what semiotician Otakar Zich calls the "stage figure." Using Cate Blanchett's star turn as Richard II in the Sydney Theatre Company's 2009 *War of the Roses*, Glen McGillivray explains that although the "Stage Figure is not Blanchett it remains, nonetheless and also, *not* not her. . . . [E]very actor onstage is both a social being and a fictional character; but in Blanchett's case stardom intensifies this juxtaposition" (159). Michael Quinn's "Celebrity and the Semiotics of Acting" makes a similar point: the "personal qualities of the individual actor dominate the perception of the actor's references to the fictional events" (155). Though McGillivray and Quinn are writing about film stars in live theatre, their descriptions of how celebrity influences audience reception are equally relevant to film acting. When actors, critics, and gossip bloggers decry the difficulty separating film and television characters from the hypervisible celebrities on the Internet and in the pages of *Hello!* and *Us Weekly*, the influence of actors' personal lives on their performances cannot be overstated. Importantly, private detail about those lives may authenticate the fictions actors present, grounding their characters' behaviours in seemingly real, verifiable referents. The realist paradigm, structuring understandings of performance for the past

---

but in our consciousness'" (Ambros 57). For more on the development of Prague School semiotics for theatre, see Ambros.

six decades, is especially inflected by what fans (think they) know about their favourite performers.

On the surface, McAdams and Oh are very different actors. Rachel McAdams is a sunny, sweet-faced girl also capable of turning on Hollywood glamour. She starred in a few Canadian film and television roles but began working almost exclusively in Hollywood with *The Hot Chick* (2002). Since that role, McAdams has mostly played honest, earnest, emotional young women like her character, Allie, in *The Notebook* (2004)—a film instrumental to the construction of her persona and her Canadianness, despite its US setting. Her films have strong commercial appeal, a characteristic McAdams embraces. In a 2009 *New York Times* interview, McAdams explained: "I try to pick movies that I want to make, that offer a challenge, but that people want to see. . . . If you act and nobody sees it, is it still acting?" (qtd. in Rozen).

In 2001 McAdams earned an Honours BFA in Theatre from York University. At York, she studied with current Professor Emeritus David Rotenberg, who founded the Professional Actor's Lab, a training centre clearly modelled on Lee Strasberg's Actors Studio. According to Rotenberg, McAdams continues to take classes at the Lab. In a 2005 *Maclean's* interview Rotenberg noted that McAdams "is grounded," a quality he attributes to her training. "We teach up at York that you've got to know where you come from—it's a big part of the training" (qtd. in Deziel). I understand Rotenberg's assertion to mean that McAdams is well-versed in the kind of emotional recall and sense memory that undergirds US versions of Method acting.

Sandra Oh is a first-generation Korean Canadian, and studied at Montreal's National Theatre School (B. Johnson, "Shooting" 66). After graduating in 1994, Oh won a Genie for her "visceral performance" as Evelyn Lau, a teenage prostitute (B. Johnson, "Double Life" 42). She worked in Canadian films, on Canadian stages, and on Canadian television before moving to Hollywood in 1995 for a supporting role in the HBO comedy *Arli$$*. Her rise was less meteoric than that of McAdams's, undoubtedly in part because of her Asian ethnic background. In 1995, she told *Maclean's* interviewer Brian Johnson how an agent had warned her that "[i]t's tough for someone like you here [in Hollywood] . . . because you look the way you do" (B. Johnson, "Shooting" 66).

Like McAdams, Oh is considered a realist actor. Her *Diary of Evelyn Lau* director, Sturla Gunnarsson, explains that she "is a rare combination of a method actor with great craft. She plays everything from the inside out" (qtd. in B. Johnson, "Double Life" 42). These components of McAdams's and Oh's biographies—their physical appearances, their Canadian roots, and their training in realist technique—trade on their femininity, ethnicity, and Canadianness to create their celebrity personae. Celebrity is always already gendered—as are discussions of the nation.

Importantly, however, the realist paradigm is not always already hegemonic. Rather, realism can be "unsafe" (untrustworthy, indefinable) as it flexes across genres and through performers. In some cases, the enabling fiction defining the realist paradigm—that the performer and the role are interchangeable—may allow some audiences to read alternative or even subversive narratives within commercial Hollywood films. For example, in 2009 McAdams starred opposite Robert Downey Jr. in *Sherlock Holmes*. On one hand, McAdams played Holmes/Downey's love interest, Irene Adler, and the two engaged in the classic antagonistic behaviour that generally denotes tremendous sexual passion and hidden true love. Audiences who primarily interpret McAdams through the lens of Canadianness, however, might also read the film as the clash between colonialist Britain (or America), symbolized by Downey, and a proudly independent Canada, as portrayed by feisty McAdams. Though few audiences will take this as the explicit meaning of a blockbuster genre film, I contend that McAdams's strong Canadian persona colours her roles, producing ambivalent characters that audiences might understand in multiple and even resistant ways.

THE REALIST PARADIGM

Most of the chapters in this book complicate Canadian stage realism. Conversely, my contribution focuses on cinematic realism. Realism's status as the paradigmatic cinematic performance style of the late twentieth century is taken for granted by most film and theatre audiences; that is, most North Americans can explain that actors use their own emotions in order to create characters, that characters are often based on components of actors' authentic selves, and that actors must "live the part" in order to convincingly play the character. These assumptions are worth untangling: the realist paradigm that structures film performance also influences audience expectations about what kinds of characters particular performers might embody as well as how their characters mean in a broader arena of cultural production.

Cinematic realist acting, a specific and historically grounded technique that seeks close correspondence between performer and character to present motivated actions and genuine emotion, sustains all other elements of the filmic illusion. Further, a complex web of performances, images, and gossip authenticate film performance by linking actor and role. Thus, movies are real, important, legitimate sources for knowledge about the world because they are based in the truth of the performers' lived physical and emotional experience. In the case of McAdams and Oh, this translates to an ideal of Canadianness available for consumption by both US and Canadian audiences, as well as the financially important global market. Oh and McAdams (rather than Anderson and Carrey) highlight how the realist paradigm structures not only film performance but also performances of citizenship and national identity, encouraging audiences to read even everyday behaviour as especially indicative of character.

During the Classical Hollywood era (roughly the 1930s–1950s, during the height of the studio system), cinematic performance was rooted in the techniques and aesthetics of theatrical realism (see Pullen). Film production during this period established standards of performance and narrative as well as film's legitimacy as art, both of which continue to resonate. Most of McAdams's and Oh's movies are best understood as Classical Hollywood film, which David Bordwell, Kristin Thompson, and Janet Staiger, discussing the Studio era, define as those movies that privilege a clear and unambiguous narrative above other elements; offer a realistic representation of people, places, and events; hide their production processes through the use of continuity editing; and present a "universal" emotional appeal that transcends individual audience differences (3).

Because actor performance is a key component of a cinematic realist illusion, Hollywood studios were invested at their outset in developing realist actors. Classical Hollywood film acting is particularly linked to the Group Theatre and Lee Strasberg's Actors Studio.[4] When the Group Theatre disbanded in 1941, many members went to Hollywood, appearing as character actors and working as drama coaches. Lee Strasberg and Stella Adler offered competing versions of Stanislavsky technique to American film and theatre actors from their base in New York City. By disseminating their ideas in acting schools, to their fellow film actors, and through studio connections, these former Group Theatre members ensured the techniques and goals of the Group were the principal influences on cinematic performance in the 1940s and 1950s. Perhaps most importantly, their influence further solidified popular understandings that film acting is always (or inherently) based in Method techniques, an assumption that remains pervasive among later generations of US film performers.

Studio publicity exerted an equally powerful influence on perceptions of cinematic performance. Publicity departments created biographies and career narratives for their stars, disseminating these stories (with accompanying photographs) through official and unofficial channels. Thus, two complementary discourses of realism structured audience perception of the correspondence between actor and character: studio publicity reinforced connections between actor and role whilst acting training focused on performers' personal, emotional connections to their characters.

In key ways, then, the realist paradigm defines successful film acting as a performance of self, one generated both inside and outside the work. As James Naremore reminds us, "the typical dramatic film . . . regards acting as an artful imitation of unmediated behavior in the real world" (18). Today, however, the collapse between performer and self is exacerbated by contemporary celebrity culture and its 24/7 gossip cycles, as an example from McAdams's

---

4   Founded in 1931 by Harold Clurman, Cheryl Crawford, and Lee Strasberg, the Group Theatre developed techniques for acting based on an understanding of Stanislavsky as taught and promoted by Richard Boleslavsky and Maria Ouspenskaya at the American Laboratory Theatre in New York City in the 1920s.

oeuvre demonstrates. At the 2005 MTV Movie Awards, Rachel McAdams and Ryan Gosling celebrated their win for Best Kiss in the film *The Notebook* by re-enacting it at the awards ceremony. McAdams took off her black jacket and hiked up her embroidered bustier as Gosling, in a white Darfur T-shirt and jeans, shook himself out like a runner before a race. They walked and then ran toward each other, McAdams launched herself into Gosling's arms, and the two clung together kissing whilst ecstatic audience members gasped and applauded. Gosling carried McAdams to the podium where they quickly accepted the award.

Links between character and performer manifest through actors' bodies. Fans of *The Notebook* had long speculated that the passion between Gosling's Noah and McAdams's Allie could not be counterfeit; their connection was so physically powerful that it had to be authentic. Of course, on its surface, the MTV performance, enacted for the audience in the Shrine Auditorium as well as for millions watching the program worldwide, suggested that their connection could, in fact, be faked. Though marked by signs of the real—Gosling's T-shirt expressing his deeply felt and oft-stated political views, McAdams's care in ensuring that she not commit an on-camera nip-slip—it was also clearly a rehearsed performance, as the two stars took their positions on opposite ends of the stage and signalled their readiness to begin. Then again: although the two Canadians had previously denied rumours that their onscreen romance in *The Notebook* carried over to their real lives, soon after the MTV Awards McAdams confirmed that they had been dating for some time. Here, at last, was proof that real love could be captured onscreen, and that movie kisses are best when the performers are actually romantically involved.

PERFORMANCE AND NATIONAL IDENTITY

It is not coincidental that both Oh and McAdams are women. Modern nation-building "is always predicated on Woman as trope, displacing historical women" and erasing individual experience in favour of gendered narratives of conquest and discovery (Alarcón, Kaplan, and Moallem 6). This trope is particularly active in US-Canadian relations, where "English Canadian nationalism habitually uses the image of Canada as the defenceless female to the American hulk" (Probyn 115). Predictably, then, Oh and McAdams have been assimilated as Canadian metonyms in the US more easily than Canadians like Jim Carrey, Ryan Reynolds, or Mike Myers. Further, as Jody Berland points out, "Canadian film, television, and popular fiction feature women protagonists fighting for recognition and selfhood" (154), while Canada's "most prominent literary hero is an orphan girl with a temper" (162). Thus, it is unsurprising that US—but especially Canadian—press coverage mobilizes *female* actors in order to construct Canadian national identity.

Though McAdams and Oh signify Canadianness in a variety of ways, their *anti*-Americanness is most constituent of their celebrity. McAdams plays candid, forthright, nice young women and is universally heralded for her down-to-earth, non-Hollywood lifestyle. Oh has achieved her greatest success playing one tile of the mosaic of racial and sexual identities on the acclaimed US television program (televised in Canada on CTV) *Grey's Anatomy*; her ease playing difference is a hallmark of her press coverage and critical reception. Further, both women are lauded for elevating formulaic genre narratives, a move that aligns their Canadianness (or un-Americanness) with quality performance.

McAdams's commercial film performances are consistently heralded for rising above the material. Her fall 2010 film *Morning Glory*, which co-starred Diane Keaton and Harrison Ford as mismatched morning show anchors with McAdams as their new producer, positioned McAdams as "An Actress on the Brink of a Blockbuster" in the words of *New York Times* reporter Leah Rozen. Though the film was negatively reviewed overall, McAdams was highly praised. In fact, the snarky *New York Magazine* posited that *Morning Glory* is "exactly the sort of rom-com trifle that would get savaged by critics if it were starring Katherine Heigl" (Paskin). But columnist Willa Paskin goes on to explain that Rachel McAdams has been nearly universally praised for making the best of bad scripts. As *Los Angeles Times* critic Kenneth Turan claimed, "Rachel McAdams gives the kind of performance we go to the movies for";

Roger Ebert remarked that "Rachel McAdams' life force illuminates" the film (both qtd. in Paskin). Manohla Dargis, writing for *The New York Times*, called McAdams "effortlessly likeable." In an odd (but not uncommon) conflation of the character and actor, Dargis concluded her review with more praise for McAdams: "As might be expected, Ms. McAdams plays her role exceptionally well: as the young actress on the verge of the big time, who can win the boy, tame the beast, flash her panties and make you smile without making you cringe, she is a natural."

McAdams's presumed depths of emotional intensity and integrity are salient indicators of her performance style. From her work in *The Notebook* on, McAdams has been heralded for the "truth" of her performances. In another tricky assessment of her ability to act at the same time as she plays herself, Michael Phillips, reviewing *Morning Glory* for *The Chicago Tribune*, said that "[w]hen she was bratting around the edges of *Mean Girls* Rachel McAdams had yet to ease into her true qualities. But now . . . [s]he has an honest, penetrating way of conveying a character's delight." These assessments of McAdams's honesty, integrity, and likeability, especially evident in the glowing reviews for *Morning Glory*, are rooted in another key performance: the construction of an "all-Canadian girl" persona.

Sandra Oh's integrity and authenticity also contribute to her "all-Canadian" performances. Oh's first major role was Jade Li in Mina Shum's 1994 film *Double Happiness*. Like Oh, Jade is an Asian Canadian actress who struggles to convince her parents that she can maintain traditional Chinese (or Korean) values whilst pursuing a film career. Many of the features and reviews of the film play up the biographical correspondences of Jade with both Oh and director Shum, such as Noreen Golfman's description of the film and character as exploring "the hyphen [as] a link preserving complementarity" with "each side of the Chinese-Canadian equation stak[ing] a claim in the national psyche" (26). Crucially, Oh's performance emphasizes the quotidian at the same time that it deploys enabling fictions of Canadian identity. When Jade breaks up with Mark, the white man with whom she has secretly fallen in love, Oh's face and voice are nearly expressionless. Delivered in a monotone, her lines explicitly say that she and Mark can't be together because she can't hurt her family by being with a Caucasian Canadian. In a paradigmatic example of how cinematic realist acting manifests emotional subtext through under-played emotion, Oh's colourless voice suggests that her life without him will be bleak indeed. Oh won a second Genie for the role and was widely praised for her work; *Times* critic Janet Maslin informed audiences that the film was good, but "[e]ven better, Ms. Oh's performance makes Jade a smart, spiky heroine you won't soon forget."

Jade Li is key to Oh's embodiment of multiracial, multicultural Canada. The autobiographical parallels as well as the performance style concretized a humble, Asian Canadian persona that was repeated in roles in *Guinevere*, *Last Night*, and *Long Life, Happiness, Prosperity*, which reunited her with director Mina Shum. These films, of course, are Canadian-produced and distribut-ed; more importantly, they are made by Oh's cohort of Canadian performers and actors. As she told *New York Times* reporter Hilary De Vries, her "friends in Canada . . . call me every four years . . . and I go up there and play a lead-ing role." Meanwhile, in the US, Oh was "in danger of being permanently labeled 'sassy'" (De Vries). Oh played the best friend/assistant in a number of Hollywood films and television programs until she appeared as sharp-tongued single mom Stephanie in the critically heralded *Sideways* (2004), directed by her then-husband, Alexander Payne. Though Oh wasn't nomi-nated for any acting awards (as her co-stars were), her "sensual" Stephanie was called a "pure delight" (Ansen). Often a juicy role in a critically acclaimed blockbuster moves an actor into another tier; when this didn't happen for Oh, she decided she "would rather work in [US] television" and play "interesting characters" (De Vries).

One such character is Dr. Cristina Yang on *Grey's Anatomy*. Though neither the program nor the character is Canadian, both might as well be. Set in Seattle (one of the geographically and culturally closest US cities to Canada), it consistently decries the US medical system that denies health care to many of its poorest citizens, and features a multicultural and pol-ysexual mosaic of characters. Since its 2005 premiere, the show has been heralded for its diverse cast; writing for *The New York Times*, Alessandra Stanley noted that

[t]here are no token blacks on "Grey's Anatomy." The three top surgeons who rule the interns with princely authority are all African-Americans, and that sign of social advancement is presented as a given, without fanfare or comment. Similarly, female doctors seem to outnumber the men, and nobody on the show finds that remarkable.

Oh's Christina Yang rounds out the multicultural production. According to executive producer and writer Shonda Rhimes, "some network executives assumed Ms. Oh's hypercompetitive character would be white," but she purposely didn't give Cristina a last name in order to leave casting open. "[S]o all it took was one 'fabulous' audition from the *Sideways* star to christen the character Cristina Yang" (qtd. in Fogel). Oh has had several compelling storylines in her pursuit of a surgical career, most notably her fraught relationship with Dr. Preston Burke (Isaiah Washington), which included an unplanned ectopic pregnancy and abandonment at the altar, and an affair with Dr. Owen Hunt (Kevin McKidd), who suffered from such a severe case of post-traumatic stress disorder that he tried to choke her to death shortly after the first time they made love. Both of these relationships were interracial, which has gone unremarked on the program.[5] Greg Braxton, writing for the *Los Angeles Times*, noted that this "represents a positive evolution demonstrating that such romances are no longer a big deal. But other[s] argue that the move toward colorblind romance oversimplifies race relations." Nevertheless, Yang's interracial relationships work to concretize Oh's performance persona by continuing a pattern of cross-racial romance in both her personal life and in her film roles.

Oh's performance on the often melodramatic *Grey's Anatomy* is critically regarded (she's been nominated for a Golden Globe, a SAG Award, and for an Emmy five times). Like McAdams, her performances are "believable" (Kuhn). Oh's celebrity authenticity is no doubt bolstered by her candour: she peppers interviews with "fuck," she cooks breakfast (B. Johnson, "Story of Oh") and

5   As editor Kim Solga noted on a draft of this essay, *Grey's Anatomy* is an anomaly on US *and* Canadian television, where the multicultural nation is rarely represented in the kind of detail *Grey's Anatomy* explores.

changes clothes (Armstrong) with reporters, and she speaks at length about the challenges of being an actress of colour in Hollywood. After playing a pivotal role in the Academy Award winning *Sideways*, she talked to *New York Times* reporter Hilary De Vries:

> I know that I don't get jobs in films by auditioning. I'm not blonde. You can't place me in movies the way you can with certain actors. . . . I know for me to be in any film over $3 million, there is someone pushing for me because I am not an easy sell.

Ten years later, while starring on *Grey's Anatomy*, she told *Maclean's* reporter Brian Johnson that though "there was a time when [I] wished [I] looked different," she's now "happy" with her Korean appearance ("Story" 56). Oh often explicitly and implicitly contrasts Hollywood practices ("Hollywood likes to put actors in boxes, and it likes to put Asian actors in really small boxes" [in B. Wilson]) with Canadian filmmaking, suggesting that the latter is more collaborative and open to non-white stories:[6] the Evelyn Lau and Jade Li roles "never would've happened if I were here in the states," she proclaimed (in Armstrong). She told *Los Angeles Times* reporter Peter McQuaid that Canadian performers have "more freedom to do and explore the things that can result in a more realized sense of craft." Clearly, her perceived honesty about the challenges facing actresses of colour *in the United States* is key to her ideal Canadianness.

Though Oh's US profiles almost always mention her Canadian citizenship (as do McAdams's) as well as her theatrical background, her ethnicity is never allowed to pass without question and comment. Of course, this is true in the US for most high-profile members of visible minority groups, whether they are performers, entrepreneurs, or politicians. Even so, the discourse

---

6   In discussions during the preparation of this chapter, Solga reminded me that English-language Canadian films are all, "essentially, art house." Their status as "quality" productions rather than blockbusters does allow them more freedom to explore other kinds of stories and storytelling. Of course, the Canadian government's continued economic support of aspects of the film industry also drives the kinds of narratives that ultimately get produced: showcasing Canada is the National Film Board's express agenda.

of multiculturalism Oh's persona mobilizes is always already tied to her national identity. Canadians are encouraged (by government, by advertising, by
social institutions of different kinds) to be proud of their multicultural policies and practices (Hayday 293), and when Oh mentions how Hollywood
offers limited opportunities for women of colour, Canadian audiences may
remind themselves of their positive difference from the US in this regard. Oh
plays specifically to her home audience, enabling the fiction of a harmoni-
ous multicultural society despite a more contentious socio-economic reality.
Sneja Gunew, for example, argues that "state multiculturalism" manages diversity by "attributing various social and economic inequalities . . . not to
systemic racism and sexism but to untouchable 'cultural differences'" (qtd. in
Knowles, "Multicultural" 77). Similarly, Neil Bissoondath suggests that "by
sanctifying the mentality of the mosaic-tile, we have succeeded in creating
mental ghettos for the various communities" that comprise the nation, and
that Canadians "come away from" celebrations of "diversity" with "stereotypes
reinforced." As these and other cultural critics (see Knowles, "Multicultural,"
and Tompkins) point out, the discourse of multiculturalism is often used as a
cover for a deeper and unexamined racism that continues to drive Canadian
politics, social structures, and popular culture representations. Thus, Oh's
championing of Canadian casting practices over those in the US solidifies
an official discourse of multiculturalism whilst eliding the socio-economic
realities of Asian Canadians who are *not* also celebrities.

If Oh's Canadianized celebrity persona depends on her embodiment
of multiculturalism, then McAdams's is predicated on her "niceness." Her
presentation of self is as grounded and down-to-earth. Profiles in *The Wall
Street Journal* and *The New York Times*, for example, both approvingly note
McAdams's penchant for taking public transportation in New York, Toronto,
and Los Angeles, suggesting that McAdams has not lost the common touch
(see Rozen; Kate Kelly). Press coverage of McAdams's life and career attributes
her solid, nice, normal persona to her Canadian heritage. For example, the *New
York Times* profile that appeared in advance of *Morning Glory* led by noting
that McAdams lives outside Toronto with her younger brother; explained that
"like virtually all Canadians, she learned to skate early;" and remarked that

she neither owns a television set nor knows how to drive (Rozen). Though the article is ostensibly about how *Morning Glory* will finally make McAdams a major star, the subtext is that she's a nice Canadian girl trying to make it in Hollywood.

Though such mainstream news profiles are crucial to the construction of celebrity aura, gossip blogs are increasingly important sources. Columnist Elaine Lui's *Lainey Gossip*, one of the most internationally popular gossip sites, and the only major Canadian one, offers a perspective on Canadian vs. Hollywood fame and a focus on Canadian stars that make her uniquely relevant here. At the same time, her attitudes toward McAdams and Oh are echoed on other sites. Lui is a particular fan of McAdams, and her coverage both implicitly and explicitly stresses the star's Canadianness. For example, in a post about how terrific McAdams looked in Spain promoting *Morning Glory*, Lui noted that she was dressed like her own mother, and that

> [a]pparently Rachel was in Creemore, Ontario over the holiday. Dropped by a local bakery . . . and took a photo with staff. . . . I love her for . . . the ongoing and deliberate small town-ness of her life despite the obvious un-small-town-ness of her job. ("Rachel in Spain")

Lui often highlights McAdams's interactions with fans, her normalcy, her support for Canadians, and her fondness for riding her bike (see "McGosling," "Designated," and "Rachel Rides").

Lui also pays close attention to Sandra Oh, an emphasis intensified by their shared ethnicity as Asian Canadians. Lui is especially dismissive of Asian celebrities like Bai Ling and Zhang Ziyi who "Hello Kitty" their way to the spotlight—that is, mobilize stereotypes of Asian submissiveness and girlishness:

> No clue what Zhang Ziyi was doing at Clive Davis's pre-Grammy party but Hello Kitty Chinagirl should have stayed home . . . ZZ walked off the boat and bought this outfit, perpetuating every massage parlour bendy sex stereotype about Asians. ("Hello Kitty at the Grammys")

Lui praises Oh for rejecting this stereotype in her clothing and her demeanour, and claims her as a "Canadian Asian sister" ("Most Disappointing"). For example, she notes that "Sandra Oh has a bite" ("Best Emmy Canadian") and "she's . . . kind of a bitch" ("People's Choice Best Black"). Importantly, Lui's Oh coverage is driven by their shared Canadian citizenship. No other gossip site mentions Oh as often or as favourably. Lui's relative focus on Oh represents her stated desire to "respect our stars" (qtd. in Schweitzer 6) and recognize their place in contemporary celebrity culture. Clearly, Lui is invested in mobilizing Oh, McAdams, and other Canadian stars as symbols of national identity and sources of national pride. In important ways, her focus on Canadian stars and their Canadianness suggests a coterie of performers whose work and lives can be understood as uniquely tied to each other and to a national ideal.

IDENTIFICATION, AMBIVALENCE, AND THE REALIST PARADIGM

Despite its roots in nineteenth-century social-problem plays, performed realism has long been critiqued for creating representations that naturalize a particular world view, usually one identified with dominant ideologies of sex and gender. Whilst this is certainly a valid critique, certain realisms—such as the acting paradigm I've explored here—may also offer alternate points of entry into texts and/or performances depending upon audience experience and context, thus generating conflicting rather than unifying readings among spectators. In the Hollywood case, audience members typically bring knowledge of a performer's personal life or previous roles to new narratives; as Marvin Carlson suggests, film audiences "are able to 'read' new works . . . only because [they] recognize within them elements that have been recycled from other structures of experience that [they] have experienced earlier" (4). Thus, when audiences "read" a Rachel McAdams or Sandra Oh performance—whether onscreen, in a print interview, or via a blog photo—they situate that performance within a set of other performances and texts. Rather than reading a single narrative or specific character, audiences *always* read performers' personae, and project meaning from those extra-filmic characterizations onto the screens in front of them. Because Oh and McAdams are so strongly identified as Canadian, their personae significantly shape—and are shaped by—ideas about Canadian national identity. Regardless of the characters they play, they also always represent "Canada," though not always in the same way.

As Carlson explains, even audiences who don't have specific, insider (or Canadian) knowledge of performers "may be affected by the operations of celebrity itself to view and experience a famous actor through an aura of expectations" (58–59). Thus, though some audience members may not read all the layers of each McAdams or Oh performance, nor experience the same intertextual pleasures as all others, they will recognize the hallmarks of authenticity and realism that structure those performances; these pleasures include recognizing "national symbols and myths" (Raney 7). For example, the McAdams *New York Times* profile that references her ice-skating in its first paragraph offers a frisson of recognition for many Canadians who also grew up in rinks even as it reinforces an enabling fiction of ruggedness, sportsmanship, and cold weather that for many stereotypically "defines" Canada. Learning that Oh finds Canadian film more open than Hollywood references Canada's multicultural policies and allows Canadian audiences to share the "deep, horizontal comradeship" (Anderson 7) that characterizes the nation as imagined community.

That said, when particular performers metonymically represent a nation, their performances may be read in contradictory ways. Barry King argues that the intertextuality of performances and personae inherently generates a dangerous "commodity-centered politics of visibility . . . that assigns and regulates the power to represent the collective" in a uni-directional way ("Stardom" 7). I argue by contrast, however, that we may be interpellated by a specific character, by the layers of previous characterization, by a generalized persona, by a particular critical or tabloid take on a star, or by a combination of all of these things, which necessarily results in *poly-directional* reception practices for "realist" movies and television programs. We may champion Sandra Oh's "bitchiness" as indicating her toughness and independence rather than her acquiescence to "Hello Kitty" stereotypes of Asian women. Based on this knowledge, audiences may read an "angry" Cristina Yang as rejecting such a negative ethnic marker. On the other hand, Cristina Yang can certainly be read as a stereotypically hypercompetitive, tightly controlled Asian. All representations are riven with ambivalence, and audience members will not always read texts in liberatory or subversive ways.

Importantly, these multiple points of identification are only enabled by a realist paradigm that has historically conflated character and performer. Realism is often critiqued for the ways in which it encourages audiences to wallow in emotion rather than activate critical thought: the "authenticity" of the onscreen representation—and the pleasure it produces—invites audiences to identify with and even aspire to conservative ideologies of sex, race, class, and gender. But this trenchant critique elides the ambivalences built into realist as well as other forms of representation. In particular, by identifying character with performer, audiences may interpret films in particularly nationalist ways, substituting their knowledge about the actor for the evidence presented by the narrative. As specifically female embodiments of Canada, McAdams's and Oh's on- and offscreen performances enable a fiction of the nation as determined, honourable, independent, and strong. Rachel McAdams's long-suffering "time traveller's wife" might be understood as embodying the patient strength of Canadian pioneer women rather than capitulating to stereotypes of passive women. Meanwhile, Sandra Oh's "sassy best friends" are like Anne Shirley: feisty, funny, and always getting themselves into awkward situations. As these examples demonstrate, counter readings are not always progressive. At the same time, however, they illustrate how realism consistently invites audience interaction and critical response. The realist paradigm structures the enabling fictions of nation and national identity in both productive and retrogressive ways; by insisting upon the ambivalences produced by actors' personae, we can interrogate how realism generates multiple performances of identity by and for both audiences and actors.

PLAITFORM CONCERNS: TREY ANTHONY'S *'DA KINK IN MY HAIR*

HARVEY YOUNG

Set in Novelette's beauty shop, a West Indian hair salon in Toronto, Trey Anthony's play *'da Kink in my hair: voices of black womyn* is comprised of a series of loosely related scenes in which seven female customers await their turns to be styled by the shop's proprietress. Upon sitting in Letty's (Novelette's) chair, each client is temporarily handed the reins of the dramatic narrative. Centred in both the salon and the play, customers, one by one, disclose a personal secret in monologue form. Their stories, prompted by their call to the chair and, more specifically, the moment that Letty touches their hair, are private acts of disclosure: secrets shared between the two women. Through Letty's touch, one customer remembers her sexual abuse by her stepfather. Another recalls the murder of her son. Yet another shares her frustration at being dumped by her black boyfriend for a white woman. In sharing these fictional stories inspired by real-life events, Anthony gives voice to the concerns of black women and presents them in a forum that ensures that they will be heard (Nestruck).

Canadian playwright Trey Anthony refers to *'da Kink in my hair* as the "little play that could" (qtd. in Crew, "Mirvishes"). Anthony's play premiered in 2001 at the Toronto Fringe Festival and proved a darling to both theatre critics and audiences. Singled out by the *Toronto Sun* as a "pick of the Fringe," *'da Kink in my hair* (hereafter "*the Kink*") was re-presented at Fringe festivals in New York and Atlanta before returning to Toronto and receiving a fully realized production at Theatre Passe Muraille in 2003. Popular among audiences, despite receiving mixed reviews, the expanded production experienced sold-out runs and attracted the attention of Mirvish Productions, a leading producer of large-scale theatrical events in the city. The following year, *the*

Kink was added to Mirvish's 2004–2005 subscription season at the Princess of Wales Theatre, making it the first Canadian play to be staged at the 2000-seat downtown space best known for hosting touring productions of Broadway and Broadway-hopeful shows (Crew, "Mirvishes").[1] Despite mixed critical reviews, *the Kink* attracted a large enough following to extend its run five times—by nearly three months. Following the success of the Mirvish production, the play transferred to London and was recognized by *The Evening Standard* as one of the top five shows running in the city in November 2006 (de Jongh 44). The following year, a television show adapted from the play premiered across Canada. The situation comedy, the first nationally broadcast television show produced by a black Canadian woman, would air for two seasons (DeMara). A decade after the Toronto Fringe Festival production, *the Kink* is widely considered to be one of the most successful plays—if not *the* most successful play—to emerge from the Fringe.

This chapter centres *the Kink* and chronicles the ways in which the play represents the experiences and concerns of black women. It begins with the origins of Anthony's play, spotlighting *the Kink*'s premiere at a local arts café in Toronto and then weaving through its subsequent stagings at the Toronto Fringe Festival and later at the Princess of Wales Theatre. It continues with an emphasis on how the play engages the conventions of realism in order to reveal the everyday abuses experienced by black women. The chapter concludes with an exploration of how the play liberates black Canadian women from a culture of silence that frequently prevents them from publicly revealing their struggles.

ORIGINS

Prior to scripting *the Kink*, Trey Anthony, a moderately successful stand-up comic and struggling actress, paid her bills by working as a counsellor for

---

1   For *the Kink* performances, the balcony of the Princess of Wales theatre was closed, reducing the 2000-seat audience capacity by half (Crew, "Mirvishes" C5).

abused women. Hearing the day-to-day struggles and sufferings of her clients, the aspiring actress was privy to the types of intimate revelations that
are shared not among family or friends (not even in private) but with non-
judging allies with whom the stakes of self-disclosure seem less high. Anthony
listened to tales of sexual assault, physical abuse, and self-hatred based upon
skin colour or bodily shape; to stories of dissatisfaction with life in Toronto;
and to the expressions of immigrants longing to return to the Caribbean. More
than merely being present for their telling, she heard and remembered those
accounts. They became a part of her, an embodied experience of others that
profoundly affected her being and outlook. According to the playwright, the
psychological toll of hearing the stories of abuse motivated her to begin writing monologues, which resembled the ones shared at the shelter, as a form of
therapeutic escape (Nestruck). The monologues, her own fictional creations
based upon the real experiences of the women with whom she interacted,
possessed the power to transform Anthony from a silent receiver of the narrated abuses of others into an active agent in their performative re-creation.
Rather than becoming the target of abuse or a passive witness to its occur-
rence, Anthony, via the monologues, played the role of survivor, author, and
protagonist in control of her own story.

The monologues also provided material for the aspiring actress to perform. A darker complexioned, plus-size black woman, Anthony quickly
realized that her desire to appear in the legitimate theatre was largely as-
pirational. Few plays featuring black characters were being written for, or
produced by, leading Canadian theatres. When those plays made it to the stage
or when colour-conscious casting was employed in productions of other texts
to create a space for black actors, lighter complexioned and/or thinner actresses were usually hired. Relegated to the stand-up and improvisatory circuit,
where the funny, "big" black role can offer sustainable employment, she eventually concluded that her only opportunities to appear on mainstream stages
would come in pieces that she herself wrote. In a 2007 interview, Anthony
recalled her frustration at not being cast as the impetus for her playwriting
career: "Writing started from that place of saying, 'Okay, no one is going to
hire me except if I hire myself'" (DeMara).

The story of how *the Kink* developed from a handful of monologues delivered by a comedienne to "pick of the Fringe" and, later, a multi-million dollar phenomenon varies slightly depending upon the source. The most accepted and widely circulating account, appearing in the preface of the published version of the play, is that Anthony first performed her monologues in February 2001 at an "open mic" night at NOW Lounge, an intimate, ninety-six-seat arts café and performance venue in Toronto (Anthony, "history" v). The capacity crowd's enthusiasm for Anthony's work and, equally importantly, for the staged experiences of black women, prompted producers to invite Anthony for a return engagement the following night. The success of the NOW Lounge shows inspired calls for the solo performer to present her work at the Toronto Fringe Festival. Anthony, seeking to expand her play from a monologue into a one-act play involving multiple actresses, recruited a few friends and alongside them devised additional characters and scenes. In the revision, the basic structure—monologues triggered by an encounter with hair—remained the same. The Toronto Fringe Festival production—buttressed by the positive word of mouth from those who either saw or heard about the NOW Lounge performance or, later, read the positive Fringe reviews—experienced sold-out runs and attracted the interest of theatre producers seeking to include the show in their subscription seasons.

An announcement that appeared in a February 2001 edition of the *Toronto Star*, however, offers a corrective to this frequently told account:

> 'da KINK IN MY HAIR Nikki Morgan hosts this event by and about black women, which features uncensored "hot topic" monologues, drama and spoken word from the intimate lives of black women. Performers include Janice Nixon, T.J. Bryan, Miranda Edwards, Debbie Young and others. Women only tonight 7:30 p.m. (includes uncensored Sista gab & Q&A), everyone welcome Fri. 7:30 p.m. ($10). NOW Lounge, 189 Church St. ("Entertainment")

Surprisingly, Anthony's name does not appear anywhere in relation to the first published mention of *the Kink*. Although the playwright may have performed

all of the monologues in the past, the NOW Lounge event description suggests that she was neither the sole nor the featured performer that evening.
By not crediting Anthony and instead spotlighting the contributions of Janice
Nixon, T.J. Bryan, Miranda Edwards, and Debbie Young (d'bi.young), as well
as asserting that the event was "by and about women," the listing offers the
impression that *the Kink* was a co-authored piece reflective of the everyday,
real experiences of black women. Although the Fringe Festival production
and all subsequent stagings of *the Kink* would list Trey Anthony as the sole
author of the work, it is difficult to divine Anthony's role in this production.[2]

The NOW Lounge announcement also reveals that *the Kink* was not an
impromptu event, an "open mic" starring a single performer. Significant preplanning had occurred. *The Kink* did not "just happen" (Anthony, "history"
v). A company of actresses had been deliberately assembled and, presumably,
rehearsed before the performance. Furthermore, *the Kink* was marketed to a
particular audience, perhaps with an aim of increasing its popular embrace.
The NOW Lounge event was advertised as a special event for women featuring "uncensored Sista gab." In effect, the venue recreated the environment of
a beauty shop, a place where women can freely express their thoughts and experiences, and thus was ideally suited as the place to workshop monologues
for, by, and about Canadian women. The reference to "Sista gab" may have
implied that the event was for, by, and about black women. In addition, it is
conceivable that *the Kink* could have already been accepted into the Toronto
Fringe Festival by the time of the NOW Lounge production. Five months before the festival, the reading gave the company of actresses an opportunity
to workshop their production. The fact that Anthony's production company,
Plaitform Entertainment, had been founded two years earlier suggests that
the playwright had producing ambitions before the NOW Lounge performance

2   The published version of the play gestures toward its multivocal origins. A section
of one monologue, "in honour of belief" (found within Stacey-Anne's monologue), is
attributed to an author other than Anthony. d'bi.young, a dubpoet, appeared in the majority
of *the Kink* productions, including the NOW Lounge workshop, as Stacey-Anne and
performed a poem about surviving childhood sexual abuse within a larger monologue
on the same topic.

and that these ambitions may have involved *the Kink* (Swartz).[3] A plait is a braid or a twist, perhaps a kink, in hair. Plaitform literally sought to give a platform to the kink in the hair.

Despite the fact that the NOW Lounge event was titled *'da Kink in my hair*, Anthony recalls that the character Novelette had yet to be created (Anthony, "history" v). The workshop revealed the necessity of adding a plot device that could bridge the other characters and their respective monologues. Letty was that bridge. Anthony herself performed the comic role of the beauty shop owner, who was named after and inspired by her actual hairstylist. Letty (the character) is funny, loud, brash, and gossipy. In many ways, she is a caricature, as evidenced by the colourful wigs that Anthony would wear in the fully realized productions, but her characterization was balanced with a well-timed delicacy of spirit and sensitivity that makes her a suitable confessor for her customers. Despite outward appearances, she possesses the power to understand her clients profoundly. Through touch, her hand on their hair, Letty gains access to the gendered, cultural, and personal experiences of her customers. The act of laying a hand on hair, which becomes analogous to a religious rite of healing, bridges the stylist and the person being styled. An exchange occurs. The personal problems and crises of her clients, the metaphorical kinks in their lives, are revealed in monologue form.

In the expanded Toronto Fringe Festival production, Anthony continued to play Letty, whose status as the conductor of the dramatic narrative became increasingly important as more monologues, a few songs, and choreographed dance sequences were added to lengthen the show. As *the Kink* grew in size—from workshop reading to Fringe Festival stage to large proscenium theatre, and from one act to two—Anthony and her core cast remained with the production. The playwright's presence as author/performer who occasionally improvised during performances gave the play a spontaneous feel that preserved the Fringe vibe in subsequent productions before more traditional theatre audiences. Despite the fact that the play tripled in length from

---

3   Plaitform is no longer in operation. Trey Anthony's current production company is Trey Anthony Studios ("Home").

the forty minute NOW Lounge reading to the Mirvish production (120 minutes), the narrative's heart remained the same: the stories of black women prompted by the touch of hair.

Although audiences continued to purchase tickets to each longer version of *the Kink*, resulting in consistently sold-out performances for every type of production, the critical response became increasingly negative with each new, expanded version of the play. At the core of these critiques was a concern that a production, originally crafted as a solo performance project and later as a chamber piece consisting of monologues, could not scale up and become a multi-actor, song-and-dance vehicle staged in a cavernous auditorium. Explaining the "severe identity crisis" of the Princess of Wales performances, theatre critic Kamal Al-Solaylee notes that Anthony and her director, Weyni Mengesha, "are only too happy to insert as many African-themed musical numbers as they can between the monologues. In fact Act 1 opens with what looks like leftover sets and sounds from *The Lion King* and ends with a number not unlike something from the ghetto scenes in *Hairspray*" ("Identity"). In addition, Anthony had transformed her play into a comedy: "*'da Kink in My Hair* is now an amusing black comedy that winks at its own blackness to its predominantly white audiences and sells it with some desperation not seen since *The Cosby Show* in the 1980s" (Al-Solaylee, "Identity"). Its commercial ambitions had compromised the perceived intimacy and sincerity of the NOW Lounge and Fringe productions. *The Kink*, the critics argued, had been stretched too thin. Ignoring the play's critics, however, audiences continued to attend the show in droves. Refuting assertions that the play had lost its authenticity were black audiences whose increasing presence at the Princess of Wales led to the play being extended multiple times. Kate Taylor, in a *Globe and Mail* article on the popularity of Anthony's play and the Mirvish extended run, notes: "At first, Mirvish subscribers—those middle-class, middle-aged white people who usually go to the theatre—filled the seats, but then word got out in the Caribbean community. Now, the audiences are more than three-quarters black" ("*'Da Kink's*").

AFFECTIVE REALISM

In a frequently recalled anecdote about the popularity of the 1959 Broadway run of Lorraine Hansberry's *A Raisin in the Sun*, Jamaican Canadian director Lloyd Richards remembers seeing a black woman, possibly a housekeeper, standing in line at the theatre's box office waiting to purchase a ticket to the play (see Young, "Influence"). Approaching the woman, he asked her why she would spend considerably more money to buy a theatre ticket when she could spend a fraction of that amount to see a film featuring Sidney Poitier, the star of the stage play. The woman, according to Richards, responded: "The word is going around in my neighborhood that there is something going on down here that concerns me, and I had to come find out what it was about" (2). A similar "concern," a rare representation of the black experience on stage, similarly attracted *the Kink* audiences and, likely, accounts for the play's tremendous commercial success at all levels. *The Kink* offered audience members an opportunity to encounter the experiences of black Canadian women. It presented a truer, more realistic depiction of black life than could be encountered anywhere else onstage.

Realist theatre seeks to portray the everyday in a manner that triggers recognition and a sense of familiarity. It is less concerned with accuracy or fidelity to an original (such as exact duplication) and more with capturing the feel of a moment in a manner that aligns with your experience or your imagination of how it should be. As a form, it is indebted to late nineteenth-century thinking about naturalism and the influence of developing research in the observational sciences on the arts. Émile Zola, an early advocate for the creation of a naturalistic theatre, acknowledged that a mirroring of everyday life in the literary arts will always appear artificial and, therefore, unreal from particular vantage points: "Any piece of work will only be a corner of nature when viewed through a certain temperament" (111). However, he implored artists not to "be content with this truth and go no further" (111). The challenge he poses to his readers is to continue to strive to develop better ways at representing the everydayness of life. Calling for the scripting and staging of stories of truth, which can be better understood as stories of day-to-day survival, Zola sought to transform the theatre into a looking glass with the power to allow societies to see and hear themselves at a distance, to encounter the everyday sufferings of people, to view the challenges and obstacles that can make subsistence difficult.

The realism of *the Kink*, a play which ultimately would expand to include so many songs and dances that one critic derisively described it as the "The Lion Kink," anchors itself in these confessional or self-revelatory moments when characters offer a glimpse at the pain and suffering that black Canadian women endure (Ouzounian, "*da Kink*"). The articulation of black concerns is noteworthy in light of the fact that they are rarely given voice in either public or private settings. A culture of silence exists within black communities, particularly among women. For "Being Strong: How Black West-Indian Canadian Women Manage Depression and Its Stigma," authors Rita Schreiber, Phyllis Noerager Stern, and Charmaine Wilson interviewed twelve women who "either immigrated or were first-born Canadians from English speaking countries of the West Indies" and concluded that black Canadian women tend to suffer privately and silently (40). Their subjects explained to them that they viewed their hardships as being no different than those experienced by others, who were able to manage their struggles without requiring therapy or other forms of assistance:

> Some women compared their lives with the lives of their mothers and other female friends and relatives, and described the struggles these women faced. When they compared their struggles with those of others, they concluded that a normal expectation in life for all women is to struggle: "Certain things in life you have to accept, you know, that you have to live with—that you can't do anything about it." Thinking that life is a struggle for all women they knew reinforced the need for private suffering. (41)

Suffering and abuse is a "normal expectation" and an everyday condition of black women. As a result, it is rarely spoken about. *The Kink* breaks this silence by airing black women's concerns in a very public setting, the theatre.

Furthermore, it presents them not only to an audience with similar troubles but also to those who may be responsible for causing black women's struggle. A 2001 *Toronto Sun* review of the Fringe production notes the power of these articulated concerns to create discomfort in men. Recalling the play's subtitle, "voices of black womyn," Jim Slotek writes, "Black or white, guys, take my advice. Do not go on a date to a play that has Womyn in the title, unless you have the sensitivity of Alan Alda. There is only one good character described in Da Kink, and he's a high school kid who gets shot by police while reaching for his wallet." The kid, Romey, is the son of Patsy, whose monologue reveals that the abuses suffered by black men also affect black women, black mothers.

In making both black women and their concerns visible on the stage, the play employs what can best be described as a form of affective realism: "To affect rather by sympathy than imitation; to display . . . the effect of things on the mind of the speaker, or of others" (Burke 332).[4] Transporting spectators to a black neighbourhood within Toronto and situating them among black folk who speak frankly about the intersectional experience of being black and female (and, often, an immigrant) living in contemporary Canada, *the Kink* offers a rare opportunity within the mainstream, commercial theatre for an audience to inhabit a non-white cultural environment. It facilitates opportunities either to identify with the characters who dwell there or, at the least, simply to be in their presence. It offers an immediacy of experience by rendering black bodies proximate and featuring monologues expressed directly to the audience.

In spotlighting embodied black experiences, *the Kink* showcases the affective power of an unflinching engagement with blackness. It creates opportunities for members of the black community, particularly black women, to recognize themselves and their pain across the play's multiple monologues.

---

4   The concept of affective realism has been explored within studies of Method acting and psychology similarly emphasizing an appeal to the emotions. Although Burke was comparing the authenticity of the poetic word and the imitated image, specifically painting (since photography had yet to be invented), his words remain the most concise definition of the concept.

It breaks the culture of silence related to black women's struggles by not only sharing it but also mobilizing a community of women both on and off stage to seek redress. This is evident in Stacey-Anne's monologue. A young Jamaican woman who was sexually abused by her Canadian stepfather, Stacey-Anne shares her experience directly with the audience. Her spoken memories gradually shift from being about her own experience to an appeal to audience members who themselves may be survivors of abuse.

> It was your fadda, my step-father, Nicole's bradda, Linda's grandfather, Tamika's teacher at school, the neighbour, the priest, Uncle Henry, Uncle Dan, Marie's cousin, the man without a name. They left you, Fearful, rejected, abused and used. Taken things not given freely but nobody would believe. Dem na believe.

> And if somebody just believed! You could become proud, strong, beautiful, please (*pause*) someone help her right the wrong. Sista, hold up your head, na badda hang it down. Look me in my eye. Erase all doubt, sweep away the shame it wasn't your fault. I said it wasn't your fault. (53)

Stacey-Anne invites audience members, her listeners, to recall their own experiences of sexual assault and the culture of silence that surrounds it. Her words speak to abuse survivors and absolve them of the guilt, shame, and trauma that they may feel as a consequence of these past encounters. Of course, the experience of abuse is not limited to black women, and a range of attendees, male and female, could potentially identify with the stories staged within the play.

The appeal of *the Kink* anchors itself in its ability to offer a glimpse into the lives of a segment of the population whose experiences are frequently overlooked, actively ignored, and rarely heard. In every iteration, the play has been about black Canadian women speaking about their day-to-day reality. In contrast to the popular rhetoric of the idyllic multiculturalism of the city of Toronto or to stories of Canada as a beacon of opportunity circulating among those residing in the Caribbean, the play's monologues reveal a shared sense of frustration and dissatisfaction with contemporary Canadian society. It is the perceived honesty of these stories that gives *the Kink* its power.

EVERYDAY CONCERNS

The amount of scholarship on black Canadians pales in comparison to the volume of critical writings on black Americans. This dearth of research has resulted in either the absenting of black Canadians within scholarly studies or the mapping of black American experiences across the lives of black Canadians under the belief that they are the same. Although similarities certainly exist among black folk on each side of the border, there are significant differences. While slavery haunts the embodied experience of black Canadians—stemming from legal slavery in the country until 1833 and, later, the arrival of black American captives seeking escape and refuge between 1833 and 1865, this history is shared among only a small fraction of Canada's black population. The majority are immigrants who arrived from the West Indies in the second half of the twentieth century. Although the transatlantic slave trade accounts for the presence of black bodies across the Americas, it is not an integral part of the Canadian experience.

The play's setting in a Jamaican Canadian beauty salon accords with the historical settlement patterns of black immigrants arriving from the West Indies. Black Canadian immigrants, like new arrivals to the country of every complexion, typically opted to live in neighbourhoods populated by people who shared their culture and customs. The existence of neighbourhoods filled with residents who possess a similar experience not only provided a sense of familiarity in a foreign environment but also offered a support system that assisted in the adaptation to and navigation of the new national environment. This explains the higher concentration of black bodies within select regions of Canada. Approximately two-thirds of Canada's black population lives in either Toronto or Montreal (Tastsoglou 97). Within these cities, ethnic-specific neighbourhoods readily exist. For example, the 2001 census reveals that approximately 3.5% of Toronto's population (or 88,305 people) were born in

Jamaica (qtd. in Saunders), but within Toronto there are several Jamaican neighbourhoods in which the percentage of Jamaican-born residents exceeds their representation within the city at large: Ward 1 (Etobicoke North) at 12.7%, Ward 42 (Scarborough Rouge) at 9.5%, and Ward 43 (Scarborough East) at 7.5%, among others (Saunders). As can be expected, these and similar neighbourhoods offer goods and services that specifically cater to the needs of immigrants and/or first- and second-generation Canadians originally from Jamaica as well as Grenada, Trinidad and Tobago, and other West Indian nations. A salon like Letty's likely resides within each of them.

The large percentage of black Canadians who were born elsewhere and the existence of communities in which black folk live side by side has helped to create a black Canadian culture which is increasingly comprised of a blending and blurring of black immigrant experiences. Perhaps the best example of this hybridization in the city of Toronto is performed in the annual Caribana Festival (which was renamed in 2011 as the Caribbean Festival Toronto), a "three-week cultural explosion of Caribbean music, cuisine, revelry as well as visual and performing arts" ("About"). The festival attracts approximately one million visitors every year and has proven to be one of the city's largest annual summer events. Despite the wide embrace of the festival, though, it would be a mistake to say that black Canadians have been fully accepted by and integrated within the cities in which they live.

Black Canadians are frequently underemployed. They regularly encounter racism and/or anti-immigrant bias. In short, their day-to-day experiences are often marked by struggle. Caribbean immigrants in Canada, especially women, frequently find that their employment possibilities are limited to domestic work, which not only ensures that they will be underemployed but also places them in situations in which abuse can and does occur unseen by others. Sociologist Evangelia Tastsoglou contends:

> Caribbean women have always been constructed in Canadian immigration legislation as fit only for domestic work, unfit or less desirable for citizenship than other immigrants, less deserving of parenthood and reproductive freedom than other women, promiscuous

and therefore morally questionable, and so forth. Racist, sexist, and class-based stereotypes have become institutionalized into law and have greatly affected the public perceptions and labor force and private experiences of this group of black Canadian women. (100–01)

With limited employment possibilities and facing routine prejudice, black women are typically hired into low-paying positions that make them vulnerable to economic and sexual exploitation.

The Kink gestures toward this grim reality in three powerful monologues. Sherelle, a Yale-trained business executive, appears successful when she first enters Novelette's salon. Well-dressed and constantly on the phone handling work and personal concerns, she appears to possess an enviable job and financial independence. However, reality soon reveals itself to be very different. Sherelle laments the biases and prejudice that exist within the corporate world and the presumed expectations of her white colleagues that black women should clean boardrooms—and not have a seat in them. Every day she works long hours in an effort to prove herself to her skeptical coworkers but finds that their perceptions are not changing. She confides:

> Try walking into a room full of stuffy old white men in outdated suits. You know, the old boys network, and try to explain to them MNAs, derivatives, calls, stocks and bonds—and then comes the looks and the unspoken questions and the polite question, "Where did you study?" Just checking to make sure the Black girl's got a high school diploma. (27–28)

In contrast to Sherelle, Shawnette cleans offices. In her monologue, she recalls how she laboured to support her boyfriend's medical school education. Her efforts were repaid with rejection and abandonment. He left her for another woman, one with "no kink to play with in her hair" (12). The ostensible reason for the breakup was that her job and limited education made it difficult for her to blend within the affluent, educated world of medical doctors. However, Sherelle's negative corporate experience serves as a reminder that even if Shawnette had a different job title and money, her blackness would still serve as an obstacle to her acceptance.

Stacey-Anne most explicitly comments upon the exploitation and vulnerability of black Canadian women, particularly immigrants. Recalling her Jamaican grandmother telling her that her new stepfather, Mr. Brown, "is the best ting which ever happen to dis ya family" and advising her to "do nothing which will make Mr. Brown mad cause him send fi onnu and him can send you right back!" (49), Stacey-Anne elects to remain silent and to suffer the indignities of rape in order to keep her family—her mother and sister—in Canada. While this monologue literally addresses the trauma of sexual assault within the family unit, it also gestures toward a broader array of related abuses that can occur as a result of significant disparities in economic and political capital between immigrants and those upon whom they depend. It hints at the fears and anxieties that domestic workers may have about reporting the inappropriate behaviour of their employers. Furthermore, it reveals Canada to be a less than idyllic place. If Mr. Brown, as George Elliott Clarke argues, exists as "a subcontractor of Canadian economic imperialism and sexual enslavement of black and brown girl and women immigrants by way of roles as domestics, nannies, and low-wage workers," then he serves as an example of how the nation exploits black Canadian women and keeps them in a cycle of dependency in which they must consent to their abuse in order to remain gainfully employed and/or within the country (8).

Black Canadian women are also subject to the everyday discrimination that exists within Canadian society at large. This prejudice stems not only from the belief that a black woman likely is (or should be) a domestic worker or a low-wage retail worker but also from the presence of global (American-influenced) stereotypes and caricatures of black bodies. The character Nia in *the Kink* most explicitly engages with the negative associations given to darker skin complexion (or recognizable blackness) when she talks about colourism, anti-black prejudice *within* the black community, by revealing her mother's active dislike of both the colour black and darker-complexioned people—"Anything too black is never good!" (56). She refers to her mother's reading of blackness as ugly—"bad hair"—and unlovable. On the occasion of her mother's funeral, Nia begins to feel liberated from the weight of anti-black oppression and to express acceptance of and pride in her blackness—her complexion, her hair, her taste in men, and even her clothes. Her gradual awakening serves as a reclamation of both herself and her community. It is not only an announcement of self-respect but also a statement of belief in the beauty and desirability of blackness. The play ends on this more hopeful note, with Nia declaring "I've been wearing black all my life" (57). Her words are repeated by each cast member as she re-enters the stage. *I've been wearing black all my life.*

PHENOMENAL WOMYN

The Kink promotes an understanding of the intersectional experiences of black Canadian women who endure societal racism, sexism, homophobia, ageism, and xenophobia. It breaks silences related to these interlocking oppressions and, in doing so, grants them a visibility rarely seen on the theatrical stage. In its centring of the stories of black women, *the Kink* resembles poet and playwright Ntozake Shange's play *For Colored Girls Who Have Considered Suicide When the Rainbow is Enuf*. A "choreopoem" consisting of poetry and movement, *For Colored Girls* premiered in 1975 and later appeared on Broadway (in 1977). A fixture in regional and university theatres throughout the late 1970s and 1980s, the play spotlights, through a series of monologues, the subjective experiences of seven differently "coloured" women. It triggered a conversation within the theatre community about the distinctive and unique struggles of black women and, alongside the poems of June Jordan and Audre Lorde, contributed to the shaping of a contemporary, post-black arts movement women's literature which would inspire the radical revision (and expansion) of feminist perspectives to include womanist concerns.

The presence of such concerns appears not only in the individual monologues of *the Kink* but also in the play's subtitle, "voices of black womyn." In electing to employ this spelling—which performatively asserts an independence from *men*—Anthony gestures toward the gender politics that inform

her play. It could also be seen as serving as either a welcoming or cautionary
banner—depending upon perspective—alerting audiences to the fact that
the play centres the day-to-day realities of women. The influence of feminist
and womanist concerns can also be seen in Trey Anthony's and d'bi.young's
decisions to change the spelling of their names, employing only lowercase
characters and, in the case of young, abbreviating her name. By the time of
the Mirvish production, Trey Anthony had become trey anthony and Debbie
Young had become d'bi.young. Although Anthony would revert to capital
letters in 2010 after a half-decade spent employing lowercase (d'bi.young
continues to employ this alternative spelling, and now adds anitafrika), each
woman's decision to adjust the way that her name appears in print hints at a
desire to embrace a more quiet (but not passive), inclusive, and more communal sense of identity possibly influenced by feminist and womanist criticism.

  The Kink also bears the influence of Djanet Sears, perhaps the most critically acclaimed black playwright working in Canada. Sears, the celebrated
author of *Harlem Duet* and *Adventures of a Black Girl in Search of God*, con-
templates the lived realities—relationship tensions between men and women
and their intersectional experiences—of black folk in her plays. Inspired by
August Wilson's 1996 call for the creation of black theatres to produce new
work, Sears co-founded the Toronto-based AfriCanadian Playwrights Festival
and Obsidian Theatre to champion the voices of emerging playwrights of
colour across Canada. Both institutions created opportunities for artists to
workshop their plays and to stage stories reflecting the concerns of black
Canadians. Since *the Kink's* production at the Toronto Fringe Festival, Anthony
and Sears have been frequent collaborators. Anthony's play first appeared
in print in an anthology, *Testifyin': Contemporary African Canadian Drama
Volume II,* edited by Sears and published in 2003. Sears wrote the "Foreword"
to the stand-alone 2005 published version of Anthony's play. There, she describes *the Kink* in the following manner:

  For a majority of women in the Black community, the hairdresser is
  the closest thing to a head doctor we ever (voluntarily) encounter.
  She / he will not only twist your dreadlocks . . . but she / he will also

listen, with the attention of a first-rate therapist, to your countless joys, and all of your woes . . . [Anthony] gives voice to the "kink," the coil, the loop, the twist, the flaw, the painful contraction, the frizz, the sharp bend produced when a loop in a line is pulled way too tight, the fit of laughter. (Sears, Foreword iv)

Sears has also assisted Anthony in developing new work by inviting her to present new plays at the AfriCanadian Playwrights Festival. In the "Acknowledgments" section of *the Kink*, Anthony formally thanks Djanet Sears "for being an inspiration and role model." In addition to serving as a mentor for Anthony, it is conceivable that Sears may have blazed the trail that led to *the Kink's* Mirvish production. Her play *Adventures of a Black Girl* was remounted at the Harbourfront Centre in Toronto in a Mirvish production during the 2003–2004 season. The success of that staging and the play's ability to attract black Canadian audiences may have inspired Mirvish producers to stage *the Kink* at the Princess of Wales in the very next season.

The Kink, much like the dramaturgy of Ntozake Shange, Djanet Sears, and numerous feminist authors, exists as part of a tradition of womanist critical writings that seeks to represent the everyday realities of black women. Its innovation within the theatrical landscape is not that it is the first play to portray the intersectional realities of black women but rather that it exists as a rare reminder to audiences of the necessity of encountering, recognizing, seeing, and hearing those realities. The staging of what I have elsewhere called "phenomenal blackness" (Young, *Embodying*) enables an appreciation of the similarities between one's own concerns and those of a larger community of black folk. The affective pull of the voice, prompted by the touch of hair, encourages an engagement with, and reflection upon, embodied black experience.

AFTER THE APPLE: POST-LAPSARIAN REALISM IN *GARDEN//SUBURBIA*—AN AUTOBIOGRAPHICAL SITE-SPECIFIC WORK

JENN STEPHENSON

If the primary intent of realism is to present in art an accurate representation of the world as we perceive it, then a work of autobiographical site-specific drama offers one of the most extreme examples of this style, as the fictional *mise en scène* is constructed from exactly the persons and objects that it seeks to represent. Examples of site-specific autobiographical performance are plentiful in the US and the UK. As a case in point, Deirdre Heddon, in her seminal book *Autobiography and Performance* (2008), devotes an entire chapter ("The Place of Self") to those autobiographical performances where not only does the performer perform as herself, but the locale is likewise co-opted to be both set and setting. To be "located" as an autobiographical performer is to be situated figuratively as a gendered, sexed, and raced subject, but in the case of site-specific work it is also to be embodied in and through specific spaces (Heddon 88). Heddon cites key works of the genre, such as: *Bubbling Tom* (2000) by Mike Pearson, a guided tour of Pearson's childhood home in Lincolnshire; Phil Smith's *The Crab Walks* (2004), which also returns to the locales of his childhood holidays on the beaches of Devon; and Bobby Baker's *Kitchen Show* (1991), which invites the audience right into Baker's own home, where she shares with us her strategies for surviving the travails of domesticity. In Canada, *Garden//Suburbia: Mapping the*

Non-Aristocratic in Lawrence Park, conceived by Melanie Bennett, created by Bennett in collaboration with Hartley Jafine and Aaron Collier, and directed by Andy Houston, constitutes a rare domestic example of the breed.[1] Under the tutelage of our guides "Melanie" (Bennett) and "Hartley" (Jafine), both residents of the area, *Garden//Suburbia* takes the form of a group walking tour of the Toronto enclave of Lawrence Park. Alternating live narration from our guides with pre-recorded audio tracks heard on personal MP3 players, the show provides commentary on community landmarks filtered through Melanie and Hartley's own autobiographical engagement with these sites.

With this example in hand, it is my intent here, first, to describe and assess the strategies employed by *Garden//Suburbia* in the erection of its fully determined realist facade, and then to consider the inherent instability of this facade as its realism acknowledges its own undoing. The ostensible aim of realism as a genre is to create an illusion of the world, an illusion so persuasive as to be absolutely transparent. Transparency, in turn, is a hallmark of knowledge and clear seeing, as it ostensibly shows us the truth of things. As Kirk Williams argues, "If the truth is empirically obvious, and all performative gestures or strategies are doomed to failure, then social or economic re-invention is equally impossible . . . Naturalism as aesthetic strategy is profoundly conservative and deeply antipathetic to change" (97–98). And yet, in the intense correlation of the world itself and its verisimilar representation, realist performance paradoxically sows the seeds of its own failure. By investing so heavily in the facticity of representation—that is, by insisting that set *is* world and character *is* performer—an autobiographical site-specific performance like *Garden//Suburbia* opens up a space to interrogate realism's facticity and ultimately question the relation between the surface representations available to our senses and the "actual truth" of things. Further, by breaking apart

---

1   *Garden//Suburbia: Mapping the Non-Aristocratic in Lawrence Park* premiered in June 2010 as part of Performance Studies international 16. Melanie Bennett and Hartley Jafine were the autobiographical performers and guides. Design of the soundtrack was by Aaron Collier. My thanks to Melanie Bennett for answering my persistent questions about details of the performance and its creation.

the determined fixity of the realistic *mise en scène* and thus prompting us to question our epistemological foundations in the world, *Garden//Suburbia* reinvests in the performative power to change the world as it is (or seems to be). Just as the autobiographical subject is open to imagining new versions of his or her self through performative self-storying—something I will explore at length below—so too the site of that performance can be re-imagined.

As a style of representation designed to communicate impressions about the world to a reader or audience, realism is founded on certain core principles. Emerging out of the ideals of the Enlightenment, the realism of novelists such as Richardson, Defoe, and Dickens is based on an unspoken agreement with the reader that there exists an autonomous, extratextual, actual world to which the work of art refers and corresponds. It is this work of referring and corresponding that constitutes the core of the realist project. As Ian Watt notes, "The novel's realism does not reside in the kind of life it presents, but in the way it presents it" (11). Moving beyond simple praise for successful lifelike representations of the world in realist work, analysis of realism as a style (among other styles) invites consideration of this constitutive process of how signs are deployed to correlate with the reality in the background. It is this double transposition from life itself to some kind of communicative medium and back to something like life again that constitutes the central challenge of realism.

Thinking about how one changes life into something life*like*, Roland Barthes (in his *S/Z*) considers a variety of literary strategies or *codes* whereby, through the arrangement of textual devices, the author can create a convincing illusion, recreating an image of the real world in the mind's eye of the reader. For example, Barthes's code of actions involves taking advantage of the recognition by the reader of common contiguous sequences from everyday life, such as answering the phone or walking to the corner to mail a letter. The shared experience of the world between the real-world reader and the fictional character cements the solidity of the realist illusion; the reader fills in the gaps in the narrative with her own experience. The author fosters this fellow feeling "by stressing at every opportunity the compatible nature of circumstance, by attaching narrated events together with a kind of logical paste" (Barthes, *S/Z* 156). The success of this particular strategy is dependent on the identification of a familiar lived experience across worlds.

Émile Zola, in his essay of first principles "Naturalism on the Stage" (1880), looks to the success of the realist novel for those definitive characteristics that he wishes to bring into the theatre. He calls for the dramaturgical style of realist plays to emulate the novel:

> I am waiting until a dramatic work free from declamations, big words, and grand sentiments has the high morality of truth, teaches the terrible lesson that belongs to all sincere inquiry. I am waiting, finally, until the evolution accomplished in the novel takes place on the stage; until they return . . . to the study of nature, to the anatomy of man, to the painting of life, in an exact reproduction, more original and powerful than any one has so far dared to place upon the boards. (143)

While a novelist in the realist style depends on a bag of literary tricks, like those described by Barthes, for imitating the sensory experience of the real world by careful arrangement of the printed word, the theatrical *metteur en scène* has at his or her disposal the actual material of that real world itself. In support of realist dramaturgy, then, the theatre holds the potential to generate a corresponding realist scenography. Zola himself can barely imagine the full extent of the gap between print and the stage; as he notes with regard to the state of stage scenery, "It is only painted pasteboard, some say; that may be so, but in a novel it is less than painted pasteboard—it is but blackened paper, notwithstanding which the illusion is produced" (152). From blackened paper to painted pasteboard, from painted pasteboard to three-dimensional scenic elements like tables and chairs on the stage, from tables and chairs on the stage to leaving the theatre building entirely and moving out into the world—at each step, the perceptual gap between the fictional world and the actual-world materials of its construction gets smaller and smaller, until in the case of autobiographical site-specific performance it reaches (almost) identity.

It is interesting to note in this context that so many pioneering novelists broke away from dependence on myths, legends, histories, and other well-known tales and instead chose to subordinate their plots to the pattern of autobiographical memoir (Watt 12–14), the genre of autobiography representing a kind of über-code of realist actions, outlining the common sequence of a whole life. Major works in this mode include *Great Expectations* by Charles Dickens, Daniel Defoe's *Moll Flanders* and *Robinson Crusoe*, and Samuel Richardson's *Pamela*. Augmenting the poetic strategies of description used to build up a faithful pictorial realism through the text, autobiography as a genre provides another kind of bridge to the world. By promising an identical connection between the textual representation of the "I" and a real-world author "I" who seems to stand behind the textual voice, autobiography operates as a tactic of Barthes's empiricism, forging extratextual links in support of a reality effect. Moving from text to performance—from the spatial field of the page to that of the stage—autobiographical performance takes that grapheme "I" and replaces it with an embodied subject. In this transubstantiation, the perceptual distance one must travel from representation to the thing represented is almost nil. Using actual-world objects as their own signs in performance seems to elide the material differences between the life-like representation in the work of art and life itself. Barthes recognizes this new "vraisemblance" in its "intention to alter the tripartite nature of the sign so as to make the descriptive notation a pure encounter between the object and its expression" ("The Reality Effect" 16). With the addition of site-specificity—in which the pictorial effect of realist description is replaced by the things themselves—to the already highly realist material of autobiographical performance, works like *Garden//Suburbia* seem to have solved the problem of realist illusion, reaching the apogee of verisimilitude.

And yet there is a critical obstacle to accepting this simple equation. No matter how close the covalent relationship between the world itself and its representation, even if the world stands in for itself, the perceptual frame of theatricality that divides the fictional world from its actual-world counterpart can never be erased or ignored. It is this perceptual frame that, making theatricality possible in the first place, does so by carving out space for the fictional world inside the surrounding, actual world, necessarily separating theatre from life (Féral 97). Anything placed within the theatrical frame is inexorably separated from its original ontological status in world[a] and transposed into a new, lower-order fictional level in world[b].[2] The security of this constitutive border around fictional worlds is troubled, however, by certain sub-genres of performance—autobiographical performance and site-specific theatre, and, in a similar vein but to a lesser extent, documentary theatre and verbatim theatre—where the same, actual objects of life[a] are used inside the frame to present life[b]. The ontological distinction still exists (it must) but it is obscured by these modes of performance.

Part and parcel of this transposition of real objects to verisimilar fictional objects is the introduction of an element of indeterminacy. Roman Ingarden distinguishes the real world from fictional worlds in terms of their relative determinacy/indeterminacy (246–54). As Ingarden explains, the real world is by necessity fully determinate; that is, the objects perceived are sensorily complete—things have colour, texture, mass, location, and so on. Fictional worlds, by contrast, are radically indeterminate. Always riddled with gaps and omissions, fictional worlds exist only partially. No matter how fully one might describe, or paint, or stage a scene, there are always elements missing: details are necessarily omitted, chunks of time skipped over, swathes of the world left blank as we jump from one location to another without detailing the landscape in between. The audience has perceptual access only to what has been rendered determinate. Even for fully ostended objects, like the autobiographical body or site-specific environment in which the set is its own setting, audience perception is still necessarily limited by our singular viewpoints, forcing things in performance to remain only a version of themselves and never exactly the fully determinate "things" we might otherwise know them to be (book, chair, desk). Even in the full phenomenological environment of the site-specific site, our impressions are still sequenced by the work,

---

2   In these terms, world[a] denotes the actual world inhabited by you and me. This is the so-called real world containing the performance as performance. World[b] is a fictional world nested inside world[a]. In the case of autobiographical site-specific performance, although these two worlds—world[a] housing the autobiographical author-subject and world[b] housing her fictional doppelgänger—may appear acutely similar, they are by necessity ontologically distinct.

rendered partial as some aspects are not made available to our experience. In many important ways, despite the acute similarity between them, the autobiographical character (a citizen of world[b]) can never be fully identical to the real-world subject (a citizen of world[a]), nor is the site-specific setting fully identical to the world it represents.

A key feature of nineteenth-century realism is the articulation of a metonymic relationship between what a person is and what her environment is. We can see this pattern in operation in the urban perambulations of Charles Dickens's alter ego, Boz, in his *Sketches by "Boz."* In the story, the stroller extrapolates his observations of inanimate objects or personal details such as clothing to a larger understanding of a person's life—both past hardships and future prospects:

> What he sees at first are things, human artifacts, streets, buildings, vehicles, objects in a pawnbroker's shop, old clothes in Monmouth Street. These objects are signs, present evidence of something absent. Boz sets himself the task of inferring from these things the life that is lived among them. Human beings are at first often seen as things among other things, more signs to decipher, present hints of that part of their lives which is past, future, or hidden. (Miller 125)

Casting himself as a kind of archaeologist of the present, Boz is able to deduce from a person's dress and demeanour his whole way of existence. We see this same pattern at work in *Garden//Suburbia* as we are led on a tour of the houses of Glengowan Road, our narrator conflating the names of the inhabitants with their house numbers:

> #54 is iconic Canadian, like the Roots brand. Quality. Longevity. Comfort. Embodies a distinctive look synonymous with a casual, athletic, hip and outdoor lifestyle. Total nature lovers and own more canoes than cars. . . . #51 is more of a Ralph Lauren type. Sturdy and long lasting. You know. The kind of style that will always be in. (Married. 1 boy. 1 girl. Oh and a golden retriever.) . . . #47 is laid

back casual. Lululemon, you know. Does yoga, eats organic, has gogi berries and almonds handy for a snack. (Their children can do no wrong). (10)

The frequent name-dropping of popular brands (lululemon, Ralph Lauren, Roots) and fashionable cultural trends (gogi berries, yoga, golden retrievers) taps into Barthes's reality effect, using his cultural code to create a web of citation in support of the realist illusion. These are things in the real world that we recognize as accurately mirrored in the realist depiction of the fictional world. But beyond this, these citations provide a shorthand to certain values. What you wear leads to what you eat and how you raise your children. To this view, each person may be defined entirely by his or her material situation—a central tenet of nineteenth-century realism.

This association of inner life with the outer trappings of that life forms the basis of much consumer culture today, which promises me a beautiful life along with my beautiful shirt, or shoes, or paint, or car. It is also a core belief of the classical stage realist project, however, that one's context (economic, cultural, political, educational, etc.) produces modes of behaviour, and thus by showing individuals in specific contexts one can reflect on the social justice of that context. In this way, Enlightenment ideals of individualism become tied to social ideals of equality and freedom from arbitrary rule. As Erich Auerbach writes in praise of Balzac,

> He not only, like Stendhal, places the human beings whose destiny he is seriously relating, in their precisely defined historical and social setting, but also conceives this connection as a necessary one: to him every milieu becomes a moral and physical atmosphere which impregnates the landscape, the dwelling, furniture, implements, clothing, physique, character, surroundings, ideas, activities, and fates of men. (417)

For the nineteenth-century realist, environment and identity become almost synonymous. In *Garden//Suburbia*, Bennett and Jafine parody this equivalence explicitly by replacing the names of the inhabitants of Glengowan Road with their street numbers.

Consistent with the preoccupation of late nineteenth- and early twentieth-century realism with social justice and economic oppression, *Garden// Suburbia* is also interested in the materialist context of a community and how the physical trappings of that community reflect the inner lives of its inhabitants. Like the impoverished London haunts of Boz (Dickens), Lawrence Park is also a kind of ghetto, riddled with class assumptions, albeit an upscale ghetto (it is one of Canada's most affluent neighbourhoods).[3] In *Stroll: Psychogeographic Walking Tours of Toronto*, Shawn Micallef refers to John Barber once calling "North Toronto, the area around Yonge and Lawrence . . . our city's only real ghetto (a rich white one)" (see also Barber). Micallef continues, "I worked up here for a while and met some of the nice ghetto denizens. They shop at the upscale supermarket Pusateri's, send their kids to Upper Canada College and, when giving me a ride to the subway, they would point out fancy homes where important wives had left important husbands. As with so many Toronto neighbourhoods, it functions like a small town, where everyone knows everyone and gossip flows through the streets" (38). Micallef's characterization may be a bit pat, but his too-cute epigram for this neighbourhood registers the clichés that Bennett and Jafine alternately enforce and puncture.

This is where realism rises up against itself. As Laura Levin observes, in the context of the specific site, "[w]e become all too aware of the world's facticity, its stubborn refusal to adhere to the theatrical illusion" (250). The hazards of outdoor performance—barking dogs, sirens, people on bicycles

---

3   The neighbourhood of Lawrence Park is bounded by Lawrence Avenue on the north, Bayview Avenue on the east, Yonge Street on the west, and the Blythwood Ravine to the south. Mount Pleasant Road runs north-south and is the main thoroughfare of the community. According to Barbara Myrvold and Lynda Moon, "The beginnings of Lawrence Park go back to 1907 when Wilfrid Servington Dinnick, the young, English-born president of a Toronto loan and mortgage company, convinced the board of directors to purchase two farm properties near Yonge Street and Lawrence Avenue East. His intention was to create a garden suburb—one of the first in Canada—for the city's middle classes" ("Historical Walking Tour").

who ride through the scene—take on a heightened meaning in the site-specific context. The hyperrealist illusion is persistently interrupted by the material of its own making as these actual elements are overcharged and refuse to be assimilated peacefully into their fictional roles. Thus the "every-day" material that contributes to our impression of reality becomes a kind of excess, escapes perceptual control, and disrupts rather than reinforces the reality-effect of the performance. The material of the realist illusion overflows its bounds, exceeding its fictional role and becoming real again. Williams identifies an anti-theatrical tendency in Naturalism which assumes "that there is an empirically verifiable subject of that discourse, or, to put it more bluntly, that it is possible to see a coherent, autonomous 'self' behind the seductive veils of theatrical dissimulation"; however, "theatre is never more theatrical, more metaphorical, than when it attempts to transcend its own conditions of representation" (Williams 101). This is precisely the bid made by autobiographical site-specific theatre as this genre takes the ideals of realist representation to their logical extreme, immersing the audience in a seemingly fully determinate environment. But by doing so, it stages its own failure. At every turn, as we are led through the planned "garden suburb" of Lawrence Park, we are confronted not with the security of knowledge in transparent representation, but with our uncertainty. Indeed, we know too much, and it is inside that knowledge that our fallen awareness takes root. For there is so much more that we do *not* see, do not hear, and cannot know. Far from being fully fleshed out, every corner illuminated plainly, the show's world is paradoxically one of lacunae, a world of secrets and shadows. And so, after tasting the apple, our epistemological foundation has been irrevocably altered. Like Adam and Eve, we are cast out from our innocent certainty of being able to equate the word with the world. The illusions of realism have become unmoored from their actual-world grounding. Yet, in their new, sadly wise self-referentiality, words have become powerful, able to create new alternate worlds and selves out of their own performative declarations.

Garden//Suburbia embraces these inevitable fluctuations and substitutions to look under the surface of Lawrence Park, question the implicit determinism of realism (in which location = destiny), and suggest alternate versions of this community. The world of Lawrence Park, authored by Bennett and Jafine (and their pseudo-fictional alter egos "Melanie" and "Hartley"), is by necessity distanced from any kind of extra-performative "truth."[4] As in much realist performance that speaks against its own realist strategies, our impressions of the world in *Garden//Suburbia* are communicated on two competing channels. On one channel, the audience receives the strong impression of a faithful pictorial realism, emanating from our 360 degree phenomenological impressions of the site and from the promise of an autobiographical account. On the other channel, the play taps into the inevitable self-referentiality that accrues to hyperrealist representation and undermines that realist illusion. Bennett and Jafine preface their performance by invoking it in the first stage direction as a "process of interpellation" (1), and this is the approach that *Garden// Suburbia* takes to the realist expectations created by its autobiographical site-specific context. By speaking into, speaking around, and speaking against the established discourses of the Lawrence Park community, the characters of "Melanie" and "Hartley" actively undermine any socially deterministic veneer to say to us scoldingly, "don't judge a book by its cover." While seeming to endorse the creation of a verisimilar facade, both characters productively use the material of that creation against itself, unravelling the strategies of realism to create new, alternate realities. Hartley and Melanie take different approaches to this deconstructive reworking: while Melanie digs under the surface, bringing unseen worlds to light, Hartley laminates new facts on top of old, fostering the proliferation of multiple worlds.

---

4   It is important throughout this discussion, as with any treatment of autobiographical work, to keep in mind that "Hartley" and "Melanie" are fictional correlatives of their real-world counterparts. Although they certainly share a physical body and likely share a significant portion of their life experiences, these two distinct ontological personae must not be conflated carelessly. I will use "Bennett" and "Jafine" to refer to the world[a] creators of the work and "Melanie" and "Hartley" to refer to their world[b] characters.

After we are welcomed to Lawrence Park and given our "Lawrence Park Survival Kits,"[5] Hartley's voice on track one of our MP3 players introduces us to the local library:

> The George Herbert Locke Memorial Library. What's to tell? It was built in 1949 in memory of the second chief librarian of Toronto. Nothing exciting. I suppose I could tell you it's the place that once housed a vast archive of photographs, letters, deeds, and maps specific to Lawrence Park. The entire collection was stolen a couple of years ago and it remains a mystery as to who did it. The librarians say the objects were of little monetary value. . . . But to local historians, the missing archive is considered a theft of the crown jewels of memories. (*Garden//Suburbia* 1)

Delivery of this speech as recorded audio, instead of as live direct address by our guides, adds significantly to the tactical repertoire of realism in *Garden// Suburbia*: the mode of delivery stages Hartley's voice as an authoritative and reliable narrator. Past experience with audio guides in art galleries, museums, and on historical walking tours primes us to accept the voice in our ears as a trustworthy repository of factual information. The speech itself, however, is anything but authoritative. Initially the voice is not sure what to tell us beyond the name of the location. It offers one fact and then concludes it was "Nothing exciting." Continuing, Hartley suggests weakly, "I suppose I could

---

5   The "Lawrence Park Survival Kits" consisted of shopping bags blazoned with the names and logos of local upscale shops. They were filled with a water bottle, a field guide featuring "facts" about Lawrence Park, and a map of the route. Also included were two contrasting postcards of 79 Dawlish Avenue: one showed a photograph of the house with a sold sign and the other showed a child's drawing of the house as an idealized place to have Christmas morning. Audience members were invited to choose their own favourite house along the route, write a message on one of the postcards (completing the phrase "This is a nice house to BLANK in"), and leave it in the mailbox. The survival kit also included baggies for collecting souvenirs along the way (pine cones, rocks, etc.), and little Canadian flags to hold during the singing of Alexander Muir's "Maple Leaf Forever" song.

tell you . . ." Finally, after this vacillating opening, our guide tells us how the whole historical archive pertaining to Lawrence Park was stolen. Apart from leaving us wondering whether this report is indeed true or not, the effect of this revelation is to sweep away in a symbolic sense any factual foundations of this community. Uncertainty abounds. Even the identity of the thief is flagged as a mystery.

Hartley then shifts from the history of the community to his own personal history in this place. But instead of offering us one story, he offers us two. His first characterization of his younger self is as a keen student spending hours in the library, cramming his head with Reaganite foreign policy, conjugations of French verbs, and Shakespeare (1). As a result, he wins early acceptance to Yale—the very picture of the successful offspring of professional privilege. Then he confesses that he has been lying to us, rejecting politics as incomprehensible, French verbs as confusing, and Shakespeare as uninteresting. Next, Hartley tells us that the library was his refuge on the day he ran away from home. Not brave enough to do something really rebellious or dangerous, he flees to the library and waits for his dad to come pick him up. Why did he run away that day? The reason offered aligns Hartley with the thief of the archives: "It was because I was accused of stealing from my stepmother. Not money. Or jewelry. Or her car. Or her phone. Or anything else of value. It was facial soap. Fucking facial soap . . . (*Pause.*) Why would I steal it? Why would I even want to steal it? But when I was accused you would've thought I stole the crown jewels" (2). Something is stolen. Something without intrinsic monetary value and yet something considered to be "the crown jewels"—Hartley uses the same phrase to describe the stolen archives and the missing soap. Hartley, in this account, both is and is not a thief. This story sets up Hartley's deconstructive modus operandi: without a repository of documentary evidence (photographs, letters, deeds, maps, or soap) tying present objects to their past, those present objects become unmoored, weightless. Fictions rush in to fill the void, and one story is as good as another.

"Lies" in this context function, then, as a performative remolding of one's self in the world in order to create new self and a new world, and from this new situation to open up other possible scenarios. Auditory

counternarratives evoke alternate possible worlds that coexist with the ones
that we can see. Our senses are divided as our embodied experience inside the "site" is troubled by another competing "world" that takes root
between our ears. As the tour continues, the local sites become less and less
about their own "real-world" history. More and more they revert to painted pasteboard, becoming the scenic backdrops for the performance of self,
a fictionalizing layering or multiplying on top of the original, "real" history. When the tour reaches the entrance to the Alexander Muir Memorial
Garden, the story that Hartley offers seems patently a lie—and yet the "truth"
of the world that our guides have been offering has already been persistently
questioned inside the frame of *Garden//Suburbia*. Indeed, the truth may not
be out there at all. Hartley begins, "Alexander (Ari) Muir was born 1905 to
Rachel and Issac Muirgold. They anglicized their family name to Muir when
they arrived here. His family immigrated to Toronto from Budapest in the
summer of 1919, right after the end of the first world war" (4). A very plausible biography, but Melanie objects: "FACT. The Protestant Alexander Muir
passed away in 1906. FACT. Muir was from Scotland, not Budapest" (4). As
the two competing biographies of Alexander Muir emerge, it becomes increasingly clear that Melanie's seems to be the truth. Her Alexander Muir is the
renowned composer of the anthem "The Maple Leaf Forever." Hartley's biography of Muir soon runs afoul of the realist strategy of non-contradiction—first
Muir is Muirgold, then later Muirstein. This Jewish-Hungarian Muir is also
a two-time winner of Wimbledon in 1926 and 1930—not impossible but increasingly implausible. Finally, Hartley claims Muir as his great-grandfather,
and his interest in the figure becomes clear. By performing an alternate biography for Muir, Hartley bifurcates the world, interpellating uncertainty
and inserting a new (albeit fictional) immigrant history into the dominant
narratives of white, Scottish Lawrence Park. In this way, as the immigrant
Muir overcomes his outsider status to achieve success in the vocabulary this
community understands—athleticism (playing tennis at the local elite club,
winning at Wimbledon) and the arts (first violin, but then as composer of a
prideful national anthem)—Hartley too finds space for himself in this community in which he both is and is not at home.

Whereas Hartley is a native son, raised in BVG and UCC, Melanie is a new arrival who shares his sense of imposture in her identity as a Lawrence Park resident.[6] In contrast to Hartley's strategy of filling gaps and proliferating multiple, alternative worlds where he might find himself reflected, Melanie's strategy is to strip away surfaces to reveal the secrets underneath. It is through these exposures and juxtapositions that Melanie limns an autobiographical account of her journey from pink-collar working-class to her present situation as a socially mobile member of the creative class. At the first landmark on our tour, Melanie responds to Hartley's story of the library, underscoring her difference from Hartley by declaring that she was thirty years old the first time she entered a public library. Like Hartley, she identifies the place as "a refuge" (1, 2), but her library is not this library. In the subsequent episodes of Melanie's autobiographical account, she breaks with the realist correlation of the site-specific environment. For Melanie, a newcomer to the neighbourhood, the places of Lawrence Park act as metonymic substitutes rather than indices to the real; that is, they do not stand in for verisimilar, specific locations from her personal history, but instead act as a stage set for her self-engendering performances.

From the library, Melanie leads us to a sandbox. Building sand structures and tracing lines in the sand, Melanie begins her own life story: "Once upon a time, there was a girl who" (2). Out of this classic opening, Melanie constructs her personal Creation myth. Etching pictograms in the sand, Melanie sketches the story of a conventional but confined woman who works as a secretary to privileged professional men, is happily married, tends to her house and her garden, but yearns for something more: "Sometimes she would feel guilty about daydreaming about silly things like becoming an actor or a teacher or a violinist or a dancer" (2). At the story's climax, the woman collapses in the middle of an elementary schoolyard. The imprisoning house-cubicle-box Melanie has sketched in the sand is obliterated. Then, as Melanie tells

---

6   BVG is Bayview Glen Day Camp. UCC is Upper Canada College. In the play, Hartley never explains what BVG is and so the reference remains impenetrable to those who are not in the know, further reinforcing the division between Lawrence Park insiders and outsiders.

us, the woman "[lay] on the pavement with a throbbing stomachache, [and] gave birth to herself as she stared up at the sky" (2). She returns home and articulates her desire to apply to university.

Breaking with the expectations of site-specificity, this children's playground is not the actual (that is, literal) setting of Melanie's story in the present. It is not doubled: there is no sandbox inside the fictional frame. Rather, using the more typical technique of theatrical transposition, this playground represents another playground elsewhere, many years ago. Outside the fictional frame, the sandbox functions as a blank page or canvas, ready to be inscribed with signs of an incipient world. The wooden frame of the sandbox literally replicates the theatrical frame, containing the world of the story. And, in the generation of her autobiographical self-story, Melanie opens herself to a performative feedback loop: experience lived once by this body is relived again. Melanie jumps into the sandbox, lying down on her back, repeating the same epiphanic gesture the woman in the story experienced in that long-ago elementary school playground, giving· birth to herself again today. The doubling of Melanie as the protagonist of her own story (who is experiencing all this for the first time) with Melanie the narrator, who writes in the sand and enacts that same story (and who has already lived through this scenario) invokes the power of performative self-telling to create a new self. In Bennett herself, we have before us the fruits born of that moment.

The archive of a life, the words of Melanie's autobiography are, in the sandbox section, erased, but the story transcends the etched symbols, re-entering her body through her actions. As Melanie re-performs her self-reinvention, her evolution is documented not in the written word, but in notes that live undercover almost to the point of invisibility. It is autobiography by stealth. "Turn to track 9 as I want to tell you something that I don't want the people here to hear" (12), she says. Then, as the audio track rolls, Melanie begins to stick pink phone-message slips to spectators' clothing. The polite business phrase "while you were out" printed on the message slips is, whispered in our ears, at first secretive, but then gradually evolves to become aggressive and accusatory. These are not just trivial things that happened while you were out, but unseen changes in social class to which Melanie's employers (and the audience) are guilty of being oblivious:

> While you were out, your son's school called and said he wasn't feel-
> ing well. While you were out, Mercedes Midtown called and said
> your car has been serviced and asked if you'd like a courtesy pick-
> up. . . . While you were out, I took a 3-hour lunch to go shopping
> with the $50 gift certificate you gave me for Secretary's Day. . . . While
> you were out, your business colleague sexually harassed me because
> you told him I was into it. While you were out I found Winner's so
> that I can afford the same designer clothing as your wife. . . . While
> you were out, I got an education and now create PowerPoint pre-
> sentations for my own career instead of yours. While you were out,
> I obtained some cultural capital and know more than you do about
> art and literature. (12–13)

Significantly, these insights come to us not by our astute perception, but only because we get "insider" information. Literally "inside" us as Melanie's record-ed voice penetrates our ears, resonating inside our heads, the phrase "while you were out" underscores the fact that we missed these things the first time and are only hearing about them after the fact. They are upheavals that would remain invisible to us otherwise—and usually do. The intense pictorial realism of site-specific autobiography proves to be just a surface: we seem to have it all, but in fact we are almost entirely in unknown and unknowable territory.

This sense of the unknown and unknowable is tied to a dynamic cycle of creative destruction and destructive creation as Melanie and Hartley lead us down the western boundary of Lawrence Park—Yonge Street. Track three features the voices of both Hartley and Melanie as they alternate telling sto-ries of Yonge Street, past and present. Hartley's narrative delivers, at least superficially, the expected historical guide, informing us of the street's cultur-al significance: "Formally known as Highway 11, Yonge Street is the longest street in the world running 1,896 km from Lake Ontario to Lake Simcoe. A conduit connecting two large bodies of water. The site of Canada's first subway line. The artery separating the East from the West" (3). The name "Toronto" is attributed to an Iroquois word meaning "a place where trees stand in water." "Except they don't," as Hartley notes. "At least not here" (3). The place where trees do stand in water is not at the south end of Yonge Street but rather at its north end, "1,886 km north of here" (3). Whether any of this is true or not is beside the point; the lesson that we learn is that there are things we cannot know, that beneath the fiction of the reality effect is more fiction, stories beneath stories.

In counterpoint to Hartley's account of the origins of Yonge Street and of the name "Toronto," Melanie marks the changes along the route, noting what was there, what is there now, and what will be there soon after what is there now is demolished. She apostrophizes each section with a cadence: "Life. Death. Transience." and "Build. Demolish. Transience" (3). Transience is an intriguing word in this context. As audience-strollers, we are transient— that is, we are in motion—but the sites we traverse wouldn't seem to be, or at least perhaps not at first. Through the reiteration of the word "transience" Melanie places emphasis not only on the instability of verifiable "facts" about the environment, but on the ephemerality of the environment itself. Through its performative storytelling, *Garden//Suburbia* makes clear that the site of Lawrence Park, as well as the autobiographical personae of Melanie and Hartley, is reinventing itself literally as we watch.

Site-specific theatre is an act of social geography. It asks the question, "How do we live in space?" It behooves us then to ask with regard to *Garden// Suburbia*: what is the audience's lived experience of the space? How do we understand that phenomenological experience in a metaphorical or thematic sense? With our "Lawrence Park Survival Kit" bags clearly visible, we try to blend in, to be unobtrusive in our strolling. But despite our efforts to pass as locals, our grouping as an audience brands us unquestionably and uncomfortably as strangers. In its depiction of a community and its stories, the play presses on this question of what it means to "belong" to a physical environment. The image of Toronto as the place where trees stand in water is prescient: it allows us to recognize that we are not an audience that circulates through a fixed environment, nor are we citizens circulating in a city whose stories have been established as facts before our arrival. The ground is not stone but water. The environment and the city are places of change and evolution, places that in their new world[b] incarnations are open to reinscription. *Garden//Suburbia*'s exploration of the interrelation of identity and place interrogates our attachments to our physical environments, paving the way for an escape from our own embedded material determinism. Environment is not heredity, as the early realists believed; through autobiographical self-storying it becomes possible not just to change my own story, but that of my self-reflexively fictionalized environment as well.

THE WORKINGS OF THE "REAL": SYSTÈME KANGOUROU'S PERFORMATIVE THEATRE

CATHERINE CYR

TRANSLATED BY JEREMY GREENWAY WITH ELISE KRUIDENIER

In 2005, over a period of several weeks, Finnish artist Laura Vuoma slipped in at night to the houses of people who had given her their keys. By flooding their bedrooms with light, the photographer would snatch them from slumber to capture on film the fleeting, liminal moment that unfolds between sleeping and waking. Entitled *Innocence*, Vuoma's series privileges the quest for truth through the seizure of these suspensive, interstitial moments. Indeed, capturing these brief, fleeting moments—perhaps the sole instance of a self-image not yet controlled, fabricated—Laura Vuoma seeks to show a naked fragility, a truth of being that would fall within the artifice of self-representation, or upon the threshold of its emergence.[1]

A few years earlier, Montreal artist Devora Neumark, asserting a similar desire for the erosion of artifice, engaged in several performative practices that, based on the encounter and the unexpected, posited art's participatory dimension, whether it takes place in a public space, a private space, or an

---

1   Merja Salo notes, "What becomes visible in Laura Vuoma's portraits is a kind of innocence. In the intimate moment of waking up we do not yet pose or pretend. We may not even remember who we are. We are vulnerable prey for the intruding camera, but also safe and secure in our unconscious state" (92).

indefinable in-between. Thus, in a performance entitled *Art of Conversation* (2000), the artist settled—in a space filled with her own furniture set up like her living room—on a street corner near Montreal's Frontenac metro station. At her bidding, passersby would sit next to her on the couch, answering her questions and asking their own; bit by bit they would pass on little life stories, approaching the borders of autofiction. As the days passed, some of the spectators—or "spect-actors"[2]—came back, sometimes bringing their own personal items (trinkets, paintings) that they incorporated into the space; even if, at the end of the day, the set-up was dismantled, the artist placing her work always in the realm of the ephemeral, of the evanescent encounter, or in the realm Yves Michaud designates—ironically—as "oeuvres d'art à l'état gazeux" ("artwork in the gaseous state"). Similarly, in *One Stitch at a Time* (2001), while participants in Neumark's performance told her stories, she would knit them little objects: the emphasis was not on the woolly and colourful materiality of the created work, nor on what it sought to represent, but rather on its participatory dimension, the transient moment during which an encounter between performer and spectator is considered to be authentic.[3]

THE "REAL" AS EVIDENCE FOR THE "TRUTH"

In the manner of Vuoma and Neumark, many practitioners of the visual arts assert a quest for authenticity that attempts, in part, to avoid representation. This is not a new development. In the sixties and seventies, performance art was already contrasting representation with the supposed "pure presence" of the

---

2   "Spect-actor" is a slightly hackneyed neologism, referring to any spectator who takes an active role in guiding the work. The spect-actor may recall the happenings and participatory utopias from the sixties and seventies, and may also be found in the derivatives of Forum theatre developed by Augusto Boal in his "Theatre of the Oppressed." When the spectator (called a non-actor) participates in these practices, however, the aim is emancipating or social, which isn't necessarily the case with contemporary practices.

3   For an overview of Neumark's unique work and process, see www.devoraneumark.com.

artist, who, often through the body, presented his work and a series of actions free of any mimesis,[4] that is, outside of any imitative dimension (or intention). Consider, for example, the work of Gina Pane or Marina Abramović, who voluntarily endangered or harmed their bodies, the work's main "flesh." And yet, since that time, the illusion of "pure presence" has crumbled. In their sociological and anthropological studies of the body, Mike Featherstone et al. and David Le Breton, among others, have clearly demonstrated how social beings are in a constant state of representation and how, in itself, the body is a medium, a screen-like surface onto which its identity constructions are projected: nomadic constructions, impermanent, always fabricated. Furthermore, while representation has been traditionally based on mimesis, or resemblance, the latter Aristotelian view has now been shaken. Thomas Patin and Jennifer McLerran argue that representation no longer means imitation, but evocation. As the authors write:

> Recently . . . our understanding of representation has been challenged by poststructuralist theory. As a result, representation can indicate any usage of material that has the ability to refer to something else, actual or imagined, visible or invisible. . . . All [these forms] are seen to have the potential to represent in some way, if not strictly mimetically. (113)

Thus displaced in the field of referentiality and evocation, representation seems no longer to be transgressible. However, still seeking to surpass or circumvent its borders (even as they are weakened or dissolved), many artists counter the artificiality of this evocative representation with the quest for a moment of "truth," or a string of these moments, snatched away, piercing holes in the

---

4   In visual arts, the term mimesis traditionally designates the figurative representation of the real world. In the theatre, in the Aristotelian tradition, it is rather "the representation of men, and particularly their actions." Therefore, it is at once "the imitation of a thing, and the observation of narrative logic" (Pavis 207). As will be examined later on, these are two meanings that are undermined in performative theatre, which is positioned at the meeting point between the visual arts and theatre.

fabric of representation. When staged skilfully, these moments of "truth" are often tied to the emergence of the unexpected, to the development of the small "music of chance."[5] They also reveal what Nicolas Bourriaud calls the "esthétique relationnelle" ("relational aesthetic"): an encounter, created however furtively, between the artist and the spectator, or the subject-participant, of the work.

In present-day theatre, one can observe a recent percolation of this search for truth and the (relational) encounter among numerous directors and companies. One company that comes to mind is Vancouver's Theatre Replacement and its plays *Box Theatre* (2006) and BIOBOXES (2009). These plays—short, one-actor shows for one spectator—are set in confined spaces reminiscent of "curiosity cabinets"; the theatre of intimacy (the material, at least in BIOBOXES, was drawn from true stories) is cinched to the experience of the one-on-one between actor and spectator, the latter being invited to participate in the unfolding action. In Europe today, there is a similar predilection for participationism and the shattering of mimetic illusion, particularly with Philippe Quesne (France) and Roger Bernat (Spain). The former, of Vivarium Studio, focuses on the development of a "laboratory-theatre" which intertwines reality and artifice, superimposes degrees of presence, and places back into question the principles of representation. His play *L'Effet de Serge* ("Serge's Effect"), presented on a conventional (proscenium) stage with a predetermined dramatic text, interposed morsels of what we might call "the real": spectators were invited to integrate with the characters' space and to comment on his actions, a delivery man appeared with a pizza to share, a dog frolicked in the background.[6] For his part, Roger Bernat revives the idea of an enlivened public space in works such as *Domaine public*, in which the participants constructed choreography by obeying instructions from a headset; the result was a provisional community born of a series of encounters among strangers.

---

5   This expression was borrowed from the title of a Paul Auster novel (1990).

6   Using animals on stage always shakes up the effects of the representation. They (paradoxically) have two effects on the performance, taking it toward hyper-naturalism and shattering it at the same time, exposing its artifice. For more on this subject, see Jacques, "Animaux."

These directors and companies, like all theatrical artists who swim in these same waters, practise a type of theatre referred to, or qualified as, performative—a scenic form affixed to the larger constellation of post-dramatic theatre. Hans-Thies Lehmann considers the latter to be "a theatre that is required to operate beyond drama, at a time 'after' the validity of the dramatic paradigm of theatre" (35). This does not mean that the text is expelled from theatrical forms under this new paradigm, only that it will no longer dominate them. Likewise, that which traditionally arises from the dramatic—in other words, mimetic illusion and its constituents, story and character—finds itself, within these forms, shaken. Post-dramatic forms are often quite similar to performance art, and for Lehmann they inhabit a different realm than that of the dramatic model; they are based on the production of other defining "signs," whether or not these signs are imbued with agency. These signs include parataxis (elimination of hierarchy between elements of representation—text, play, set design), simultaneity of onstage actions, exacerbated corporeality, and irruption of the real, among others. This latter "sign" can be problematic. Indeed, some, like Amelia Jones, are careful not to refer to the "real," as the various meanings of the word are at once fluctuating, vast, and limiting. For Jones, "there is no such thing as 'the real'" (20), but rather different experiences of reality separated by the blurred boundaries on which many artists are pleased to play. So she willingly swaps the "real" for the "not-fake": "By not-fake, then, I do not mean to suggest a definitively determinable category. . . . Rather, I want to point to a kind of . . . art gesture that pushes in the direction of what may seem to be not-fake (by posing itself as 'authentic')" (20). Moreover, the not-fake does not cover, in the case of post-dramatic theatre, all manifestations of "authentic" elements in the representation: accidents, or the recourse of randomness during the course of half-composed, half-improvised scenes, exceed such a framework. Also, it is tenable to consider the not-fake as a particular form of irruption of the "real," which, in post-dramatic theatre, can manifest in many ways, even if it only gives the illusion of such manifestation.

The irruption of the "real" can be found at the heart of performative theatre. Located in what Lehmann designates as "the field between" theatre and performance art, performative theatre, through a refusal of the realistic illusion, and by privileging a breach of the story or an erosion of character—and sometimes by reviving the mirage of "pure presence" from its ashes—develops the theatrical experiences that lend their quest for "truth" to performative practices. In Québec, the emerging troupe Système Kangourou has developed a performative theatre that relies on the immanent presence of actor-performers who are no longer tied to a role; rather, they "personify" themselves while engaging the spectator to the work in progress by filling the space with a series of actions, often determined randomly. From *Au détour de mai, en plein coeur des ambivalences* (2006) to *Mobycool* (2010), through *C'est comme un photomaton . . . mais en mieux* (2006), *40% de déséquilibre* (2007), and *Bricolages pour femme et ours polaire* (2008), the company, led by directors Anne-Marie Guilmaine and Claudine Robillard, has developed a hybrid stage language over time by weaving borrowings from performance art—in which "le plus radical . . . consiste en un refus: celui d'une réalité référentielle imaginaire" ("the most radical . . . consists of a refusal: that of an imaginary referential reality") (Guilmaine 8)—into a decidedly theatrical fabric.

As part of this discussion, I will probe the works *Bricolages pour femme et ours polaire* and *40% de déséquilibre* in particular. The first is a work that director Anne-Marie Guilmaine designates as a "solo déambulatoire de théâtre performatif" ("solo perambulatory performance of performative theatre"). Like the abundant itinerant works of today,[7] it recalls the *stationendrama* of German expressionists—artists who, in their time, "responded" to theatrical realism through scenic forms that fancied themselves more "real" than it. The second play presents itself as a series of tableaux in which, in a succession of actions, the actor-performers explore the jamming of identities as well as the taking of risks. Both works, like those in contemporary art based on relational

---

7   For several years, artists have been staging theatrical *parcours*, in which the spectator passes through the space from one "station" to the other. Examples include *L'Ardent désir des fleurs de cacao*, written and directed by Dominique Leduc (Momentum, 2006), or, more recently, the "initiatory path" of *La porte du non-retour*, developed by Philippe Ducros (Maison de la culture Frontenac, 2011).

aesthetics, focus on the experience of the encounter with the spectator. I will address here some of the modalities of the disappearance of mimesis in favour of bursts of fragmented "truths" in these two works—"truths" pertaining to the dissolution of character and play ("jeu"), to the irruption of the "real" and chance, and to integration and the apprenticeship of the spectator in the "body of work." Ultimately, I will also bring to light certain paradoxes, or zones of indecisiveness, that arise under an aesthetic approach of this nature.

THE ACTOR-PERFORMER, OR THE EROSION OF THE CHARACTER AND PLAY ("JEU")

Presented in 2008 at the Bain St-Michel in Montreal, *Bricolages pour femme et ours polaire*, directed by Anne-Marie Guilmaine, split off into a litany of little tableaux scattered in all corners of the old bathhouse. Tracing a theatrical pathway that explored the imagination of memory and childhood, the show invited the spectator to follow the footsteps of Marie-Ève Dubé, lone actress embarking on this remarkable route. Apparently stripped of the shackles of character, refusing mimetic play in favour of actions and encounters with the Other, the actress progressively wove a complicit connection with the spectator: "Qu'il s'agisse d'un échange de confidences saugrenues entre les murs d'un cabinet de toilettes . . . en compagnie d'un spectateur évoquant ses désarrois amoureux, d'une danse partagée ou d'un chaotique toast d'anniversaire, le 'déambulatoire' se décline, ainsi, en un chapelet de petits moments où se nouent des connivences passagères" ("Whether it is an exchange of outlandish secrets between the walls of a bathroom stall . . . with a spectator evoking his romantic distresses, of a shared dance or a chaotic birthday toast, the 'itinerant' declines, consequently, in small moments tied together by a string of transitory collusions") (Cyr, "Solo" 136). The dissolution of the theatrical character lies at the heart of these collusions, seeming to arise as a condition of their emergence—an essential erosion, according to the creators of the show, for the outgrowth of the "real," or a fragment of the "real," in the theatrical operative. "En jouant autrement," they seek "une qualité de présence,

un haut degré de vivant, un échantillon de réel coupé-collé" ("By acting differently," they seek "a quality of presence, a higher degree of living, a sample
of the cut-and-pasted real") (Guilmaine and Robillard 135).

Of course, the undermining of theatrical character is not unique to
Système Kangourou nor to performative theatre more broadly. In recurring
fashion, since the beginning of the modern period, diverse theatrical practices
have sought to abolish the character, or to place it in crisis, contributing to its
erasure or its embrittlement. I am thinking, for example, of different choral
forms, explored in particular by Maeterlinck from the end of the nineteenth
century onward; these forms abound today in dramatic art as well as on the
theatrical stage. Indeed, in choral arrangement, what Christophe Triau calls
a veritable "effet fantôme de choeur" (a "ghostly choral effect") occurs when
speech is spread among evanescent characters, who appear as "subjectivités
parlantes" ("speaking subjectivities") (Dupré 88), as enunciated instances
with blurred, shifting contours—what Jean-Pierre Sarrazac neatly terms in
French "impersonnages"[8] ("non-characters") or, similarly, what Julie Sermon
calls "énonciateurs incertains" ("uncertain speakers").

Yet, while choral forms, in their erosion of character, tend to separate representation from the "real," creating a more or less pronounced
estrangement, performative theatre uses the character's disappearance as

---

8   "L'impersonnage," writes Sarrazac, "se présente à nous comme le lieu de passage et de
métamorphose de tous les visages, de tous les masques ('nus') qui font la vie d'un homme
[sic]. Cet impersonnage est, au sens musilien, 'sans qualités.' Ce qui signifie paradoxale-
ment qu'il est pourvu de mille qualités mais d'aucune unité ni substance identitaire. Que,
dès lors, il paraît voué à ce nomadisme et à ce caméléonisme—changer de place en place
d'identité—qui l'oblige à jouer tous les rôles, ce qui lui permet de ne se dérober à aucun"
(48). ("The 'uncharacter,'" writes Sarrazac, "presents himself to us as the passage and meta-
morphosis of all faces, of all ['bare'] masks that make up a man's life. This uncharacter
is, in the musilian sense, 'without qualities.' This paradoxically means that he has a thousand qualities, but no unity or identifying substance. From there, he seems destined to be
a nomad and a chameleon—changing place and identity—which obliges him to play all
roles, allows him not to reveal himself to anyone"). Translator's note: the expression "impersonnage" is a play on "impersonnel" (impersonal) and "personnage" (character); it can
be rendered as "uncharacter" in English.

the essential ingredient for the inscription of a *surplus* of "reality" in the show. In *Bricolages pour femme et ours polaire*, as I said above, a relational dynamic is established between the spectator and the actor, who is relieved of the weight of the character. Is this to say, however, that the "pure pres- ence" of the young woman is asserted, that she bares herself, unadorned and without artifice, without the recourse of play, of the invented, of the slip- page or the swelling of Self-representation? Are we fully in the territory of the not-fake, as described above? From tableau to tableau, while the specta- tors took part in the actions concocted for them by Dubé (dancing, singing, answering more or less preposterous or intrusive questions, dialoguing, cut- ting up patterns of paper), this impression collapsed convulsively. Thus, the sequence of meticulously choreographed movements, the sequence of a vo- cal effect, an intended glance, a pregnant pause, all pierced—or appeared to pierce—the artifice of play, to add a degree to it, to one-up it. The solo performative body appeared to unfold in a blurred territory, in a space of indecisiveness where different degrees of representation cohabited courte- sy of the being and the doing of the actress.

This was a desired cohabitation. For the director, it allowed for more than merely the exploration of intimacy in favour of a weaving of the indi- vidual and the collective. She writes:

> Jouer autrement, c'est s'exposer sur scène en tant que soi-même, sans l'apparat d'un personnage. Mais encore là, c'est un soi "déca- lé." Les contours de la personnalité réelle de l'acteur sont brouillés, le vrai et le faux, floués, de manière à composer une "personnali- té scénique" qui ait du chien. Oui, parce que derrière cette idée de se jouer soi-même se cache non pas le désir de s'exhiber gratuite- ment, mais celui de mettre à jour une réalité plus grande que soi. Les morceaux intimes que nous cherchons à mettre en scène sont choisis selon leur capacité à parler du collectif, à témoigner du réel . . . L'acteur . . . ne se révèle que dans la mesure où son expérien- ce peut rejoindre celle des autres. (Guilmaine and Robillard 137)

(Playing differently is to expose oneself on stage as one is, without the
trappings of a character. But even so, this is a self that is "displaced."
The contours of the actor's real personality are scrambled, the true
and the false fiddled with, so as to constitute a "stage personality"
that has some zest. Yes, because playing oneself is not a desire for
gratuitous self-exhibition, but rather a desire to bring to light a reality that is larger than oneself. The intimate pieces that we seek to
stage are chosen based on their ability to speak of the collective, to
witness the real . . . The actor . . . reveals himself only to the extent
that his experience can reach the experiences of others.)

Moreover, sometimes an ambiguity hovers around these "morceaux intimes" ("intimate parts") that appear in each Système Kangourou piece. In *40%
de déséquilibre*, staged in the spring of 2007 in the La Chapelle theatre with a
rough, construction-site backdrop—cement blocks, gravel, ropes, ladder—the
five actor-performers (professionals and non-professionals mixed indiscrim-
inately) confided in the audience a series of desires and fears. Retaining the
main markers of their identities (first name, personality traits, gestures),
speaking directly to spectators rather than sidekicks, they disclosed their
appetite for risk-taking, their need to put themselves in danger to feel alive,
or their fear of solitude. In another scene, playing (or not playing) lovers,
Claudine Robillard and Xavier Malo, in the manner of two "Petit Poucets,"
marked long paths of pebbles leading them toward each other; throughout
their journey, they also confided in each other, this time about their past
loves, from childhood to present. Which of these confidences were not-fake?
Which were invented, or belonged to another player? Which combined the
"real" and the imaginary in a finely woven fabric, impossible to untangle?
Hard to know. In performative theatre, the actor-performer, and with him
his identity and his tales, is firmly inscribed in the paradox of one who "joue
à être vrai" ("plays it real").[9] Anne-Marie Guilmaine conveys this paradoxical

---

9   This is quite a different "paradox of acting" than the one theorized by Diderot in the
eighteenth century. Diderot posited that the convincing actor is one who can express an

dimension by stating that this is "un jeu sur l'identité de l'acteur-performeur: il se joue lui-même, c'est-à-dire qu'il joue les différents morceaux qui le composent, ou même ceux qui ne le composent pas, passant subrepticement du réel à la fiction, mais en s'exposant toujours en tant que lui-même" ("a play on the identity of the actor-performer: he plays himself, that is to say that he plays his different constitutive parts, or even the parts that do not constitute him, passing surreptitiously from the 'real' to fiction, but always exposing himself as himself") (28). The director continues:

> Il revient ainsi aux spectateurs de tenter le jeu du discernement entre le vrai et le faux dans ce qui est dit, ou bien entre le dramatique fictionnel et le performatif autoreprésentationnel. En exposant autant de points de vue sur ce qu'est ou peut être l'acteur-performeur, il s'agit ici de mettre en scène une "multiplicité de coexistences virtuelles," comme le dit Gilles Deleuze. (qtd. in Batt 81)

> (It falls to spectators to play the discerning game between the true and the false of what is said, or between the fictional drama and the auto-representational performative. By exposing so many versions of what is or what could be the actor-performer, a "multiplicity of virtual coexistences" is staged, in the words of Gilles Deleuze.)

In addition to the actor-performer's ambiguous playing, which presses upon and eventually cracks open the idea of "character" in this piece, mimetic illusion is similarly undermined in the work of Système Kangourou: representation succumbs to the emergence of chance and explosions of the real, and the self and the spectator are put to the test.

---

emotion that he does not feel.

IRRUPTION OF CHANCE, FRAGMENTS
OF "THE REAL"

Traditionally, says Lehmann, "l'idée . . . du théâtre part du principe d'un cosmos fictif clos" ("the idea . . . of theatre assumes a closed fictive cosmos") (157).
And yet, in many post-dramatic theatrical forms this assumption is doubly
shaken: first, the "fictive cosmos" is, in many ways, traversed by non-fictive
elements, or all form of fiction is apparently removed in favour of reality (the
real "situation" is substituted for the dramatic fable). Then, the "barrier" of the
work is often deconstructed by the contributions of the spectators who are
invited to take part in the action, and the border separating the actors from
the spectators dissolves in the creation of a shared space, establishing an essentially relational theatrical dynamic. Each time, the goal is not to renounce
all theatricality, nor to eradicate mimetic illusion and its artificial charge entirely, but rather to play with the limits, the interstices, the zones in-between.
Moving along the fine "ligne qui marque la frontière entre la représentation et
la situation" ("line that demarcates the boundary between representation and
situation") (Guilmaine 201), the post-dramatic stage likes to bring forth the
not-fake in theatrical pretence just as it appears out of the "composé" ("composite") or the "bricolé" ("tinkered") in the fragments of reality it depicts
(201). An experience of ambivalence and uncertainty, post-dramatic theatre—
especially in its performative form—stands as a permanent oscillation, "un
chavirement continu . . . d'une contiguïté 'réelle' (connexion avec la réalité)
et d'une construction 'mise en scène'" ("a continuous capsizing . . . of a 'real'
contiguity [connection with reality] and a 'staged' construction") (Lehmann
162). In the works of Système Kangourou, this coexistence "de moments pré-
définis et d'instants spontanés" ("of predefined moments and spontaneous
instances") (199), which blur the boundaries between fake and not-fake, is
manifested and actualized in particular in the irruption of chance and the
integration of fragments of the "real" (which are never the same) into the
fabric of representation.

    In the first tableau of the performance of *Bricolages pour femme et ours
polaire*, which takes place in the cloakroom of the Bain St-Michel, Marie-Ève

Dubé puts on some of the spectators' coats that had been hung on hangers, and she empties the contents of their pockets. The objects that are removed—keys, crumpled papers, photographs, ticket stubs—are not accessories made for the performance with a predetermined symbolic meaning: they come straight from the "real"; they belong to the lived world, the intimate territory of the spectators.

The sudden appearance in the show of these bits and pieces from the everyday, outside world are like little bursts of reality. Indeed, although, as noted above, the actress is not playing a role, she displays a certain level of artifice or "amplification" during different moments on the perambulatory path. This appearance of artifice is tempered by the spectators' personal objects, which are taken from their universe, from their candid histories, and projected into space. However, the "real" to which these objects are attached will be quickly replaced, drawn toward the space of the imaginary and the artificial. Indeed, having chosen at random an eclectic assortment of objects, the actress then begins to invent their histories, improvising a micro-narrative for each one. Then, by intersecting these stories, she teases out, bit by bit, a portrait—fictive, of course—of the coat's owner—cinema buff, traveller, jilted lover, distracted and clumsy student, and so on. Becoming, in spite of himself, the protagonist of the story, the spectator is then gradually integrated into the show while the actress asks him questions, invites him to talk about himself, and, like Devora Neumark "knitting" the speech of the other, she weaves into the presentation the self-narrative that he wants to tell. As the spectator espouses multiple identity constructions, he becomes, in a noteworthy reversal, that which the actress is trying not to embody: a character.

At the discretion of objects drawn at random, and at the discretion of this intertwining of tiny fables and self-narratives (which also contain, no doubt, their share of invention or embellishment, like any autofiction),[10] the show unfolds in an ambiguous area, in a space of indeterminacy where borders between true and false, between the not-fake and the fake, fray. Provided

10   On the subject of autofiction and what kind of "fiction" it contains, see L. Leroux, *Le Québec*, and Jacques, "La tentation autobiographique."

that complicity develops between the actress and the spectator, the element of truth would reside here, at least according to the director, in the exchange secured between them, at the heart of relational dynamics—dynamics in which, notably, the unexpected is essential, is necessary for the establishment of temporary intimacies. In fact, chance is one of the main ingredients in Système Kangourou's method. In an article entitled "Trouver un confetti dans une craque de trottoir et le garder dans sa poche, pour toujours," which is a text written as a dialogue between Claudine Robillard and Anne-Marie Guilmaine, the latter affirms:

> J'aime laisser entrer le hasard sur la scène. Je lui réserve des encla-ves, comme on creuse volontairement un trou dans un terrain bien aménagé. Le hasard prend la forme d'une structure aléatoire, mais surtout d'un appel aux spectateurs. Tu [Claudine Robillard] leur as demandé de te prendre dans leurs bras ou de sortir faire le tour du bloc avec toi . . . Au cœur de ces trous-là, je ne contrôle plus rien comme metteure en scène, tout peut arriver ou presque. Du beau, du drôle, du terriblement ennuyant aussi. Dans la régie, j'ai toujours peur, mais c'est le jeu. (Guilmaine and Robillard 136).

> (I like to let chance onto the stage. I save a place for it, just like when you dig a hole in the middle of a nicely kept plot of land. Chance has an erratic pattern, but also an appeal to the audience. You [Claudine Robillard] have asked them to take you into their arms or to take a walk around the block with you[11] . . . in the core of those holes, I do not control anything as a director, almost anything can happen. The beautiful, the funny, the incredibly boring, too. When I am back-stage, I am always afraid, but that is the game.)

---

11   *40% de déséquilibre* (2007). All parts of Système Kangourou are random, to a greater or lesser extent.

According to the director, "il y a, dans cet aléatoire du contact avec le spectateur, une honnêteté, une part de vérité qu'on ne trouve pas ailleurs" ("In this random contact with the spectator, there is an honesty, an element of truth that is not found elsewhere") (Cyr, "Solo" 136). In *Bricolages pour femme et ours polaire*, this element of truth, whether skimmed or saturated to varying degrees by highly fictional details, is quite an interesting paradox. For Système Kangourou, truth is always woven from fiction and it is for the spectator to untangle the web—or not. Indeed, for the director, "[q]ue le spectateur devine si tel ou tel moment est réellement inventé ou non a peu d'importance. C'est précisément ce doute qui est recherché" ("It is of little importance whether the spectator guesses that any one moment is actually invented or not. This doubt is precisely what is sought") (Guilmaine 45).

SELF AND SPECTATOR PUT TO THE TEST

In Système Kangourou's approach, the appearance of chance and explosions of the "real" are also linked to the notion of risk-taking. Since the 1960s, risk-taking has been at the heart of performance art, as it often employs the body as an object of genuine self-endangerment. In certain cases, this endangerment has relied on audience participation: in one of her performances, Marina Abramović asked her spectators to do what they wanted with her, even to hold a loaded gun to her temple; in another performance, Yoko Ono offered up a large pair of scissors so that participants could cut up her clothes, exposing herself to the sharp blades that, bit by bit, laid bare her flesh. Though perhaps less perilous, the risk-takings that pepper each Système Kangourou production follow similar performative practices and, likewise, are most often tied to audience participation. In *40% de déséquilibre*, for example, after a series of tableaux that waver ambiguously between "composé et imprévisible" ("composed and unpredictable") (Guilmaine 45), the action stops abruptly and the five actor-performers invite the spectators to participate in a reinvented version of the ever-popular Truth or Dare? In a shared space and time, with the border between scene and room shattered, the spectators can ask the actors indiscreet questions or instruct them to perform any dare they can devise. Most often in performance, the spectators chose the dare and this is, for the actor-performer, a challenge, a test of the self—generally physical: jumping, spinning around, running full speed toward a brick wall, letting oneself fall from dizzying heights, hanging oneself by the feet from the rungs of a tall ladder, and so on. In each of these moments, when the bodies of the actor-performers were invested in diversely dangerous equities, mimetic illusion, or its ensuing ambiguity, seemed to disappear in favour of the "real" situation. The requests from the audience were impossible to predict, and thus instilled chance and randomness into the performance. The actor-performers' risk-taking appeared to eradicate, for a moment, any mimetic illusion: they did not "act" like they put their bodies in danger, but rather they threw themselves into the prescribed action (of course, they also had the opportunity to refuse if it appeared too perilous or if it exceeded their physical limitations). The audience's intervention and the corporeal response of the actor-performers helped "ménager une place à la réalité" ("to make room for reality") (Guilmaine 4) at the heart of theatrical set-up, which, further, cultivated ambiguity between the "real" and the effect of the "real." As the director explains:

> Paradoxalement, l'une des quêtes du performatif est justement d'obtenir un effet de réel et une qualité de présence si forts dans l'exécution d'une action qu'ils relèguent au second plan le caractère composite composé/imprévisible au profit d'une énergie brute, intense, souvent risquée ou dangereuse, transcendant "l'arrangement." Par une composition si précise que surgit le naturel ou par un *effet* de spontanéité qui tend à préserver le naturel, le but poursuivi est le même: une présence au plus près du vivant, d'une intensité brute, violente, qui rend les corps prêts à réagir. (Guilmaine 45)

> (Paradoxically, one of the quests of the performative is precisely to obtain an effect of the "real" and a quality of presence so strong in the execution of an action that they relegate the composed/unpredictable composite character to the background in favour of a raw,

intense, and often risky energy that transcends the "arrangement." Whether a composition is so precise that the natural emerges, or it uses an *effect* of spontaneity that tends to preserve the natural, the goal is the same: a presence as close as possible to living—a rough, violent intensity that prepares the bodies to react.)

On the other hand, while the actor-performers' actions in instances such as Truth or Dare? are connected to their bodies, it should be noted that the actions in which they engaged all came from the audience's imagination. The spectators' ideas were projected onto the interpreters, where they found a provisional incarnation; their ideas, their fantasies, the intimate imagery that lives in them, contributed to the (brief) birth of characters or fragments of characters. On stage, while fleeting figurations of the intrepid child, of the warrior or the kamikaze, appeared and disappeared, a form of mimetic representation returned for a time, created by the encounter between the spectator's imagination and the acting actor's body. Thus, while the actors executed the actions via their bodies rather than through their acting, these actions performed on stage were not completely devoid of artifice or the potentiality of its emergence. As they cultivated an ontological ambiguity, the "impersonnages" ("non-characters") that appeared briefly in this section of the play—even though the bodies at risk were *not* playing—never stopped planting doubt as to the nature, and to the different degrees, of the "real" and the invented that inhabited them.

The actors' bodies are not the only ones implicated in Système Kangourou's performances. Sometimes, the spectators' bodies are also involved. In one tableau from *40% de déséquilibre,* two of the actor-performers, standing before a screen on which winter scenes were projected—poetic images, detached from their evocative context—grilled sausages on a small portable barbecue. Slowly, aromas began to emanate from the cooking food and spilled over the stage area to invade the spectator's sensorial space—soaking by smell. Rarely summoned to the stage, smell behaves, here, as a surplus of the "real" while paradoxically infusing the scene with a dose of the imaginary. Indeed, as anthropologist David Le Breton argues, odours are never neutral: they arise from the roots of carnal thought, intimate symbols of the memory. Posing as "petites incisions dans le temps" ("little slits in time") (268), their meaning depends on the context in which they appear, which can then be revisited by olfactory memory, itself "tissée d'imaginaire" ("woven from the imaginary") (294), a place where personal stories, memories, and real and imagined perceptions intertwine. As I have discussed elsewhere, "au théâtre . . . les manifestations de cet imaginaire olfactif ne sont pas sans affecter l'expérience de la représentation. Et pour le spectateur, la déstabilisation agit à même le corps" (Cyr, "Représentation" 130) ("in the theatre . . . the manifestations of this olfactory imagination are not without an effect on the experience of representation. This destabilization works directly on the spectator's body"), which is penetrated by odours it cannot evade physiologically. Thus,

> envahissantes, les émanations lui font expérimenter, comme le remarque Eleanor Margolies, une sorte d'effritement des frontières usuelles entre ce qui se joue sur la scène et ce qui est perçu par son corps. Par ailleurs, sa perception du temps se trouve également perturbée puisque la sensation olfactive inscrit le spectateur à la fois dans la fugacité du présent de l'œuvre en scène et dans une durée indéterminée, cotonneuse, faite de l'enchevêtrement des souvenirs et des affects associés à une odeur particulière. (131)

(as Eleanor Margolies notes,[12] the invasive emanations cause one to experience the erosion of the usual borders between what is playing on stage and what one's body perceives. Moreover, one's perception of time is also impaired as the olfactory sensation places the spectator at once in the transient present of the piece and in an indefinite, fluffy duration, made of the entanglement of memories and affects associated with a particular odour.)

12　See Margolies.

Therefore, the experience of smell in *40% de déséquilibre* perturbs the perception of the unfolding representation, simultaneously leading the viewer toward immediate and tangible sensations and drawing him away from the experience of the show, toward more intimate, embedded territories in a fleeting moment of pure self-presence. Thus, if Système Kangourou's performative theatre privileges the encounter with the Other, it also favours a different type of encounter—with the self. And yet, if this encounter can borrow the body's channels and sensorial perception, it can also manifest itself in other ways, through the rhythm of the show itself. For example, in *Bricolages pour femme et ours polaire*, as the actress withdraws from the space several times, only to reappear a little later, another form of self-encounter gradually takes place. Scattered with silent displacements and transitory moments, *Bricolages pour femme et ours polaire* is filled with vacant periods, deploying a suspended temporality in which it is permissible for the spectator, absorbed among the toys and objects of childhood—spinning tops, dolls, teddy bears, school books—to encounter himself through his own memories and his own imagination. There, in the silence, for a moment alone with himself, and immersed in himself, he moves through the realm of intimate memory, which is made, always, from an inextricable entanglement of the "real" and the invented. In Système Kangourou's performative theatre, the experience of the "real" may reside, in part, in these little bursts of pure self-presence, strung throughout the show, whether they manifest themselves in suspended moments of time or in sensory intensification. Grafted to the (partial) refusal of character, to the (planned) emergence of chance and to the testing put forth by the spectator, this self-presence opens up a space for dreaming and forces the dissolution, or the permanent blurring, in the reading of the work, of the borders between past and present, between the "real" and the invented. It is in this enduring tension, in this cohabiting of contraries and, finally, in this space of perpetual irresolution that, for Système Kangourou, the workings of the "real" are afoot.

FROM *LANGUE* TO BODY: THE QUEST FOR THE "REAL" IN QUÉBÉCOIS THEATRE

LOUIS PATRICK LEROUX

Language has historically been the constituting *action* of Québec drama—its very raison-d'être—serving as one of the key markers of theatrical verisimilitude in the province. As Lucie Robert insists, theatre "was the first speech act of Quebec literature and its very first subject was precisely that of language" (112). But language has also served to authenticate Québec drama's distinctiveness, with marginalized characters—workers, orphans, bastards, women, homosexuals, transsexuals—held up as metonymic mirrors to *québécitude*.[1] Yet which is more "realistic": the stylized *joual* of Michel Tremblay's choral set pieces (starting with *Les Belles Soeurs*), or Larry Tremblay's mirror plays (most notably in *Le problème avec moi*, *La hache*, and *The Dragonfly of Chicoutimi*), featuring characters who dangerously and violently desire their doubles? Both authors have playfully teased audiences with autofictional glimpses on the one hand (see Michel Tremblay's famous Flaubertian assertions such as, "Sandra, c'est moi") and auto*frictional* taunts on the other (Larry Tremblay's homoerotics featuring panicked men before their body doubles).[2] In this essay, I

---

1   *Québécitude* could translate roughly as "Québec rootedness." Jocelyn Létourneau defines "québécitude" as the "romantic project of Québec as a country and nation stemming from its singular historical roots, its traditions, secular heritage, its unshakeable essence and its inalterable memory," as opposed to "québécité," which may be defined as a "process of (re)construction of Québec which is developed in reaction, if not in opposition to the [Canadian multicultural] project" (158–59, my translation).

2   I have developed the notion of *autofriction* in a few articles, but more fully in my doctoral dissertation *Le Québec en autoreprésentation: le passage d'une dramaturgie de*

will consider how the sense of the "real" has shifted in recent Québec theatre from iconic representation of an audience's likeness (in language and in
culture), to an embodied (re)presentation of contemporary authors. Larry
Tremblay writes that "[t]he individual can belong to many social identifiers
which aren't necessarily simultaneously played out. If the individual reduces
himself, ideologically, to a single dimension, he imperils his very physical
integrity" (20, my translation). He feels that an "unchallenged" identity is as
uninteresting on stage as in life. Contemporary Québec theatre takes up this
very invitation to challenge identity: rather than affirming an "unchallenged"
sense of cultural or linguistic self through traditional audience identification,
it renders the perception of the self as physical—embodied, in all of its difficulty, multiplicity, complexity.

The firm hold language has had on Québec theatre led to a conception
of realism that privileged linguistic mimesis; however, this very focus on language allowed a parallel dance scene to emerge that integrated theatre and
performance art, not to mention a theatre-influenced but non-dramatic form
of contemporary circus. In these forms, the performing body speaks more
eloquently than words. The audience becomes concerned with its inevitable
movement and physical integrity, and when either is challenged spectators
may react with awe, unease, or maybe even perverse anticipation of the body's
fall or collapse.[3] The movement toward a hyperembodied realism calls for a
post-dramatic displacement of audience empathy (and identification) away
from characters and onto performing bodies, achieved through the ability
to encapsulate and heighten our own sense of reality through the dizzying

---

l'identitaire vers celle de l'individu (Sorbonne nouvelle, 2009). Auto*friction* plays with
Serge Doubrovsky's own hybrid genre, that of "autofiction," which can be defined as an
"oxymoric pact" with the reader that seeks to create a sense of verisimilitude rather than
of truth itself. If autofiction relies on fiction to heighten or alter biographical elements for
the sake of the story, auto*friction* might then be the staging of a conscious tension between
the real and the verisimilar, drawing attention to the artifice of self-representation and
focusing the reader's attention on the occurring battle.

3   See Erin Hurley's "Les corps multiples du Cirque du Soleil."

possibilities of performances that go beyond our own physical or moral limitations (see Lehmann). In the second half of this essay I explore contemporary theatrical cross-genre performances and processes that play on audience expectations of authenticity and verisimilitude through a refocusing of the site of identification onto the performative body. In Théâtre Momentum's *Les Laboratoires Crête*, this body becomes an experimental testing ground, a Barthesian degree zero of reality onto which one may either project or inflict pain, pleasure, or ecstasy. The theoretical questions raised by such experiments become my major focus in the final part of my discussion, which considers the spectator's complex experience of the autothanatological dance-theatre works in which artist Dave St-Pierre invites us to gaze indiscreetly onto his dying body and plays into our deference (and ethical trouble) before the sacrificial and holy body. In these instances, language becomes an untrustworthy guide to interpreting the bodily reality before us. Instead, it morphs into a tool for theatrical artifice, while the body becomes a performative space to invest and investigate as "real."

A BRIEF HISTORY OF STAGE REALISM(S) IN QUÉBEC

Realism in Québec drama emerged and reigned through language and anecdote. From Joseph Quesnel's *L'Anglomanie ou le diner à l'anglaise* (1802) onward, speech acts have functioned as empowering calls to action and to resistance against a foreboding sense of impeding cultural and linguistic assimilation. Society playwrights of the late nineteenth and early twentieth centuries such as Félix-Gabriel Marchand and Louis Fréchette emulated European dramaturgical models, habits, and speech while drawing upon Romantic versions of patriotism and applying them to French Canadian liberal society or bourgeois contexts. Meanwhile, popular entertainments privileged vaudeville and sketch comedy in the Québec slang of the time. From Tizoune to Gratien Gélinas's Fridolin and Tit-Coq, anti-heroes with whom French Canadians could and did identify, language and mores functioned as clear markers of a perceived verisimilitude, albeit one generated via the usual conventions of the nineteenth- and twentieth-century realist stage.

Quotidian language, use of anecdote, and overwrought pathos were also to be found in melodramas based on real-life events, such as *Aurore, l'enfant martyre*, first produced in 1921. *Aurore* was based on a famous trial heard in February 1920, and featured an indifferent father and an abusive stepmother whose torment and eventual murder of young Aurore left very little room for empathy. The pre-radio, pre-television audience's appetite for live pathos was whetted by a Manichean feast of a child's innocence and virtue before the uncompromising evil of terrible parents. The play by Léon Petitjean and Henri Rollin reconstituting these tragic events toured Québec for years and was often replayed and adapted (in other plays, television, radio, and two film adaptations).[4] Most importantly, it provided a model for the kind of naturalistic, cathartic melodrama spoken in a plain, popular tongue that would thrive during the heyday of realism on Québec stages between 1948 and 1968. It would also serve as a cornerstone for popular Québec radio and television drama following the same model. The maintenance of realistic illusion was material to the staging of *Aurore*, as was its basis in an "authentic" story. The audience's empathy for the abused child and identification with her plight were further compounded by the aura of anecdotal verisimilitude surrounding the stage version, as it echoed documented horrors.

Aurore was seen by many as "macabre theatre," but Jacques Ferron, in a 1950 conference on Québécois theatre, remained unimpressed by its illusion of reality. "What is the reality of theatre?" he asked, rhetorically: "Theatre's truthfulness is to be found in the audience, not on stage" (qtd. in Petitjean and Rollin 109, my translation). Rather than getting caught up in judicial or morbid particulars, or even reading the play as a political allegory (with Québec as

---

4   The Théâtre National offered its own version of *L'Enfant de la marâtre* starting in 1925; in 1927 Henry Deyglun offered *Le Martyre de la petite Aurore*, which ran simultaneously with *Aurore, l'enfant martyre* at the Ouimetoscope. A film, *La petite Aurore, l'enfant martyre*, based on the Petitjean-Rollin play, was released in 1952. The most recent film version, *Aurore*, was released as late as 2005. A telefilm was also released in 1994, as was a radio play in 1986.

the helpless child abandoned by Mother France, neglected by Father England, and actively abused by Stepmother Canada), Ferron instead focused on a social reading of the audience's identification with all of the characters—its appropriate empathy for Aurore, but also, in an era of poverty, neglect, and chronic childhood deaths, its fundamental recognition of the collective failure to ensure a proper livelihood for its own children. *Aurore* was not mere melodrama for an audience that identified with such a communal tragedy. For Ferron and other audience members, its social realism was utterly convincing and heartbreaking.

As Jean Cléo Godin has argued, the sixties and seventies saw the emergence of various forms of "realism" in Québec: Michel Garneau's cast-inspired collective creations, which one might qualify as "poetic realism"; Marie Laberge's "pathetic realism" based on melodrama; and of course Michel Tremblay's "absurdist realism" (65–72). In his preface to the first edition of the play, Jean-Claude Germain hailed *Les Belles Soeurs* as a work with mirror-like qualities reflecting a Québec society that was changing very quickly. The 1968 audience could laugh appreciatively and recognize the fundamental social changes of the previous decade as Tremblay's fifteen women gathered in the small kitchen for a coupon party and recited the rosary before the radio. Germain wrote that Tremblay's women were depicted as though spied on from behind the kitchen window, with both an anthropologist's eye for detail and an intimate knowledge of the clan (6). This work, without being conventionally "realist" in its construction and premise, or in its use of highly stylized *joual*, choral speech, soliloquies, and asides, nevertheless proved to be both a convincing example of sociological authenticity and an exploration of otherness through the author's gaze. Michel Tremblay, ever conscious of his active role in constructing an oeuvre both social and genealogical, would later explicitly reflect upon the implications of replicating real life in his masterful impromptu *The Real World?* (see L. Leroux, "Tremblay's").

Although the movement within Michel Tremblay's own oeuvre from plays that mirror "realistic" characters, language, and situations to work that explicitly explores the creative process and individual creative concerns reflects a general progression in later twentieth-century Québec drama, one specific historical event (or series of events) has been a vital and continuing source of political realism over the course of the past few decades. The collective psychodrama of October 1970, referred to either as the "October Crisis" or, in nationalistic circles, as the more euphemistic "events of October," sanctioned what many saw as state terrorism with the imposition of the War Measures Act that suppressed individual rights for many months.[5] The crisis produced an onslaught of plays, films, poems, and novels, each addressing a very "real" series of events as they were experienced from varying perspectives. The dominant position adopted in works of literature and theatre[6] was that of the over four hundred imprisoned

---

5   After years of covert action targeting federal or "imperial" symbols, placing bombs in mailboxes or in army recruitment centres, and staging bank heists in order to fund its socialist and anti-imperial activities, the Front de libération du Québec (FLQ) came to prominence on October 5, 1970, when one of its guerrilla cells kidnapped British commercial envoy James Cross and demanded, in exchange for his release, a number of concessions, including that all FLQ political prisoners be freed. They also demanded that their anti-capitalistic and anti-imperialistic manifesto be read on the air on a Radio-Canada television broadcast. On October 10 the provincial government announced that it refused to negotiate with terrorists. Within thirty minutes of the press conference, another cell kidnapped Québec deputy premier and minister of labour, Pierre Laporte. Within days, the Québec government and the city of Montreal, overwhelmed and fearing the worst, requested that the federal government intervene. On the night of October 15, Prime Minister Pierre Elliot Trudeau sent military troupes to Québec and declared the War Measures Act to be in effect, suspending all civil rights. From the early hours of October 16, 450 activists, writers, intellectuals, and union leaders were rounded up by Montreal police and detained without warrant or accusation, in some cases for weeks. Many of those arrested would later write about the events, questioning the government's heavy-handed response. In time, the memory and political trauma of the War Measures Act came to supersede the actual assassination of Pierre Laporte by the Chénier cell on October 17. See Bouthilier and Cloutier and M. Leroux.

6   These works included, among others, Jacques Ferron's novel *Le salut de l'Irlande* (revised as the events were unfolding and rushed to publication in December 1970), Victor-Lévy Beaulieu's 1977 play *Cérémonial pour l'assassinat d'un ministre*, Robert Gurik's *Les tas de sièges* (1970), Jean-Claude Germain's *Les tourtereaux ou la vieillesse frappe à la porte* (1974), and André Major's *Une soirée en octobre* (1975). A second wave of plays looking

artists whose iconic and sympathetic capital was raised overnight by their participation in the crisis. These artists, along with other intellectuals, union leaders, and "troublesome elements" experienced state repression first-hand and vowed to fight back. Consequently, the focus of the theatrical works born from the events of October 1970 was neither on the kidnapping and death of then deputy premier and minister of labour Pierre Laporte by the FLQ, nor on any of their acts of terror, but rather on the swift police repression of an entire population: an action that collectively reminded the community of the British government's swift, bloody response to the Patriote rebellions of 1838 and of the later publication of Lord Durham's Report calling for a policy of assimilation and political containment.

One play stood out in this context. *Le procès des cinq*, "authored" by FLQ members Michel Chartrand, Pierre Vallières, Charles Gagnon, Robert Lemieux, and Jacques Larue-Langlois and published by the Mouvement pour la défense des prisonniers politiques québécois,[7] presented a dramatized, heavily edited version of the 619-page court transcription of their trial for "seditious conspiracy" against the state. The play mostly charts the almost comical turning of the tables by the accused through their refusal to play along with the judicial system in the wake of the trauma of the War Measures Act. Edited from real-life materials (though its rhetoric is often larger than life), the piece allowed readers a shorthand version of Canadian justice on trial by *felquistes* members who were not directly involved in the kidnappings or murder and who were eventually acquitted. Here was Erwin Piscator's "Political Theatre" made up of "hard" documentary materials any

---

back on October 1970 from the vantage of the 1990s include Anne Legault's *Conte d'hiver 70* (1992); Dominique Champagne's *La cité interdite* (1992); Champagne, Jean-Frédéric Messier, Pascale Rafie, and Jean-François Caron's euphoric and cathartic *Cabarets neiges noires* (1994); and a segment of Robert Lepage's *Seven Streams of the River Ota* (1997), later reprised independently as its own film, *Nò* (1998).

7   The play was re-edited by Lux in 2010 with a significant preface by novelist Louis Hamelin. It was also read publicly at the National Theatre School by popular political satire troupe Les Zapartistes in 2010.

positivist would have sanctioned, though it featured much posturing and explicit theatrics.

Following a few decades where realism in Québec drama moved more consistently toward poetic forms—with orally-inflected speech ceding to the literary, or speech being evacuated and minimized by the object and image theatres of Robert Lepage and Gilles Maheu on one hand, and the cross-genre formal experiments of Denis Marleau and Édouard Lock on the other—*Les Cahiers de théâtre Jeu* published an issue in 1997 on the state of realistic theatre in Québec. It featured general meditations on realism as an unlikely, yet consistent, prompter of aesthetic revolution in the province, arguing that artists had always sought, in essence, to represent reality, but not always through realistic illusion. The "realism" dossier in *Jeu* 85 also offered examples of theatrical practices that tested the limits of typical stage realism. For example, Robert Gravel's "non-acting," which pushed unexpressive American stage acting to the extreme, raised the question of where acting ends and the performative act begins: if you ask an actor to go up on stage and "not" act, won't he just be playing at non-acting? Various "solutions" were explored, including ignoring the audience when staging the play and drinking real alcohol on stage. Other tantalizing examples of the theatrical "real" included François Archambault's *15 secondes*, in which Dave Richer, an actor with cerebral palsy for whom the play was written, played a similarly disabled character. The thrill of the performance lay in the tension arising from the audience's understanding that, while Richer was acting, his disability was authentic and he was somehow overcoming it in order to act. Or was he? The actor kept insisting in interviews that he wasn't acting,[8] and some commentators feared that the work might feed a dangerous return to exhibitionistic spectacle, drawing upon audiences' fascinations with an otherness that, in this case, was brought closer to them by the exemplary display of the actor's ability not to perform

---

8   The playwright was very much troubled by the actor's assertion, insisting that the story had been *crafted* and that the Dave Richer he saw on stage was very different from the off-stage Dave Richer (Archambault 74).

despite his disability, but rather to perform it as such.[9] Yet the performer also embodied the character's pain, not merely playing it or channelling it for us. As François Archambault himself would later realize:

> During an hour and forty-five minutes, we go on in this play about the difficulty of being handicapped. But, once the curtain's down, Dave can't just leave his character behind. It's the same when he plays his character, he can't not be himself. . . . Other actors can remove their Cyrano de Bergerac nose, he cannot; he returns to life moving like his character does. (Archambault 74, my translation)

The confusion of character and performer—able-bodied or otherwise—is nothing new in Québec, and plays an important role in ongoing debates over the performance of the real. This confusion is fuelled in Québec by its established star system, bolstering a constant presence of recognizable personalities across the media. Actors are seen as characters on television and on stage, but they also host radio and television shows or are regular participants on them, essentially playing themselves. They sing, try out recipes on cooking shows, and write columns in newspapers. In this context, theatrical character is perceived as but a temporary layer, another mask before the very familiar face we've come to know. This is not surprising in a society that admires singularity and values exceptionalism while insisting on the interconnectedness of individuals. The individual performing his or her role (perhaps principally that of *performer*) in the Québec star system will be constantly confronted by the public display of his or her persona. Paradoxically, in this context, the characters pale before both the performance *and* the performer. The audience responds to the truthfulness of the theatrical conceit but also to the "risk" (moral or physical) assumed by the performer him or herself. Even in the case of relatively unknown performers, it becomes difficult

9   A 2007 production of the play at Ottawa's Théâtre du Trillium starring an able-bodied actor, Benjamin Gaillard, played up the cerebral palsy, raising compelling ethical questions. These were not, to my knowledge, taken up publically in reaction to the performance.

to abstain from considering the person before us, his or her ethos and physical integrity, when assessing the degree of the "real" in any performance. This fluctuating sense of the "real" allows us now to turn to the increasing examples of self-representation on the Québec stage.

NEW QUÉBEC REALISMS: QUESTIONS AND EXPERIMENTS

Despite the many strengths of early, often political, realist work in Québec, the "traditional" model in which the theatre was seen as a mirror of the province's singularity and as a possible tool to assert its distinct identity no longer corresponds to its contemporary performance reality. Over the course of the 1980s and 1990s Québec theatre shifted its attention to both image and object (through the works of Robert Lepage, Gilles Maheu, Denis Marleau, and Édouard Lock, for example), but also, in playwriting, to biographical work, and more specifically to the projection of the artist's identity onto multiple stage personas. This new preoccupation with the individual, in this case the writer/performer as individual artist, was pursued in a series of autobiographical variations from theatrical self-portraiture to staged confession.

The history of Québécois realism appears thus to lead us away from the search for authentic language and toward a search for an authentic self, located in the body and actions of the performer of autobiographical work. Yet, can the authentic "I" exist at all in theatre—even in this explicitly autobiographical and relentlessly physical form? Theatre necessarily imposes fictions, masks, layers of artistic and aesthetic meddling, from the director to the designers and actors through to the audience. Plato's rejection of actors as mere imitators established a fundamental anxiety that remains with us to this day. How can you trust someone who can imitate sincerity? If the authentic "I" is diluted in a series of interpretations of interpretations, what remains "real" in this labyrinthine mirroring of a past experience? The present moment? The body? Maybe the very process of revealing oneself to the audience?

In Aristotelian praxis, the real is action, and the real "I" can only be performative. The character is engaged in a quest (a movement toward the object of desire) and theatre offers the stage for the representation of that action. In post-dramatic theatre, conversely, action is not *between* bodies but is brought *onto* bodies themselves. The scenic body performing itself essentially requires the performer's active engagement in the autobiographical act both as a reconstitution of the past and as a perpetually present projection into the future. This representational body is not only engaged in mimesis, it is a reminder, by virtue of its autobiographical ethos, that it has taken the dramatic action onto itself. The "authentic I" is an unsteady subject: it can fall victim to delusion, sublimation, transfer, and misinterpretation. The autobiographical subject engaged in an autobiographical process, on the other hand, has become the ideal "realistic" character insofar as it is engaged in an authentic doing or remembering.

But isn't it human nature to lie—ever so slightly—about the extent and depth of one's process? Autobiographers confabulate, contrive, invent; they playfully hide true motivations (and sometimes don't fully realize their scope); they rearrange biographical facts; they are often more interested in ideal verisimilitude than in truth. We assume that the unguarded body itself cannot lie. Or can it? In 2001, theatrical "misfit" Stéphane Crête raised this question by staging a series of four laboratory experiments, the *Laboratoires Crête*, where he played the role of a proto-scientist while actually experimenting with both actors and the audience. The performance asked the central question of which actors might be "faking it" and which were truly "in" a particular state induced by the work. Crête invited actors to partake in a series of "consciousness-altering" exercises using Claude Bernard's "experimental method in medical research," which relies on a systematic verification of hypotheses as one element at a time is eliminated or controlled to measure the effect of the modification.[10] A registered nurse oversaw the health and safety of the cast (administering the drugs, for instance) and ensured scientific control.

---

10   For an in-depth discussion of Claude Bernard's experimental method as applied to experimental theatre in Québec, see Cyr, "Ronfard."

In the first lab Crête, playing the scientific researcher to a fault, asked actors to perform scenes while in controlled pain. In the second, he used hypnosis; in the third, actual mind-altering drugs; and in the fourth, he brought various sexual devices (dildos, anal plugs, clitoral vibrators) for the actors to use or insert during performances. Interestingly, not all of the actors were in actual pain, states of hypnosis, drugged, or poked and prodded sexually during performances. The audience often guessed wrongly as to which actors were literally suffering these indignities and which were performing them.

The pieces attracted a wide variety of performers, from Sylvie Moreau to Marie Brassard, but Brigitte Poupart was the only actress to participate in all four *Laboratoires*. In an interview that acted as a kind of hall of mirrors with Crête's academic alter ego, Gunther de Villier (who in turn interviewed his own scientific alter ego "*le Docteur Crête*"), Poupart revealed that she had, in fact, not faked a dildo's penetration, nor the administration of Valium (which she admitted altered her state for three days), and that she had only "performed" pain in one of the four labs. She concluded that there is no pleasure in seeing actors in pain, and that inflicting this pain for entertainment is akin to watching (and to assisting in) torture. Many spectators refused to accept that there was actual pain involved in the shows; many, she noted, remained convinced that they had seen only a display of robust and nuanced acting. Indeed, Poupart suggested that the most convincing moments of the labs on a theatrical level were those the actors *performed* rather than experienced: "It was interesting to realize to what extent fakery was more convincing (to the audience) than the actual experience" (Poupart, qtd. in de Villier 130, my translation).[11]

Limit-performances such as these remain relatively closed and allow select audiences to ponder ethical issues pertaining to performance, the actor's

---

11   The book, published in 2008, is richly illustrated and includes material elements from the experiments. While its jocular tone and mocking of intellectuals might confuse an unsuspecting reader, the book includes actual evidence of serious research into altered performance states. A documentary by Vali Fugulin and Sonia Vigneault accompanies the book and examines the backstage preparatory work to the laboratory-performances.

craft, and the audience's expectation of a certain degree of convention-bound conceit. Yet autobiographical performances in theatre and crossover dance-theatre explore some of the same themes; in Québec, these performances have been very much integrated into the cultural mainstream, gaining acceptance as a valid form of creative self-portraiture in which audiences are willing to accept a certain measure of "narcissistic ambiguity," to borrow a term from Vincent Colonna (see Hubier 124), as to what is reality and what is representation.

SELF-PORTRAIT OF AN ARTIST DYING

Self-portraiture has given us countless examples in Québec of self-representational plays flirting with our desire for sincerity and authenticity, offering up a taste of the "real," and featuring magisterial and explicit "performances of the self." They include Pol Pelletier's demonstration of her acting technique in *Or* (1997), Jean-Pierre Ronfard and Robert Gravel's autofictional illustration of their creative process and relationship in *Tête à tête* (1994), and Marcel Pomerlo's confessional elegy *L'Inoublié* (2002). Yet perhaps the most fascinating recent examples emerge from the grey zones between theatre and performance art and between theatre and dance, and particularly from the work of *enfant terrible* choreographer Dave St-Pierre, who is known in Québec and Europe for his provocative dance pieces featuring dozens of naked, sexualized bodies. His two major dance-theatre performances, *La pornographie des âmes* (*Bare Naked Souls*) and *Un peu de tendresse, bordel de merde!* (*A little tenderness, for crying out loud!*), have featured a sequential narrative of transgression, testing the audience's comfort before the naked body in all of its shapes and sizes and challenging the limits of what is acceptable and presentable. He is the artistic child of Jan Fabre, Pina Bausch, and Rodrigo García, sometimes to a fault, and has explicitly referenced his masters by integrating García's texts into his latest work, *Cycle de la boucherie* (2011), and by citing Jan Fabre's *Je suis sang*. By flying in, *deus ex machina*-style, Pina Bausch's red dress in *What's Next?* (2011), he created a metonymic object from the German choreographer's original "ready-made," allowing it to be "reframed" and inscribed in dance history by a Québécois choreographer whose works are regularly produced in Europe.

Dave St-Pierre has cystic fibrosis, which confines his life expectancy to thirty-seven years; pushing into his thirties, he has made a point of dancing in his shows. For him, dancing is a lifeline; with it he resists death's embrace, but he also refuses to wax poetic on his moribund state. In *Over My Dead Body* (2009), St-Pierre walks onto the stage tied to and flanked by his respirator and oxygen tank. He flatly states: "I will never live a long life" (St-Pierre, *Over*). The audience might wonder: is this metaphor, hyperbole, or mere statement of fact? Is he so sick that he actually needs the respirator or is it a dubious prop? Those in the know are aware of his critical state and almost two-year wait for a double lung transplant. The theme of the show will be death and the dancer-choreographer's daily overcoming of Thanatos. This is not fiction; the "real" is present before us. It is Dave St-Pierre, struggling to breathe, pushing back death nightly, surrounding himself with friends. Confessional drama usually involves a single performer, but in this case, St-Pierre calls upon three faithful collaborators, Éric Robidoux, Julie Perron, and Alexis Lefebvre, to play his allegorical alter egos. What is Narcissus without Echo?

Rather than explore the tragedy of his impending death, St-Pierre asks Éric Robidoux to play the dumb blond character who previously appeared in *Un peu de tendresse, bordel de merde!* The naked and bewigged Robidoux repeatedly asks in a falsetto voice: "Are you dead yet Dave Saint-Père?" mispronouncing St-Pierre as "Saint-Père" or Holy Father. The pathos is played up to instill discomfort in the audience, yet the uninhibited burlesque quality of the interaction as St-Pierre lies there, half buried, creates a sense of sardonic humor. At the Gates of Paradise, St-Pierre meets Céline Dion, the patron (saint?) of the Canadian Cystic Fibrosis Foundation. Céline makes a show of her heavy-hitting emotional labour (see Hurley, *National Performance*), as befits her status as diva and icon, but can't help overemphasizing her *Pietà*-inspired empathy, taking centre stage as a performing, majestic *pleureuse* (tearful mourner). St-Pierre, breathing heavily, is buried and resurrected: he bares his body and opens it up to scrutiny, exposing his anus as one would the deepest secrets of the soul.

In spite of its physical exhibitionism, the fundamental immodesty of *Over My Dead Body* rests on the dying performer's refusal to die while simultaneously letting us into the spectacle of his stifled body.

The naked man donning the blond wig, the same actor/dancer putting on a giant rabbit head, the caricature of Céline Dion—none of this is *realistic*, of course, but the very proposition of a pièce de résistance where the focus of the action is fully transferred onto the moribund dancing body before us provokes the question of how much "real" the spectator can actually take. *Le Devoir* critic Catherine Lalonde felt that St-Pierre's piece was egotistical and that little of his emotional roller-coaster ride could be experienced by the audience; to her, it seemed first and foremost a cathartic device for its creator. One might argue to the contrary, however, that St-Pierre uses the likelihood of audience discomfort as a material, a tool to allow us to tap into a sense of the "real" easily lost in our hyperstimulated, hypermodern society. To fully achieve this, St-Pierre might need to compromise the audience's own sense of physical safety, as he did in *Un peu de tendresse, bordel de merde!*, where actor-dancers thrust their genitals and buttocks in the faces of spectators, and sometimes sat on them.[12]

In her article on staging the suffering body, Tamar Tembeck places St-Pierre's work alongside American performance artist Bob Flanagan's, not only because of their shared cystic fibrosis, but also because of their explicit staging of the impeding ascension of their suffering bodies. In *Visiting Hours* (1992, 1994, and 1995; the artist died in 1996), Flanagan invited spectators into a reconstituted children's hospital room in which they observed him being periodically lifted by the ankles up to the ceiling, as though presenting them "with an inversed and premature ascension of the artist's body" (Tembeck 42, my translation). Naked, hanging by his feet for long minutes, breathing with difficulty,

---

12   While these provocations were taken with a certain bemused distance or engaged playfulness in Québec and most of Europe, German audiences and British critics in particular did not accept the breaks in decorum very readily. The headline to Luke Jennings's *Guardian* review reads: "Spat at by a naked dancer: In its crass attempt to shock, this Sadler's Wells show provided the most unpleasant moment I've ever experienced in the theatre."

his face reddened alarmingly for the troubled audience members unable to assist him. Tembeck sees both performers' work not as "victim art," to use Arlene Croce's term (see also Szporer), but rather as a conscious use of ironic performance strategies, notably the personification of martyrdom through religious iconography (Flanagan's bodily ascension, St-Pierre's oft-mentioned "*christic* fibrosis") and the tongue-in-cheek representation of autopathography, both of which draw on our empathy yet also call on our thinly veiled *schadenfreude*.

How is this not simply a sideshow? In her work on freaks and cultural imagination, Rachel Adams has argued that "part of the sideshow's frisson arises from the audience's recognition of the ease with which [the categories of] freak and normal may slide unsteadily into one another" (9). In short, it is the carnival mirror effect—the frightful replication of the self—that is at the heart of our fascination with freaks. The same might be said of our fascination with artists such as St-Pierre and Flanagan. Yet, I would argue that sideshow acts generally have little agency, while no one forces confessional monologues on playwrights or actors. No one forced Dave St-Pierre to create *Over My Dead Body*, especially as his previous work as choreographer of dance pieces for Cirque du Soleil's *Zumanity* and *Love* ensures him some financial independence. Rather than losing agency, St-Pierre is actively recovering what disease is taking from him. He uses his body not as freakish spectacle but rather as a site at which we may recognize and anticipate our own inevitable decay. If he or she has past experiences with St-Pierre's work, the spectator knows that his or her own physicality might be compromised at any point in the performance by any of the performers, yet it is St-Pierre's own gaze upon his deathly body that most disarms us. The choreographer whose credo is to "disarm the spectator" admits that with *Over My Dead Body* he is engaging in his most subversive performance ("Désarmer" 116). He insists that it is through cheating (with conventions) that one can really touch upon truthfulness. He is "real," tangibly real, yet all the while he is performing for us and calling upon his friends to act as artistic alter egos or pathetic foils to his dying grace. There is some abnegation in this creative act, but it is mostly the resistance that we see, both in his humour and in his very stage presence. This ethos of resistance, a posture made possible through the continuous action of the dancing body and through St-Pierre's self-portrait as a dying man, is also a call to a common resistance of artifice.[13]

Is the spectacularization of a dying body more "real" in this case than its sublimation through a work that might equally have drawn upon pathos but instead presented a fictional alternative? In his unexpected (but dramaturgically inevitable) dance solo in *Over My Dead Body*, St-Pierre explores this question by shedding his allegorical characters (naked rabbit-man, the dumb blond, proto-Céline). This passage was referred to by critics as the "only real dance in the show" (Szporer). He challenges his body, gravity, fate. He pushes himself to the jubilatory limits of exertion, even if ever so briefly, reconnecting with Pina Bausch's earlier tests in performer endurance. Dave St-Pierre never seems so morbidly full of life as during the energetic solo when he defies his body with elegance and abandon. Earlier, when he tries to aim carrots at the anus of the rabbit-headed dancer but fails to reach the target—a sad reflection of his inability to sustain his previously accurate aim—he is tapping into pathos, rather than dancing pathetically, through his resistance to suffering but also through his body's exertion. He is not transcending his condition; he dances in spite of it and maybe even alongside it. Dave St-Pierre alone on stage exhibiting his dying body would have proven insufferable, but his solo dance is rather a duet in which he confronts his sickly double, and wins again, one night at a time.

As such work suggests, Québec's new realism isn't necessarily linguistic; it is corporeal and, as always, existential. The body politic has turned its attention to the seemingly "apolitical" body of individuals, subversive through the virtue of their unleashed energy. Does the emerging discourse of carnal authenticity

---

13   St-Pierre's *What's Next?* was produced in 2011, after the artist underwent a successful lung transplant, and was conceived and performed in tandem with experimental theatre actress and director Brigitte Poupart, a close friend (and scenic soulmate). In February 2012, Poupart released her documentary feature titled *Over My Dead Body*, which includes parts of the eponymous theatre-dance piece, but especially follows Dave St-Pierre's daily life as he waits for the call for his lung transplant.

defy the usual discourses of Québec cultural production (and their expected stances on language and culture)? After all, culture itself is corporeal as
well as linguistic. As changing social mores enable devil-may-care creativity
that pushes the limits of our understanding of the value and function of the
"real" in contemporary performance, the site of Québécois reality has shifted
from Michel Tremblay's rue Fabre *parler-vrai* (authentic speech) to the site of
St-Pierre and his dancers' bodies, subversive through their very human acts
of resistance and survival. It has moved away from the realist melodrama of
Aurore, l'enfant martyre to rather embrace the body's playful refusal to take
part in the pathos of the spectacle of death. Death is but a threat, an inevitable circumstance. The site of tension and of engaging, immediate reality is
now to be found on the pulsating body.

DEVISING REALISMS
(AN EXCHANGE)

EVAN WEBBER, ALEX McLEAN, AND BRUCE BARTON

Devising and Realism are commonly thought of as mutually exclusive, even antithetical theatrical approaches. Yet while it is seductive to envision them as irreconcilable camps skirmishing along the front lines of contemporary theatre, to do so is to confuse what is essentially a method of creation (devising) with a formal aesthetic (Realism). Granted, many devising practitioners exhibit an uneasy skepticism about the tenets underpinning Realism, but this aversion manifests itself in diverse ways that express a spectrum of artistic and ideological positions. What follows is a gently revised Google Doc exchange in which we reflect upon our practices and discuss our varied, sometimes conflicting relationships to both the work of devising and the cluster of realit(ies) that surrounds the Realist aesthetic.

FIRST: DEVISING

EW: Devising is not a word that any of us tend to use much when we're working. It's a word I use to try to signal my outsider-ness or my stance of resistance. And usually when I hear other people use it, I feel like we're signalling the same thing: a mutual desire to make art in theatre that does something other than affirm the intractability of the prevailing culture in the way that it's made, presented, and discussed. So I don't particularly like the word "devising" but in certain contexts it's useful as a kind of portable barricade—in a conversation about Realism, for example. Pointing outwards, it defends the morality of the work that's going on inside: a frequently messy search for accountability in practice and in conversation with audiences and other participants.

Like other barricades, its defensibility is weak—for one, it's easy to encircle—but its visibility as landmark provides certain small advantages, too; one can fly a flag there, or maybe meet one's friends, try to get a sense of what you're all up against.

BB: Truth be told, I *do* use the word "devising" in my work on occasion. But usually it is in an effort to either describe or assert what my work is *not*—or at least what I don't want it to be. Often I use it as a challenge to all of us in the room to come up with more precise ways to think about what we're doing. While the term is understood in many different ways, I suspect it owes its traction to this specific quality, this usefulness as a spacer: not as a divider between spaces but as a tool to claim space. Basically, I think of devising as a site—of activity, of contention, of negotiation—and I particularly appreciate the term's explicit incongruity in the context of artistic creation, given its proximity to others such as "contrived" and "manufactured." I suppose it is, in this sense, almost always offered as a gentle but clear provocation to more specifically and concretely fill the space the term opens up (before something else does, something more familiar). Admittedly, one can only use the same provocation so many times before it begins to lose its bite, and the current ubiquity and generality of the devising discussion is clearly dulling its teeth. But, on the level of utility, a wrench doesn't stop being a wrench just because it comes in many different shapes and sizes and everybody owns one.

To me, "devising" suggests *doing*, and I suppose this is where it parts ways with "contrived" and "manufactured," both of which place the emphasis on products and outcomes. I have read a lot, and written a fair bit, about what people understand devising to *do*, what it has the potential to do.[1] Much of the available discussion is pretty abstract and demonstrates an anxiety about words pinning living things to a wall. I have some sympathy for that apprehension. But some of the best writing about devising strains in the opposite

---

1   See, for example, my introduction to *Collective Creation, Collaboration and Devising*.

direction and is quite methodical (if not entirely methodological, to borrow Alison Oddey's term [11]). It's these efforts, the ones that say, "This is what devising means *to me*," that I find most enlightening and useful and inspiring. Of course, what devising means to me, at any particular moment and in any particular process, may look quite different than what it did or will mean in an entirely different context. But what does, I hope, remain fairly constant is that when I "devise" theatre I am looking for concrete solutions, tools, strategies—ways of doing things—and, perhaps even more importantly, that the value of these activities lies primarily in their doing, rather than in their service to a pre-existing text or theme or idea (like, say, Realism). Texts and themes and ideas are, almost invariably, at play, but they might just as likely emerge out of the doing as inspire it.

SECOND: (THE) REAL

AM: "Real" is another tricky word. Like "culture," it refers to something that we sense, something of which we have an impression and something to which we have an implied but elusive relationship. We are somehow a part of it *and* affected by it *and* its progenitors. We move on shaky ground.

"Real" is a word I use quite a bit when making a show. For me, it has a lot to do with consequence and intimacy. When I was a dishwasher, I loved seeing the pile of clean dishes and the basin of dirty water at the end of a shift. It is a simple but important pleasure, I think, to see that your presence in the world has not gone unmarked—that you have had some *effect*. A theatre space becomes a place of actual possibility for me when it contains an actor ducking a stick that is swung at her/his head, or sharing a drink with a member of the audience. Moments like this are hard to keep within quotation marks. They compel response, engagement, and thus evade abstract categorization.

Intimacy, I think, is something you allow for rather than create. It is something I can feel with performers I am watching and with fellow audience members. I have always been drawn to theatre that brings its audience into close proximity with performers, that catches me in the wind of a moving body.

Recently, when I saw Toneelgroep Amsterdam's *Roman Tragedies* (Festival Transamériques, Montreal, May 2010), I was surprised by the intimacy I felt in the room even while watching actors on television screens.[2] This feeling was fuelled, I think, by the fact that I was sitting on the stage and that I knew the actor onscreen was somewhere in the space behind me. Also, though, I felt some kind of kinship with the other audience members who had accepted the invitation to sit amidst the action. We were receiving and responding to the experience together. It was happening in our world.

EW: And when you say "real," Alex, is it a good thing? As in, "That part of the show feels real"? What you're describing—consequence and intimacy, as in the *Roman Tragedies* experience—it's like my idealized imagination of what politics is, or how political demands come into being: through a group of people sharing space and time, reflecting together on the fabric of their social imaginary. And through this process they come to a recognition that their demands overlap, that their seemingly individual desires are in fact parts of some greater demand—for more justice, for more safety, for more humility, etc.

I like this, but it's not what I'm talking about when I'm talking about the real in art. For me, the consequence and intimacy of political action is always in relation, if not in opposition, to what prevails, to what is normal (or what defines normalcy). That's the real. The world groans under the weight of it.

I suppose this sounds laboriously poetic. I don't want it to. I just mean that as the conditions under which we live and relate to each other are not entirely satisfactory, I don't want to reinscribe their normalcy in performance. The last thing I want to do is make art that feels real in this sense.

AM: The "real" that I describe is something other than the aesthetic form we know as Realism. Realism, it seems to me, is based on the belief that there is an *objective reality* that artists are morally obliged to access and show to others.

---

2   Text, photos, and video about this production are available at http://www.toneelgroepamsterdam.nl/default.asp?path=sqrgjlo3.

In my view, a critique of Realism must suggest one or a combination of the following: a) that there *is not* or *may not* be an objective reality; b) that there may in fact be *multiple*, conflicting realities; c) that nobody is capable of seeing an objective reality even if it exists; and d) that too much is lost in translation between receiving objective reality and transmitting it to others. The final three points are, in my view, the ones upon which our ethical stance as artists must be based. The "real" theatrical moments to which I refer above can usefully accentuate the difference between what is *actually* happening in the *presence* of the audience and what is being *represented* in the aesthetic context of Realism. However, I have come to believe that entirely evading the troubled territory opened up by Realism is an abdication of responsibility.

BB: I agree that it's important, if nearly impossible in any absolute sense, to distinguish between Realism and realism and "the real." Realism, with a capital "R," I understand as a historically and culturally specific phenomenon, a systematic relationship to conventions, theatrical and otherwise, that initially reflected the emerging ideological framework of Western culture as it rounded the nineteenth century on its way into the twentieth. By contrast, realism, our contemporary, despite the loss of capitalization, is something much broader and more pervasive in scope, more diverse and elastic in form, and more covert and insidious in operation. Capital "R" Realism is explicit, a distinct and overt aesthetic perspective; realism, by contrast, is implicit—and all the more persuasive as a result—within our entertainments, our pedagogies, our economies, our politics, and our art. Many of the tenets of historical Realism live on in contemporary realism's self-articulation—which is a good thing. These tenets mark what is otherwise very difficult to discern, assess, critique, or contest. But the overt trademarks of Realism largely constitute the bottle of conventions that the genie of realism as social practice moves freely within and beyond.

It's the third term in this sequence, however, that enters consciously and intentionally into my practice. I suppose my understanding of "the real" is a correlate of my understanding of devising, in that it reflects a particular kind of *doing*. All sorts of things are done in theatre contexts, and on at least one level it's a dubious suggestion that any are more real than any others. Material gets moved around, physical exertion is involved, furniture gets dented, shins get bruised, whether in the service of Stanislavsky, Boal, or Etchells. So, as with devising, the definition of real in these contexts is contingent, subjective, and utilitarian. Often, I think, we call something "real" when we want to promote its worth and when we want to assign priority to its particular kind of affect. My understanding (my preference) in terms of "the real" in theatre doesn't have much to do with efforts to discover something unique and essential in live performance. But I do think live performance is a particularly good place to go for evidence of it—precisely because it is so accommodating to, and conventionally associated with, the potential for intimacy. In this sense, I think, the "real" of performance is noteworthy more in degree than in kind. It refers to an uncommon level of intensity and minimizing of distraction. Otherwise, though, I suppose it involves the same characteristics of experience that feel real to me outside the theatre—that is, the experience of being challenged, of being a bit off balance, of finding myself in only partly recognizable conditions on only partly familiar terrain. I don't mean extreme vertigo or complete submersion or utter alienation; those experiences tend to strike me as quite unreal, or surreal. I tend to forcibly resist or simply give up in those situations. No, I mean situations where I know I'm being tested and where I'm not sure I've done enough homework—or, more precisely, the *right* homework—to pass. Then things feel real to me, whether or not I'm in the theatre.

Which, I guess, is why I don't find any contradiction in the use of both "devising" and "real" in my work, in that the former seems to me a means to the latter—much the same way that I think we're in part responsible for/complicit in the ongoing construction of our realities outside the theatre. We may have slightly more control over our "devising" in the theatre, but I think the projects are closely related. This is why I find it so challenging—and so rewarding—to explore intersections between what I and my collaborators do, what we're pretty good at (or, at least, comfortable with), and what we can't do very well, or at all, or have never done. For instance, bringing aerial movement together with physical performance or with puppetry, the way we've been attempting with our *Vertical City* work,[3] ensures that no one can stay in their comfort zone; everyone is off balance. Often, the performers' responses to the things I ask them to try amount to "Are you for real?" That's when I know I'm on to something.

EW: Real is a word I use a lot too when I'm working. When a performance feels real all of a sudden when it didn't before—that's interesting: when I suddenly recognize something that appeared strange in one moment as being, in the next, *experientially*, normal. I try to make way for these moments. But it's not that I'm wanting to create something real or effect some conjuration; it's more like trying to find the essence of the bare realness that's already there: my realism. The more I work the more I'm starting to believe or trust that whatever I am capable of doing in the theatre is always already real—and, more, real-istic. So I try to keep looking inward, to make these constant little adjustments to stay close to the place of bare realism where things are always already happening—but without claiming anything and, hence, reinscribing it. Inspiring intimate consequence, by way of either a stick swinging at my head or a forceful emotive gesture—or, equally, being "myself" as a performer—is missing the territory I want to explore. Instead I try to work in that bare state, so that the real—my sense of it, at least—becomes a material to be worked with, a figure to be seen more clearly. Maybe this can be a way to prepare for consequence and intimacy, for politics. Groundwork. But it's personal too: the experience an audience has when a work isn't claiming anything is something like the state of awareness I would like to be in all the time.

THIRD: DANGERS

AM: I, too, believe that a certain dominant strain of theatre is complicit with the worst aspects of our culture. I attempt to avoid reinscribing normalcy in work, and acknowledge that classical Realism does something very

---

3   *Vertical City* is a dramaturgy-driven hub for contemporary performance that brings aerial movement into interdisciplinary exchange. See Solga.

dangerous by positing a certain state as "real" above others. This is surely the conundrum of Realism and what perhaps caused its swift eclipse by
other forms with supposedly radical aims in the twentieth century. And
yet it lingers. . . .

I am not drawn as you are, Evan, to the notion of work that "isn't claiming anything." I wonder if our difference in this is rooted in contrasting
sociological positions. I think it is likely necessary to always define ourselves, at least partially, in opposition to something. Many of us "devise"
work that attempts in one way or another to resist the assumptions of a perceived aesthetic norm. Where perhaps we differ is on the notion of unity,
which I find highly suspect. First of all, countercultural positions too often assume a unified dominant culture whereas, I think, what we perceive
as such is actually multiple conflicting voices. Secondly, you describe individuals with fundamentally compatible desires—a complicity I think is
fictional. Except when we struggle to be citizens rather than subjects (as is
happening in a very pronounced and *real* way in the Arab world right now
[2011]), and for what are essentially liberal notions of social justice, I think
our desires are not complicit. I tend to view social interaction as Strindberg
does in *A Dream Play*, as largely defined by "contradictions, irresolution,
discord" (54). All we can do is take positions and—importantly—establish
spaces within which those positions can be taken. I wonder if you think
that a space that makes no claims is one that allows people to find what you
see as our natural unity.

In response to your direct question a while back: yes, when I say something "feels real," I mean it in a good way. I say so in response to being affected
by something that is happening in front of me and not strictly as a function of
some suspension of disbelief. When an actor eats a raw onion onstage, even
though it may be representing something, I also know it is happening in the
actor's body. To me this is of interest and is an example of what I call "real" in
performance. My primary motivation for seeking this is that I find it pleasurable. However, for such a thing to be pleasurable, I feel the actor must have
agency and a degree of control. Once, my colleague Stewart broke his foot in
a show, but my response was not to say, "That feels real."

EW: To clarify: I know our desires are not complicit. But inasmuch as our desires ever find voice as political demands they must be *made* to seem complicit under the umbrella of certain language—often Realist language. Not because it's more accurate but because, as Boris Groys has written, politics long ago "situated itself in the aesthetic field" and set about producing a "real" with intimacy and consequence far exceeding the productive capacity of artists. So in contrast to, and even against this, I try to make a space that makes no claims where one might recognize the un-naturalness of one's unities and disunities—to choose again.

BB: I agree that the assumption of a unified dominant culture is flawed, and that the assertion that there is a basic commonality (of interest, of process, of aesthetic) among countercultural efforts is equally seductive and equally misleading. It's in the face of this reality that the elasticity of the term "devising," while potentially elusive and frustrating, makes some sense. Among the few common aspects of many devising practices is that they, themselves, can be potentially and *intentionally* elusive and frustrating; beyond that, the range of intentions, approaches, and results is very wide. In this sense devising, as well as a way of doing things, is also a way of positioning oneself. Certainly implicitly, and often explicitly, it's a way to announce a countercultural position without buying into any specific alternative. On a preliminary level, then, devising represents resistance without obligation: no wonder it's ubiquitous.

But if we keep alive in the conversation devising's focus on *doing* then it's impossible to content ourselves with a generalized oppositional stance. A focus on doing forces us to articulate—to ourselves, at least, but also to others—what we're doing and how we're doing it. And when we do this, we're usually not talking about commonalities; rather, the conversations usually revolve around differences. Consider, for instance, the distance between Alex's swinging sticks and Evan's "bare realness." But, despite the conceptual distinctions between these approaches, what they share is that both are composite, both display inner tensions and contradictions. Unlike classic Realism, which had a deep investment in articulating an inner cohesion and consistent logic (without marking either overtly), most approaches to devising invest in a plurality of form and simultaneity of meaning that is foregrounded in performance.

On face value, this can seem to run the risk of indulged indecision—of a lot of frenetic theatrical activity that actually reflects the paralysis of perpetual ideological vacillation (a very different form of "not claiming anything"). However, in my experience much devising is primarily concerned with the sites at which these composite forms and contents butt up against one another, the sometimes hard and sometimes porous places where the disparate intentions and expressions of different devising processes confront and trouble one another. Much devising is, to quote Evan, "All Seams" (see Webber et al.): processes that rely upon juxtaposition and montage for meaning, in which the congregation of agonistic perspectives critique and complicate, as well as complement, one another. I don't think this is about avoiding the obligation to take a position so much as it's a necessary concession that to do so is "unnatural"—to do so requires an *act*, one that is immediately open to assessment and adjustment, a *doing* that is vulnerable to contamination.

AM: As Bruce writes, given that performance is something that happens in the fabric of reality, it can *only* be real. Therefore, to debate the "realness" of something is to assume some additional criteria. Hence my discussion of the ethical claims of Realism versus those concepts of "intimacy" and "consequence"—those theatrical experiences that do not require a suspension of disbelief.

Yes: in the theatre I suppose that "real" is a "particular kind of *doing*." I, too, seek an experience of being off balance, in the midst of something both foreign and familiar. It brings about what I consider to be a productive state of consciousness. In such a state, it seems to me, it is harder to succumb to cliché or thoughtless consensus.

Yet, despite the contingency of "the real" in theatre, there is something quite fascinating to me about early "Realism" and/or "Naturalism." All of the performance training that I have done, in some way, has been based in a refutation of Realist ideals. I have mostly encountered the name Stanislavsky, for example, as a target of derision. The work that I have done is less formally Realistic or Naturalistic than most theatre in Canada. Nonetheless, there is something quite compelling to me about the audacious artists of those movements and their aspirations. Like their contemporaries Darwin, Marx, and Freud, they make great claims on reality, the refutations of which have provided a raison d'être for many in diverse fields in the last hundred years. But something still resonates. We cannot quite be rid of these looming monsters. And I wonder which of us would banish them if given the opportunity.

The Realists sought through theatrical representation to refer to the material reality of the world. Poverty is *real*. The multiple forms of inequality are *real*. As has been duly stressed, by tackling such things directly, one risks reinscribing the very conditions one seeks to critique. Nonetheless, when I watch David Simon's HBO television series *The Wire* (firmly in the tradition of Zola and Ibsen), I think that more good is being done than harm. It feels "real." Why? I have never been to Baltimore, I have never been a cop or drug dealer, but the way people affect one another in the show is like the way people I know in the world do. It is foreign and familiar. It poses a certain challenge that I cannot just wish away or relegate to a place on a bookshelf. I can hear it grinding away at the quotation marks within which I lazily seek to contain it.

Some watered-down form of Realism has long been the prevailing norm in the theatre, which surely contributes to why so many of us have been inclined to move in other directions. This prevailing norm rarely leaves us off balance. I was surprised when I learned the degree to which opinion was divided amongst those nineteenth-/early-twentieth-century artists as to whether the well-made play structure served to aide or impede the exploration of the "real." A deviser at heart, I'm inclined to side with those who wanted to avoid prescribed structures. But a theatre that points to the observable world is still one that I can get behind; it seems to me as necessary as ever. Still, how to point without reinscribing negative conditions? That's a big question for me.

FOURTH: REFLEXIVITY

EW: I wonder if it isn't the big question for everyone making theatre at this point in history. It reminds me of this Destroyer lyric:

> For someone so beautifully scarred
> I imagine it must be hard to stay away
> from a life of public relations
> but try girl! You gotta try!
> You've got to stay critical or die! ("Beggars Might Ride")

Realism's objective promise nests snugly with the complex of premises, some apparently emancipatory, some clearly harmful, that support the Western notion of progress. No surprise that it's come to be the dominant global artistic style. For Ibsen and Zola, drawing attention to material conditions was an ethical responsibility. I don't know about HBO. Though I wouldn't be surprised to hear their executives espouse many nineteenth-century progressive ideals, maybe even compelling ones, I'm also not sure that those ideals approach the contemporary ethico-aesthetic situation. More than half of what a typical urban human sees and hears is constructed with the intention of selling a product or opinion; money is no longer tied to labour or material; Realism's potential as a humanizing force has collapsed. Not failed, but flattened. Realism is the ground, so the question starts to become: are you going to try to point out the inconsistencies in the system? Or are you going to try to embrace it wholeheartedly, or reject the whole premise, or operate, aesthetically, poetically, outside it? (This takes us back to where devising starts to be relevant as a spacer.)

But however one might want to situate oneself or one's work, there is, I think, another problem to deal with first, and this is the problem concerning pointing and violence. There's got to be something to the fact that we titled this piece with the present participle, as if to say: the concretizing of the belief that the real can be represented according to any one system is happening now and is a form of violence that we are all complicit in. Beware.

I think that pointing to a world that is observable (again, whether that's a performer's abject body, or "real experience," or a careful reconstruction of material circumstances) inevitably does a form of violence—engages in instruction that reiterates the basic inequality of experience. When I said that the last thing I want to do is make something that is real, that gesture of pointing is what I was referring to: the last thing I want to do is make work that claims reality is any particular way and that I am in possession of this knowledge of what is "real" prior to the moment in which the performance is happening. The problem of violence is a teaching problem and it's in the very syntax of Realism. Given this, I think it makes sense to engage with Realism, not so much as form, but as subject. Maybe that's what devising realism is about.

Practically, following the intention of doing no violence in the context of performance has placed lots of constraints on me, but it's also provided access to surprising freedoms. That's the bare realness I was trying to get at before. I want to see, and thus try to make, art that is soft enough that it stages an absence. The absence invites expectation, recognition, feeling, but, ideally, is never filled in completely. Various responses can appear without closure providing the aesthetic signal of one or the other being "real." The space between them then becomes free, available.

BB: I'm intrigued by the notion that Realism is the "ground," in that it both describes and inscribes our experience. Discussing literary prose, James Wood has suggested that "Realism, seen broadly, cannot be only a genre; instead, it makes other forms of fiction seem like subgenres. For realism teaches everyone else. It schools its own truants." Yet the concepts of "fore" and "ground" are learned perspectives, and while refuting and/or unlearning dominant perspectives is never simple nor easy (nor, arguably, complete), there is historical precedence for the effort.[4]

---

4   I suspect, for instance, that some members of the Futurist and Dadaist movements—those like Sophie Taeuber-Arp, whose relationship to the absolutism of manifestos was troubled by complicating factors such as interdisciplinarity and gender—made a pretty

Ultimately, the *idea* of Realism as ground is expressed through *contextualized* conventions. Thus, while most contemporary "alternative" theatre practitioners are bombarded by Realist conventions in television, film, and commercial media in general, these same practitioners likely also do a pretty good job of putting Realist *theatrical* practice and product at arm's length. For many working in theatrical devising, Realist conventions are experienced a bit like conservative political ideology—that is, via a form of "alienation effect" that highlights capital "R" Realism's consolidating otherness at the same time that it concedes small "r" realism's diversity and ubiquity. And just as they are forced to come to terms with their own, often unwitting, collusion with conservative ideology, so too are they made aware of their own participation in realist priorities. The matrix may, in the end, be constructed on realist values via Realist conventional strategies, and it may be impossible to get entirely outside the system, but one can become increasingly aware of and savvy about one's own complicity.[5]

AM: I think we should stop avoiding the dialectic and make work that somehow invites response, not by claiming little but by claiming a lot and being open to a return volley. I am suspicious of work that absorbs its own critique. It seems to me that if we see Realism for what it is—a construct—it can be very useful. That said, I agree that we should be opening spaces and "staging absence" in our work. We are well beyond the point at which Realism can be ethically embraced without explicitly acknowledging its holes and potential treachery. When we point to the world, we should direct attention to the gaps as well as the solids. Realism plus space.

---

consistent effort to put Realism at a healthy distance in their day-to-day lives (without assuming naive isolation from realism's effects).

5   An excellent example of this can be found in Guillermo Verdecchia's *Fronteras Americanas*. See Hansen.

LAST: CURIOSITY

BB: I think Alex's question—*can* we point without reinscribing negative conditions?—speaks, in part, to your concerns about teaching and violence, Evan; it's my query, too. Emmanuel Levinas spent his life wrestling with this dilemma—the violence that the "said" inevitably inflicts upon the potential of "saying."[6] From this perspective all actions are *betrayals*—yet, paradoxically, also the unavoidable alternative to stasis, inertia, procrastination. I don't think that stasis and inertia are what you're proposing, Evan, but avoidance and betrayal are often understood as the only two options. This is why Realism loves heroes—because they have the nerve to do the necessary violence. But what does a theatre (a stance) that refuses to engage in the economy of doing and teaching, without simply throwing in the towel, look like?

EW: Let me just say that the word "stance," the theatre being a kind of stance, makes a lot of sense to me because we're talking about art, so we're first of all talking about the choice of making certain signs and positioning ourselves within a whole field of possibilities. "Stance" also connotes a little bit of the swaying that happens in any live encounter; "betrayal" might be another word for this sway. I acknowledge a certain amount of betrayal in every interaction. I mean, you can't be doing anything—anything!—ethically if you are not willing to take a stand somewhere. But this reminds me of another reason why I like performance: it's easier to forgive yourself (and others) for the betrayal if you're working through a problem in real time.

I'm trying to work up some nerve to answer your question, Bruce. I can say that I know I've seen that kind of theatre before in important and understated works. I think that Richard Maxwell's work on affect-less archetypes does this, like *Ode to the Man Who Kneels* and *Neutral Hero*. I think that STO Union and PME-ART do this, especially with *Revolutions in Therapy* and the *Hospitality* series, respectively. It's something I try to work with, too, as a principle, and it's a big preoccupation of many of the artists I work with, which is heartening.

---

6   See Alford, "Levinas," and Waldenfels.

When I think about the qualities of performance demonstrated by the artists above, I'm struck by how much their non-violent stance is an embodiment of thinking. The stance that can be adopted in the theatre is a deeply observant, critical, open, receptive one. This requires a certain fearlessness when it comes to doing very little, like a certain hunger for the productive boredom of meditation. And curiosity. In my own work I'm interested in how we might adopt and maintain (or struggle to maintain) this stance while speaking the words of the script of the world we inhabit. This is a script that was written largely by Westerners in the nineteenth and twentieth centuries, and it continues to be read now. We all know it. We know it very well. We all know it has problems. But it's very interesting to stage it in the stance of non-violence, to see how much non-violence this script can accommodate. This seems like meaningful ground to work on, to be devising on.

BB: Chasing after your thoughts, Evan, I find myself running alongside a body of troubled water that I'm curious about, drawn to, but suspicious of, all at the same time. I'm not convinced that much of it is as deep as I want it to be. The paradox is a key one: why is it so hard to imagine a theatre that earns a spectator's attention to "doing nothing"? How does one perform the productive boredom of meditation? I know it can be done; I've experienced it, too (in the theatre, but more often elsewhere). But when it happened it never felt systematic or premeditated. What does the *practice* that results in this experience look like?

Devising emerges, at least in part, from resistance to authoritarianism, from a desire for heightened collaboration and the admirable fantasy of democracy. But it is also commonly associated with pronounced *activity*—conspicuous, even exaggerated *doing*—as if many of its advocates feel a need to emphasize its collaborative nature by making sure that everyone involved does a lot and does it writ large. "Look, we're collaborating!" Very often this can result in counter-violence, in an intentional betrayal in order to seek a new balance. Affirmative action, of a sort. And in this, I think, devising shares a lot with Realism. Realism equally feels (now, to me) like it's pushing deep into my personal space, insisting that I note and participate in its cultural and ethical assumptions and preconceptions. I guess I hope devising isn't trading so heavily in the unnamed, in the taken for granted, in the implicit. But it is often still intrusive. Tracing back part of its mongrel pedigree to popular and political theatre movements, much devising is motivated by a lack of confidence in meditation and productive boredom holding their own in an oppressive world.

For my part, I recognize that heritage in my own work and in that of many of my collaborators. But my practice is also tempered by a suspicion of inherited enthusiasm and shaped by a hunger for contemporary relevance—the trump card played so vigorously by Realism. Picking up on your thoughts about form and subject, Evan, I suppose what I'm especially curious about are the ways that Realism can be utilized within devising as a means to an end, without it surreptitiously becoming an end to the means. I think the latter happens when devising unintentionally surrenders the "ground" to Realism, when Realism becomes the base upon which larger-than-Realist movement and sound are layered. Devising as accentuation, or filter, or disguise. But I think the former is also possible, particularly when devising isn't afraid of or antagonistic to Realism, but rather when devising is curious about Realism—as a form, as the expression of a philosophy, as the framework of a key mode of interpreting social and political realities. Take, for example, Zuppa Theatre's *Penny Dreadful* (2007), which wrestles with Realism as a subject (in its allusions to Ibsen's *Ghosts*, in its flirtation with sensationalism, in its reluctant pull toward narrative closure) without surrendering to Realism as a form. I think that, for me, this is a key source of tension in that show.

EW: Doing text, speaking words that are written for us, with the addition, as you said, Alex, of *space*—that seems like one of the ways Realism can be utilized within devising. Working with text is key to this. It's become the basis of my work in theatre: *people* doing *plays*, with as little as possible in between—making room for an ethical encounter between individuals. This all points away from a concern with the aesthetic experience: with message, teaching, and drawing attention. I don't know how far this goes.

I certainly observe a lack of confidence in this direction, especially from theatre-makers, but whether it's boring, productive, or otherwise, I think only poetics will hold its own in contest with the real: a poetic logic of creation and survival. And so that's the invitation I want to extend to everyone through what I do.

Heiner Müller wrote about this before he died, just after Germany was reunified: "The point now is not ideas, but rather realities." Nonetheless, he concluded, "You have to learn—and this is the essence of emancipation—to bear being alone" (141).

AM: I agree with your above statement, Evan, but I will also echo the suspicion that colours Bruce's enthusiasm. I think that an ethical encounter is impossible if we pretend there is little or no distance between us, or that we can do anything without "drawing attention." I think this is apathy in disguise. I see no alternative to pointing, and find myself seeking a way of doing so for *this* particular moment. I think that theatre can only exist on shaky ground.

Clearly, we should never return to the aesthetic assumptions of nineteenth-century Realism. But I feel we are at a particular crossroads right now—one that became apparent to me, as I mentioned above, watching *The Wire*. I certainly cannot speak to HBO's motives or even those of the show's creators, but it seemed to me as I watched that something quite compelling was happening to me, in my consciousness. I left the experience wondering if this piece of slightly unusual mass culture was not in fact more subversive than the vast majority of publicly funded specialist art. Admittedly, "subversive" is another tricky word in a culture that has become so habitually self-reflexive, but I mean it to refer to an act that provides us with a tool—one that can be used upon the structures of thought and the institutions with which we are familiar.

Unquestionably, *The Wire* teaches. Whether you agree with it or not, the series is a polemic, advancing a very negative view of how American institutions function at this point in time. It forced me to think about institutional life as I experience it—in art institutions, institutions of higher education, etc. It made claims that I now have to test and it made me think about how I structure the world around myself. It seems absurd not to utilize this capacity of Realism, especially as institutions are being interrogated before us [in 2011].

I sometimes wonder if we would benefit from considering every word to be in quotation marks. I don't think I'm being reactionary when I say that surely a certain era of stories about telling stories and performances about making performances is coming to an end. There is something tiresome now about work that constantly refers to its frame. The all-absorbing, self-reflective cautiousness of the late twentieth century must have run its course, and is probably no more welcoming to rookie players than that which it replaced. Something of the late-twentieth-century critique will likely always be with us, but I *would* suggest that we need to engage in the dialectic more openly again—and that has some affinity with Realism.

As for devising, Bruce, I think you are right when you identify the dangers of demonstrating "collaboration." Devising of this sort has become very banal, at least for those of us to whom it has become familiar. But I don't believe there is much that is fearless about doing nothing and, indeed, I don't think that one *can* do nothing.

BB: Your comments, Alex, bring to mind those of Carol Martin in her introduction to the recent collection of essays *Dramaturgy of the Real on the World Stage*:

> Despite the postmodern assertion that the truth is not entirely verifiable, most people live guided by convictions about what they believe to be true. It's this world—the world where truth is championed even as we experience our failure to ever know it with absolute finality— that theatre of the real attempts to stage. Its assertion is that there is something to be known in addition to the dizzying kaleidoscopic array of competing truths. Skepticism and irony are still present but no longer center stage. A new generation of artists and scholars is committed to understanding theatre as an act of positive consequence. (3–4)

For my part, I get uneasy around the talk of crossroads and of finding ourselves in a particular moment of change. I recognize the utility of the gesture, which can provide a sense of focus and urgency when the current is strong and the water unclear. But change happens so fast and so slowly. I often have the experience of having a brand new conversation for the umpteenth time, and I'm often amazed by our general ability to unask questions. I agree that we've moved both beyond the naive adoption of Realism as "ground zero" *and* beyond a naive assumption that we can simply draw upon realism as a single, equally available and compliant tool for composition and performance (and living, for that matter). Not surprisingly, I usually find myself somewhere along a sliding continuum between these two positions (although rarely in the same place twice).

Ultimately, to indulge in generalizations (another, perhaps necessary, betrayal at times), I understand Realism as an attempt to construct the perfect *container* for the real—one that grants the real absolute authority at the same time that it tries to define, control, and exhibit it. Conversely, I understand devising as the building of frames (to look and pass back and forth through, to isolate and orient): practical strategies for approaching the real without attempting to contain it *or* concede it absolute authority. In short: yes, I suppose we're devising realisms, plural.

AM: I am loath to attempt an easy consensus, but I can endorse the desire to follow one's curiosity. That simple formulation proposes a different set of possibilities than are made available by acquiescing to a received standard. Curiosity has been a fundamental condition of devising for me, just as curiosity about the world will always make Realism have some influence on me.

Play in the troubled water. Play in the troubled water.

REALISMS OF REDRESS: ALAMEDA THEATRE AND THE FORMATION OF A LATINA/O-CANADIAN THEATRE AND POLITICS

NATALIE ALVAREZ

I'd like to begin by echoing the questions that launch E. Patrick Johnson's investigation of performing blackness, though from a distinct perspective, one taken from the edges of a Latina/o-Canadian theatre culture in formation: "What happens when [Latinidad] is embodied? What are the cultural, social and political consequences of that embodiment in a racist society? What is at stake when race or [Latinidad] is theorized discursively, and the material reality of the [Latina/o] is occluded? Indeed, what happens in those moments when ["Latina/o-ness"] takes on corporeality?" (2). Moreover, what are the consequences of this embodiment under the concerns and tacit givens of realism?

Galvanized by the experimental theatre movement of the 1960s and 1970s, cultural and materialist feminists responded to what they perceived as the consolidation of realism's aesthetic "givens" with its post-WWII entrenchment as the dominant form of the modern American theatre. The cultural feminist critique of realism was targeted at both its content and form. The realist canon not only revealed a "relentless plotting toward a white, middle-class, male privilege the history of dramatic texts maintained" (Dolan, *Feminist Spectator* 85), but its formal features also succeeded in obfuscating this very particular ideological position through an airtight illusionism, which naturalized this position in the seeming transparency of its representational system.

Realism was seen as a conservative and "prescriptive" form that reproduced and reified, as Jill Dolan put it, "the dominant culture's inscription of traditional power relations between gender and classes" (84).

But this resounding renunciation of the form among feminist critics in the 1980s had its own consolidating effects, eclipsing other feminist positions, which tried to recuperate realism's potential for highly visible social critique as mainstream fare, or to remind us of other *kinds* of realism that productively unsettle the view of mimesis as merely imitative and reproductive. In *Unmaking Mimesis*, Elin Diamond returns to the work of the late nineteenth- and early twentieth-century realists in order to reveal realism's paradoxes, its "hysteria," and to complicate a totalizing, neo-Platonic view of the limitations of mimesis, arguing that mimesis is a "political practice, inseparable from interpretation and contestation" (viii). It is, arguably, necessary to recover this critical perspective of realism's multiplicities and its potential as a site of paradox and contestation in order to create a critical opening for the subject positions that have been historically marginalized by its aesthetic system. This critical opening is particularly crucial in light of the fact that the very attributes cultural feminists identify as the source of realism's ideological dangers account for its capacity to serve an important function of "reflection and validation," as Jill Dolan asserts, for marginalized communities who have been "disenfranchised at dominant cultural production sites" (*Presence* 26). For Latin-Canadian company Alameda Theatre, realism serves this very particular aesthetic and political function of "reflection and validation."

Due, in part, to realism's legacy as an aesthetic bearer of the white bourgeois subject and the systemic disenfranchisement to which Dolan alludes, visible minorities have historically been estranged from participating in its aesthetic system. The casting of visible minorities in realism's repertoire, whether it be through "colour-blind" or "non-traditional" casting, is often seen as a dissonant sign that throws open the codes of its operations, rupturing its illusionism. This paper seeks to dig deeper into the problem of realism's apparent incapacity to "accommodate people of colour" (Dolan, *Presence* 139) and asks whether a redressive realism that aims to integrate Latina/o actors into this aesthetic system is desirable or even possible politically.

On the surface, this essay interrogates the casting challenges that a Latina/o-Canadian theatre culture in formation is now facing, and in this regard may seem to present a return to questions that pervaded theatre scholarship in the 1980s. But judging from an important recent issue of *alt.theatre*, it seems these questions have resurfaced. The September 2009 issue featured letters to the editor of the *Vancouver Plays* blog, Jerry Wasserman, on the subject of diversity on Canadian stages. In response to this thread, Camyar Chai writes, "I can't believe we are still discussing this issue." I can't believe we are either. But a crisis of representation of Latinas/os on Canadian stages is precisely what induced Chilean-Canadian actor, playwright, and producer Marilo Nuñez to form Alameda Theatre and it's a topic that is very much at the forefront of discussions among the artistic directors, directors, and producers of Latina/o theatre in Canada.[1]

The event that induced Marilo Nuñez to form Alameda Theatre is an infamous one to Canadian theatre scholars and practitioners. In a recent interview, she rehearsed the scene: she arrived at the first read-through of Ken Gass's 2003 Factory Theatre production of Carmen Aguirre's *The Refugee Hotel*, a play about Chilean refugees who arrive in Vancouver after the coup in Chile, only to discover that not only was she the only non-white actor cast in the play, but she was cast in the role of La Calladita (the Quiet One), its only mute character. Refusing to remain "calladita" about it, Marilo spoke out against Gass's casting choices, which he justified on the grounds that there is a dearth of experienced, trained, and competent Latina/o-Canadian performers to take on these roles.[2] Aguirre withdrew the play from Factory's 2003 season on the grounds of what she referred to as Gass's "racial and cultural insensitivity" (Crew, "Factory Theatre"). The experience prompted Nuñez to launch

---

1   In an interview, Nuñez informed me that conversations between her, Beatriz Pizano of Aluna Theatre, and playwright/director Carmen Aguirre often turn to questions concerning casting and become quite charged as they wrestle with the issues this paper, in part, aims to examine.

2   For an examination of Gass's position and the cultural barriers preventing visible minorities from getting cast in Canadian theatre, see K. Taylor, "Fix."

Alameda Theatre, designed to give opportunities to Latina/o-Canadian artists, in the belief that with time and experience not only will Latina/o-Canadian actors be hired to play the roles of Latina/o-Canadian characters, but they will also be cast in leading roles regardless of ethnicity.[3]

In its efforts to forge a distinctly Latina/o-Canadian theatre culture in Toronto, Alameda Theatre engages in what might be called a "realism of redress," recuperating representations of the Latin-American diaspora, which had been elided both by a predominantly Anglo theatrical tradition in Toronto and by destructive stereotypes. Alameda's aim is to redress this elision from within, integrating well-trained and talented Latina/o actors into the dominant realist aesthetics of Canada's premiere professional stages, but *as* Latina/o actors who, unlike in their experiences in acting school, as Nuñez notes,[4] are not forced to erase the physical and vocal markers of their Latinidad and "pass" in the roles dictated by a predominantly Western, Anglo canon. Rather, Alameda aims to create opportunities for its actors to participate in this canon, as well as in their own stories, *as* Latinas/os. In turn, Alameda has adopted a political mandate to cast, wherever possible, from within the Latin-American diaspora—a mandate that Nuñez herself refers to as unapologetically and explicitly political. The purpose of my investigation here is twofold: first, I want to examine what this implicitly identity-based, testimonial casting reveals about an economy of desire at play in realism made evident in the deployment of a particular form of performative authorization; second, I want to investigate the implications— and complications—of these "authorized embodiments" for the formation of a Latina/o-Canadian theatrical culture.

---

3   This comes at the issue from the opposite angle of what frustrated Nuñez in the first place: she hopes casting will be colour-blind in the future, if that means that Latina/os are widely cast.

4   In an interview, Nuñez recounted how her acting teachers encouraged her to "get rid of her accent" (Nuñez) if she wanted to pursue a career in acting.

THE DOMINANT AESTHETIC AND THE DISSONANT SIGN: AN OVERVIEW OF THE DEBATES

The vibrant debates on ethnicity and casting that permeated theatre studies scholarship in the 1980s and 1990s can be seen as an unfurling of the identity politics spawned by the social movements of the 1960s and 1970s. In stride with the Civil Rights Movement in the US, Canada witnessed a similar turn toward anti-establishment politics in the 1960s and 1970s, which helped catalyze the formation of alternative theatres in Canada dedicated to finding a distinctly Canadian artistic identity in the shadows of the cultural hegemony of the Mother Country. But the project of national identity formation, kindled by Canada's 1967 Centennial celebrations and the creation of Canada's official multicultural policy in 1971, consolidated that identity under the rubric of its officially sanctioned charter groups—French and English—relegating the stories and practices of the "ethnic Canadian" or "visible minority," as Sharon Pollock has argued, to the status of inconsequential "folk art" or "craft" ("Evolution" 121). The "ethnic Canadian" became the colonized of the colonized and her artistic practices were contained within the policy's preservationist discourse as "cultural heritage."[5]

Despite the best efforts of the early mavericks forging a distinctly Canadian theatre in the wake of these idyllic nationalist and multicultural turns, the work of alternative theatres did not, Pollock argues, "reflect the diverse multi-racial and cultural nature of Canada, no more than did the playwrights' names, or the faces seen and the voices heard on stages" (120). Reflecting on her own efforts to become an actor in Canada in the 1960s, Pollock notes, "it was always necessary for me to assume another voice":

---

5   For a trenchant analysis of the "multicultural script" and overview of its most prominent critiques, see Ric Knowles, "Multicultural Text, Intercultural Performance," as well as Knowles's introduction to his special issue on intercultural theatre for *Theatre Research in Canada/Recherches Théâtrales au Canada*, in which he examines the impact of multicultural policy on non-Western cultural practices.

One used a range of appropriate British accents for plays set in Great Britain, similarly so for plays set in the United States, and what was referred to within the profession as a "mid-Atlantic" (translation: upper-class educated English) accent for all other plays although they clearly were not set in the mid-Atlantic but in places like Russia, France, Italy, Spain, Germany, Scandinavia, or in some imaginary location. The only voice and accent one never used was the Canadian voice and accent[.] [T]he Canadian voice as it was heard when it fell from the lips of white Canadians. . . . (116)

Pollock's account reveals how the body on Canadian stages in the 1960s carried the physical and vocal markers of the colonizer, centralizing the dominant Caucasian subject and further eclipsing the "visible minority" within the national theatrical landscape.

The invisibility of "visible minorities" on Canadian stages persisted in the 1980s, even as Canadians witnessed Trudeau's White Paper on multiculturalism pass into the Charter of Rights and Freedoms and the Canadian legal system. This persistent and systemic exclusion was made evident in the call for a forum on the subject, and in 1988 the Canadian Actors' Equity Association, under the leadership of Brenda Kamino and Dirk McLean, organized the first national symposium on non-traditional and cross-cultural casting. The term "non-traditional casting" had been gaining currency in the US with the formation of the Non-Traditional Casting Project (NTCP) in 1986, following the more commonplace usage of "colour-blind" casting in the 1950s and 1960s. While "colour-blind" served a specific strategy of racial integration in stride with the anti-segregation movements across the US in the 1950s, and 1960s, the term "non-traditional casting" reflected the NTCP's broader efforts to promote the inclusion not merely of ethnic minorities, but also of women and the disabled.[6]

In the late 1980s and early 1990s, just as noted feminist scholars such as Elin Diamond, Jill Dolan, Sue-Ellen Case, and Teresa de Lauretis began

---

6   On the history of these terminologies and the non-traditional casting movement in the US, see Pao 3–6.

interrogating realism as an invisible apparatus of hegemonic culture, debates around "non-traditional" casting practices served, too, to question
the assumptions safeguarding realism as the dominant aesthetic. Non-
traditional casting, in which the ethnicity, gender, or physicality of the
performer does not coincide with the character represented, became a
cipher through which realism and its attendant conventions were decod-
ed and scrutinized. In a 1989 issue of *TDR*, Richard Schechner lamented
that "the stage . . . enforces its own especially binding naturalistic rigor"
("Race Free" 6), allowing little room for a rethinking of the performer-
character dyad that non-traditional casting affords and of the "stringent
requirement" that there be "a close fit between the representers and the
represented" (6). Schechner called for a radical form of "race free, gender
free, body-type free, age free casting" that allows flexibility for "situation-
specific decisions" as to "when to use, when to ignore, and when not to
see race, gender, age, and body type" (10); in turn, this flexibility will allow for "different kinds of responses"—times when race, gender, etc. are
and are not perceived—"because spectators have been trained to be race,
gender, age, and body-type 'blind'" (9).

While Schechner is careful to point out that he is not advocating for the
re-imposition of "the melting pot" and "mainstream mid-American values"
(10), the notion of training the spectator to become "blind" to the markers
of race and gender does present potentially regressive implications and questions about its viability (and desirability). Richard Hornby, in his 1989 essay,
"Interracial Casting," expresses doubt about the possibility of colour-blind
casting "unless our society itself becomes colour-blind, which is not only
unlikely but probably undesirable" (460). Instead, Hornby calls for "colour-
neutral casting, in which we accept the conventionalized nature of the stage,
and suspend concern about the race of an actor unless the play itself stresses it" (460). He adds that the best way to "achieve colour-neutral casting on
stage is to practice it as often as possible" (460). But the logic that underpins
colour-blind casting is not altogether altered with Hornby's notion of "colour-neutral casting," nor are the problems it presents circumvented. Despite
the progressive pluralism colour-blind or "colour-neutral" casting potentially

promotes, it also, as Benny Ambush argues in a 1989 *American Theatre* article, "whitewashes aesthetically different people" (5), promulgating the sense
that ethnic difference and "cultural specificities do not 'matter'" (Gilbert and
Lo 33). In Helen Gilbert and Jacqueline Lo's reading, these casting practices have the potential to sustain "a familiar view of the world by subsuming
the defamiliarizing potential created by the lack of 'fit' between actor and
role into the normative conventions of Western theatrical realism" (33–34).

The disputes over the merits of colour-blind casting were reignited in
the 1990s, when Pulitzer Prize–winning playwright August Wilson made an
incendiary keynote address at the Theatre Communications Group's bienni-
al conference at Princeton University in 1996, later published in *American
Theatre* as "The Ground On Which I Stand." In this piece, Wilson argued
that colour-blind casting served as an affirmative-action strategy by mainstream (read: white) theatres to secure financial and governmental support
that would be more effectively imparted to black theatre and its emerging
artists. Wilson referred to colour-blind casting as

> an aberrant idea that has never had any validity other than as a tool
> of the Cultural Imperialists who view American culture, rooted in
> the icons of European culture, as beyond reproach in its perfection.
> It is inconceivable to them that life could be lived and enriched with-
> out knowing Shakespeare and Mozart. Their gods, their manners,
> their being, are the only true and correct representations of human-
> kind. They refuse to recognize black conduct and manners as part
> of a system that is fueled by its own philosophy, mythology, history,
> creative motif, social organization and ethos. . . . For a black actor to
> stand on the stage as part of a social milieu that has denied him his
> gods, his culture, his humanity, his mores, his idea of himself and
> the world he lives in, is to be in league with a thousand naysayers
> who wish to corrupt the vigor and spirit of his heart.

Wilson's remarks ignited a flurry of responses, most notably from his principal detractor, American Repertory Theater (ARP) artistic director Robert

Brustein, which were published in the pages of *American Theatre*. Among these responses, Schechner rose to the defense of colour-blind casting once again, arguing that "to always cast according to type—racial type, especially—is a stupid, short-sighted and inartistic thing to do" (Schechner, "In Praise of Promiscuity").[7]

Meanwhile, in Canada in the 1990s, the pages of *Canadian Theatre Review* were lit up by artists and advocates who, in the spirit of Wilson's hard look at Caucasian monoculture, lamented the homogenous representations of a white Canada on its stages. As the late Lorena Gale, founder of the Program for the Professional Development of Artists of Colour in the Theatre, asserted,

> The ethnic make-up of Canada has changed, but Canadian theatre has remained the same. Too cowardly to risk reflecting the cultural richness and diversity of post-modern society, it serves a dying white audience a tasteless unnourishing gruel of the same theatrical fare it dined on centuries ago, not realizing, as it races backwards towards extinction, that Darwin's theory of evolution also applies to artistic form—adapt or perish. (18)

Canadian theatre's staid artistic forms, Gale's remarks imply, coincided (and still do) with a dearth of diversity on its stages. The dominant aesthetic here, once bent on high British culture, is now homologous with a Caucasian Canadian tradition.

Following the Factory Theatre debacle with Aguirre's *Refugee Hotel*, another high-profile debate concerning the lack of diversity on Canadian stages surfaced again in 2008, this time centring on actor and Chalmers-winning playwright Andrew Moodie and Shaw Festival artistic director Jackie Maxwell. After Moodie submitted a play to the festival for consideration, a play that was otherwise compatible with the Shaw Festival mandate,

---

7   The number of articles published in the 1980s and 1990s on the question of colour-blind casting are too numerous for me to list in full here. See, for example, Fichandler; Newman; Schultz; and E.P. Walker.

he was told by "an employee of the company" that the play "would never get produced at Shaw because the cast had too many people of colour" (Moodie, "My Open Letter"). Moodie subsequently initiated a Facebook campaign and website, called "Share the Stage," devoted to diversity issues in Canadian theatre. In one thread of the Facebook page, members took up the thorny question of colour-blind casting. Queen's professor Craig Walker attempted to defend the dearth of visible minorities on Shaw Festival stages by considering "facets of the mandate which make colour-blind casting more problematic." He writes,

> The Modernist period is first and foremost the period of Realism and Naturalism, which uses real settings at real historical periods amidst real political questions. As opposed to most Shakespearean plays, which, being set primarily in a realm of ideas, are abstract enough from specific roots to allow setting and casting to be shifted at will, a Realist play is much more likely to demand the evocation of a very particular social milieu. In short, in Realism and Naturalism, surfaces and appearances matter. So colour-blind casting sometimes can be a little more complicated in such circumstances: not impossible, of course, but just a little more complicated.

Moodie responded to Walker's reasoning with the following: "Realism and naturalism should not be used as code words for racial exclusion" (Moodie, "Colour-blind"). Walker's post prompted another member of the site by the name of Patrick Cieslar to arrive at the following question: "Would not the inclusion of a diverse range of actors of visible minorities (although perhaps violating the stringencies of Realism, albeit no more than inviting a 21st century Ontario audience to believe they have been magically transported to Victorian England for an afternoon) create a meaningful, modern variation on the very same social criticism that Shaw directed at his own audience?" (Cieslar).

The sheer number of posts generated by this thread is itself evidence that concerns about colour-blind and non-traditional casting continue. Add to this the recent meeting in November 2010 of the Canadian Theatre Critics Association, which hosted a debate on the subject of non-traditional casting—featuring Djanet Sears, Andrew Moodie, Antoni Cimolino, and Kamal Al-Solaylee—and a speech, given by Richard Schechner in June 2010, printed as "Casting Without Limits" in the pages of *American Theatre* once again, in which he revisits some of the core arguments of his 1989 essay. Evidently, the problem persists, and its persistence raises the spectre of realism's historical limits, and perhaps also its potential, as a mode capable of representing difference.

AUTHORIZED EMBODIMENTS: ICONICITY, LEGIBILITY, AND THE THEORETICAL KNOT

As the work of theorists such as Diamond reminds us, realism has a classically mimetic and epistemological function that operates on the "expectation of resemblance" ("Brechtian Theory" 84). Realism's particular exchange economy trades on the actor's body, which becomes "laminated" to the character in the convention of what semioticians refer to as "iconicity." Charles Sanders Peirce was the first to introduce the notion of iconicity within his general theory of semiotics as a sign vehicle that denotes an object "by virtue of some common ingredient or similarity" or "by likeness" (2.254, 255); "[i]t is," simply put, "like that thing and used as a sign of it" (2.247). Its likeness serves to summon into the onlooker's imagination the idea of a similar object and, as a consequence, the icon always carries with it an idea or an assertion that draws upon a socialized knowledge to be recognized (2.278). In the context of stage realism and mimetic performance, iconicity serves to capture how the conventions of its casting practices operate. As Diamond describes it, iconicity refers to "the mimetic property of acting" in which "the performer's body conventionally resembles the object (or character) to which it refers" ("Brechtian" 84).

This property of iconicity is precisely why feminist performance strategies that redeploy Brechtian staging devices can be so effective, since they

can, by contrast with illusionistic realism, create an "indexical" relation between representer and represented, prying the actor away from character and
denaturalizing normative constructions of gender—and race—that realist
performance otherwise conceals. In Peirce's formulation, the indexical sign
operates in dynamic relation to the object it indicates and directs our attention to it. Unlike iconicity, "the action of indices depends upon association
by contiguity, and not upon association by resemblance" (2.306). Indexicality
calls our attention to the object without subsuming it. In an indexical relation with character, the actor, as Brecht explains it in "The Street Scene,"
"never forgets, nor does he [sic] allow it to be forgotten, that he is not the
subject but the demonstrator" (125). Indexicality, importantly, relies on the
"expectation of resemblance," however it disrupts this expectation and fore-
grounds it, exposing the ideological constructions of race and gender in turn.
Conventional realist stage practices, by contrast, often foster an uninterrupt-
ed identification with representation through iconicity, in a virtuosic fusion
of demonstrator and subject, and its pleasures and desires arguably turn on
the mutual enterprise shared by spectators and performers of consolidating
and reaffirming the familiar.

When it comes to the question of the representation of minorities in realist frameworks, iconicity presents an unwieldy problem. On the one hand,
for minoritized subjects, iconicity provides a vocabulary for identifying what
is wrong when, for example, a heterosexual woman plays a lesbian or a white
actor plays a Latino. For example, appealing to the logic of iconicity, Nuñez
finds it nonsensical that it would be okay for a white actor to play the role of a
Chilean in a production of *The Refugee Hotel* when it doesn't work in the other
direction. In the case of minoritized representations, these breaches of iconicity run the risk of "usurp[ing] a minority voice"; moreover, the heterosexual
or white actor "becomes an imposter, organizing an alien experience under
the rubric of her heterosexual [or white] privilege" (Dolan, *Presence* 145).

On the other hand, the appeal for continuity between actor and character
in the logic of iconicity runs the risk of re-entrenching essentializing representations and obfuscating difference. The potential obfuscation of difference
becomes especially apparent in cases such as Alameda's 2009 production of

The Refugee Hotel at Theatre Passe Muraille. Actors from Columbia, Argentina, and Mexico were cast to play Chilean characters even though, from Nuñez's point of view, under ideal circumstances the cast would have been comprised of Chilean actors exclusively in order to allow the actors' expressive functions as Chileans to fund the performances in the form of an iconic and validating testimonial. The question that iconicity poses is how to form a theatrical culture that recognizes difference without making oneself *reducible* to that difference and obfuscating what Alicia Arrizón describes as "the cultural plurality that defines the configuration of Latina/o identity" (xvii). To put this another way, in the words of Jacqueline Lo and Helen Gilbert: "How [are we] to avoid essentialist constructions of race and gender while still accounting for the irreducible specificity of certain bodies and body behaviours" (47)? Is iconicity nimble enough as a performance strategy to handle this balancing act?

　　Consider Carmen Aguirre's casting choice of Cheri Maracle, a First Nations actor, in the role of *The Refugee Hotel*'s Christina, an Indigenous Mapuche of south-central Chile. According to Nuñez, this was a deliberate strategy on the part of Aguirre who wanted to underscore the continuity between "the plight of the Mapuches [and] the plight of the First Nations here" (Nuñez). This strategic rupture of iconicity generated a powerful semantic layer that reverberated in the confrontational scene between Christina and Fat Jorge. Christina rails against Jorge's faith in those who have remained in Chile to resist the Pinochet regime: "I've come to the conclusion," Christina says, "that our country is a country of cowards," a country that "turns the other way when their neighbours are being taken away," beaten, abused (Aguirre 70–71). When pressed by Jorge as to why she left Chile instead of staying to join the underground resistance, Christina confesses her fear: "You may know a little bit about fear," she says to Jorge, "But I know a lot about it. I am a Mapuche. We've lived in fear for 450 years" (75). She alludes to a history of struggle against conquering forces beginning with the Inca, followed in turn by the Spanish and the Chilean government. Christina's words uttered by Maracle created a powerful testimonial of transindigeneity, constellating the conditions of the Mapuche with those of First Nations in Canada, such that the apathy Christina describes in her country describes our own in the face of Canada's history of de facto apartheid in its treatment of First Nations peoples and reservation lands, and in the legacy of the residential school system.

But is this a case of productively ruptured iconicity that creates a critical opening for recognition across boundaries? Or does it result in a conflation of indigeneity that flattens the distinctions that make the plight of the culturally diverse Mapuche different from that of the culturally diverse First Nations in Canada—a conflation that the expectation for iconicity produces? What "irreducible specificities," to borrow Gilbert and Lo's phrase, are lost in this casting choice in favour of what is inarguably a powerful moment of recognition across difference?

The thorny issue of iconicity looms under the darker shadows cast by realism as an aesthetic bearer of a dominant ideology. In *Presence and Desire*, Jill Dolan asks whether or not realism "can accommodate people of colour" (139) precisely because its dominant (white and male) ideology tends to be obscured by the genre's illusionism and its assumption of neutrality. Within this aesthetic system, the white, Anglo actor often operates as a compatibly neutral sign able to participate easily in a larger network of "dissimulated conventions" (Diamond, *Performance* 5). The tradition that conceives of whiteness as a neutral, unracialized category might explain why Anglo actors have, historically, stood in the place of minoritized identities without query, when minoritized actors can never be anything on stage other than themselves within this dominant aesthetic due to the fact that their ethnicity is "clearly legible in the sign system that governs how bodies are represented in performance" (Dolan, *Presence* 138). In light of this conundrum, Alameda's mandate seems to be driven by a desire for visibility in the face of the visible markers that make Latinas/os "legible in the sign system," embracing the "legibility" that has historically barred them from participating in realism's codes of iconicity as a means of redressing the *in*visibility of marginalized identities on Canadian stages. But this is a visibility that accedes to—and indeed, desires to meet—the terms and criteria of the dominant aesthetic: with enough experience and Stanislavskian-derived training, the thinking goes, Latina/o-Canadian actors will be good enough

to play "themselves" and perhaps even "not-themselves" on Canada's premiere professional stages.

Nuñez has come under fire for comments that often read as an apo-
logia for Latina/o actors as, in the words of Bernard Shaw, "unpracticed
executant[s]" (200). In Alameda's blogumentary leading up to the opening
night of *The Refugee Hotel*, Nuñez seemed anxious to pre-empt any criticisms,
and to address the prejudices she has encountered from artistic directors and
producers about "inexperienced" Latina/o actors, when she enjoined view-
ers to consider the fact that these actors are never given a chance, and that
while the show may not seem as good as others, these kinds of opportunities
will ensure that the actors will get better.[8] According to Donna-Michelle St.
Bernard, however, Nuñez's comments served to reinforce "the reason actors
of colour are often not even auditioned—the perception that they are somehow collectively less as a community of artists"—to which she adds, "do work
that makes your people look good, dude," a rejoinder that contains within it
an invitation to think outside the *a priori* forms of the dominant aesthetic.
But what does it mean to look good, when ideas of what constitutes "looking good" are often determined on the standards of virtuosity governed by
the legacy of realism as a dominant aesthetic—an aesthetic whose very structure, as Dolan implies, estranges ethnic minorities?

Critiques of Nuñez's comments aside, one can perhaps understand the
drives that underpin them: namely, a refusal to accept that Latina/o performers cannot succeed according to the terms and criteria of the dominant
aesthetic, despite—and perhaps in the face of—Dolan's arguments about the
inability of realism to accommodate difference. Nuñez refuses to give up the
possibility that traditional mimesis can serve as a means of making visible
those who are otherwise invisible. Iconicity is, for Nuñez, the corrective. The
problem here is the appeal to iconicity as a way of overcoming the very problems that iconicity has produced; Alameda's mandate puts back into operation
the problems of iconicity, leaving them unquestioned.

---

8   See Part 1 of the blogumentary for *The Refugee Hotel* at www.refugeehotel.blogspot.
com.

But in the face of this desire for representation, for visibility, theoriz-
ing the implications of Latinidad on stage discursively through a critique
of iconicity seems a luxury and risks veiling the lived, material realities of
Latina/o-Canadian artists who simply want to work without feeling as though
they have to erase any and all traces of what makes their ethnicity "legible"
in order to participate in mainstream theatre culture. This very article risks
exacerbating the dilemma, entrapping minoritized artists in a double bind
between the demands of the dominant aesthetic and those of a politico-aca-
demic discourse that, in its romance with the avant-garde, might position this
desire as an insufficiently critical or oppositional acquiescence. Keeping this
potentiality in mind, however, I do feel these are important problems to address (discursively), if only because they continue to grip discussions among
Latin-Canadian artists, and it's important to ask whether or not, at this crucial stage of formation, a Latina/o-Canadian theatre culture can proceed on
the grounds of visibility in and through iconicity. As Peggy Phelan cautions,
"visibility and invisibility are crucially bound . . . Gaining visibility for the
politically under-represented without scrutinizing the power of who is required to display what to whom is an impoverished political agenda" (26).

Questions as to who can or is required to display *what* to *whom* and, in
turn, what exactly is visible to whom (and under what conditions of performance) point to the structures of power and desire that operate in iconicity.
Iconicity is, one could argue, the means by which performativity operates in
performance through a collective authorization of who can perform what and
for whom. If we turn to performativity's linguistic roots, we are reminded that
J.L. Austin identifies the contours and components of a felicitous performative
on the basis, in part, of proper authorization; that is, the particular person ut-
tering the performative must be appropriate for the invocation and authorized
to make it. The lack of proper authorization may not simply be "a matter of
'incapacity'" but may be a case "where the . . . 'performer' is of the wrong kind
or type" (34–35). Such performatives, which *do* things with words, are "hol-
low," "void," and "without effect" because "I was not the proper person . . . to
perform it" (24). "Part of the procedure" of ensuring a felicitous performative, Austin adds, "is getting oneself appointed" (24). To appropriate Austin's

words crudely, "getting oneself appointed" might be one way of expressing the drives of Latina/o-Canadian theatre companies that aim to forge spaces within the Canadian theatrical landscape for self-representation in plays written by and performed by members of the Latina/o diaspora: as Nuñez would have it, the goal is to put *their* words in *their* mouths, where they belong.

Situating questions of proper authorization in the realm of performance might be one way of describing the desires at work in iconicity, a desire for correlation and continuity that entitles one to speak. For Austin, performative authorization forestalls falsehood and insincerity (except, of course, when uttered in performance), qualities against which realism also safeguards itself in order to hermetically and hermeneutically seal its illusionism. The particular viewing procedures of stage realism depend on correlation and sincerity, which, when met successfully, reassure the onlooker that what they see is continuous with what they hear, generating a fulfillment in recognition. The affective powers of correlation and sincerity cannot be dismissed since these are the means by which cultural identities are both instantiated and validated in the process of recognition. Nuñez has apparently received a number of emails from spectators describing the palpable emotions they felt among fellow audience members in Alameda productions (which attract members of the Latin-American diaspora), responses that for Nuñez are not surprising: they are, she says, "seeing themselves on stage"—in some cases for the first time.

But what exactly is seen when iconicity and proper authorization succeed on the basis of a reaffirmation of the familiar? Performativity and its authorization share the same structure as iconicity, in that they are determined on the basis of a consistency with the familiar or, as Judith Butler puts it, "prior actions": "A performative provisionally succeeds . . . because that action echoes prior actions, and *accumulates the force of authority through the repetition or citation of a prior, authoritative set of practices*" (*Bodies That Matter* 227, emphasis in original). Iconicity and authorization are performative in the sense that they are governed by a set of norms that regulate the scene of recognition, which is precisely the problem some feminist critics have had with realism.

In the context of her search for an ethical philosophy in *Giving An Account of Oneself*, Butler's reflections on the ways in which recognition serves to constitute subjectivities is certainly pertinent to the challenges a Latina/o theatre culture in formation faces. "The norms by which I recognize another or, indeed, myself are not mine alone," Butler asserts, "They function to the extent that they are social, exceeding every dyadic exchange that they condition. . . . Some would doubtless argue that norms must already be in place for recognition to become possible" (24). It might also be argued that the norms of recognition are responsible for generating a sense of cultural intimacy and validation that is crucial for the development of specific theatre cultures in formation. But in the scene of recognition that iconicity allows, what does this "horizon of normativity" obscure from our vision?

Perhaps the way forward in examining the problem of iconicity and ethnicity is to ask after the possibilities of an indexical realism,[9] one in which Latina/o and other "visible minorities" can participate in realism's aesthetic criteria without having to render themselves "illegible" within its sign system, but also without ceding to a referential system that always already governs the scene of recognition. There is, as the debates outlined in this paper have demonstrated, something productively recalcitrant about "race"[10] within the conventions of realism and its repertoire. The inability of visible minorities to be subsumed within realism's dynamics of iconicity and therefore preserve its illusionism suggests that visible minorities on realist stages inevitably introduce indexical forms of representation. The contingent "fact" of one's race is always being indexed within realism's illusionism precisely because it is a contingent fact—one to which one belongs but to which one doesn't wish to be reduced.

An indexical realism would embrace this facticity and the radical singularity of the Latina/o actor who stands before the audience with all of her

9   For this question I am indebted to Ric Knowles and his thoughtful responses to my paper at the New Canadian Realisms symposium, where these arguments were first presented.

10   I place "race" in quotation marks here in order to acknowledge the ways in which this category has been complicated by historians and scholars of race theory and dismantled by biologists and geneticists.

"irreducible specificities," apart from the referential "idea" of Latinidad that the realist text might otherwise prefigure. This "failure" to live up to the notional might serve as the ground upon which realism's politics of visibility are revised, enjoining the spectator to take account of what is always missing and never wholly recuperable in representation. An indexical realism might, in effect, point to all those "rhetorically unmarked aspects of identity," to borrow from Phelan (26), that cannot be accounted for or legible within the sign systems that govern how bodies "are read." As a device that ruptures illusionism and exposes the mechanics of realism's operations, it could be argued that an indexical form of representation cannot, therefore, be understood as realism according to the terms by which realism has been cast in cultural feminist criticism. But the queries I have launched and rehearsed here, including those that presently govern the troubled territory of so-called "colour-blind casting," seem to beg for a return to realism's paradoxes and a fuller understanding of the genre's own complexities and contradictions in order to mine its potential as a site of "interpretation and contestation," to echo Diamond's phrase. Perhaps an indexical realism might allow us to renegotiate not only realism's aesthetic criteria, but also how ethnicity is "read" in realist performance, presenting a critical opening for a truly viable "realism of redress."

DRAMA AS SURGICAL ACT: OPERATIVE REALISM AND THE CHINESE CANADIAN REDRESS

PARIE LEUNG

On 22 June 2006, the Canadian government, led by Prime Minister Stephen Harper, apologized to the Chinese Canadian community for the "race-based financial measures" and exclusionary immigration policies "aimed solely at the Chinese [that were] implemented with deliberation by the Canadian state" between 1885 and 1947.[1] Since the Chinese Canadian National Council (CCNC) had begun a campaign for redress over the Chinese Head Tax and Exclusion Act in 1984, the apology and attendant symbolic payments to the few remaining Head Tax payers and their spouses were hard-earned, and, for many, the realization of a long-fought-for dream. As part of this official apology, the government also sought to "establish funds to help finance community projects aimed at acknowledging the impact of past wartime measures and immigration restrictions on ethno-cultural communities" ("Address by").

When such a moment of redress occurs, argues Roy Miki, members of the community in question experience a complex and immediate loss of a long-held identity position:

---

1   This began with the Chinese Head Tax at $50 per head in 1885, increasing to $100 per head in 1900 and then to $500 per head in 1903. (This amount was equivalent to two years' wages.) In 1923, the passing of the Chinese Exclusion Act prevented all Chinese from entering Canada, except for certain students, diplomats, merchants, and clergy. In this way, the labourers who had helped build the Canadian Pacific Railway were systematically prevented from bringing over their wives and in some cases children to join them ("Chinese Head Tax").

When you're dealing with this notion of a wounded identity, as long
as you're in the state of the wound, you're always moving toward a future where you imagine the pain to be resolved. The paradox is that,
if you ever get to that future, you can no longer occupy that condition of consciousness. (qtd. in Beauregard 73)

Miki asserts that the achievement of redress renders the language and voice
created around its championing unnecessary. Further, in the redressed state
the injured community's history "is both [theirs] and no longer [theirs]" because "that history [has been] absorbed into the official history of . . . the
state" (qtd. in Beauregard 73). In this paper, I investigate David Yee's *lady in
the red dress* (2009) and Alan Bau and Kathy Leung's *Red Letters* (2010) as responses to the historical and contemporary realities surrounding the Chinese
Canadian call for redress, but also as performative acts that trouble the "before" and "after" spaces of consciousness that Miki describes.[2] Ineluctably
bound up with the social implications of these artistic works are the broader
politics surrounding the status of Asian Canadian theatre creation and reception in the English Canadian theatrical landscape. Within this context, I
ask whether realism, as a representational strategy, is adequate to the task of
addressing historical events and their repercussions, especially with regard
to the ownership of perceived narrative truth. In these cases, where reviewers often expected a conventional realism underpinned by the "one-to-one
concordance [that] can be recognised between words and world" (Morris
5), Yee, Bau, and Leung offered productions that deliberately "failed" to sub-
scribe to conventional realist mimesis. Instead, both works interwove realist
approaches with non-realist devices, a strategy that not only complicated their
portrayals of the Head Tax and its contemporary resolution but also served to

---

2   Playwrights Canada Press published Yee's play in 2010. I did not see Nina Lee Aquino's
2009 production of *lady in the red dress* for fu-GEN Theatre; my analysis in this paper is
based on the published text. The musical book of *Red Letters*, conversely, has not yet been
published; my analysis is based on the 2010 production by the Vancouver Asian Canadian
Theatre company.

destabilize perceptions of "Chineseness" within the Asian Canadian context.[3]
If realism, given its nomenclatural link with "reality," is by default the theatrical frame most called upon for the purpose of portraying what we perceive
to be truthful experiences, then the conflict between mainstream reviewers'
opinions and artists' strategies demonstrates that assumptions about what
constitutes effective theatrical realism should be adjusted when "real" historical events, particularly those implicated in cultural violence and matters
of redress, are at stake. In such situations, I argue, historical events and their
contemporary resonances may be more effectively represented through what
I describe as "operative realism." In place of conventional mimicry, the model
of operative realism allows theatre artists to "operate on" reality by mobilizing
realist conventions in disruptive ways, shaping new realities that challenge
the mainstream social order.

Viewed through the lens of theatre and performance studies, realism has
been both lauded for class-conscious politics and criticized for perpetuating
the status quo, especially with regards to white, heterosexual male privilege.
Cultural critic Catherine Belsey and feminist scholar Jill Dolan agree that realism is "predominantly conservative" (Dolan, *Feminist Spectator* 84; Belsey,
Critical Practice 47). According to Belsey, "the experience of reading a realist text is ultimately reassuring, however harrowing the events of the story,
because the world evoked in the fiction, its patterns of cause and effect, of social relationships and moral values, largely confirm the patterns of the world
we seem to know" (47). Further, for Dolan, "the crisis that propels the realist plot is resolved when the elements that create the textual disturbance are
reinstated within a culturally defined system of order at the narrative's end"
(84). Its frequent movement toward the resolution of crisis and its confirma-
tion of familiar time and space makes realism a form that often signals what
Belsey calls "closure" (69), disengaging the desire and ability to create change.

Lately, however, Dolan has somewhat revised this strong criticism. In a
recent article, she writes:

---

3   See Aquino and Knowles for the identity politics surrounding the construction of
"Asian Canadian" identity.

While realism might never achieve the cutting critical edge of more
Brechtian epic drama, playwrights [now] more frequently fragment
its once coherent characters with touches of expressionism and the
absurd. Because television and the new media have splintered spectators' attention spans and required us to move our focus among
multiple, conflicting screens and images simultaneously, contemporary realism can't afford to be as static and definitive—performatively
or ideologically—as it once was. ("Feminist Performance" 455)

Richard Hornby offers a context for Dolan's new insight when he reminds
us that "no plays, however 'realistic,' reflect life directly; all plays, however 'unrealistic,' are semiological devices for categorizing and measuring life
indirectly" (*Drama* 14). Hence, he asserts, "we should not view drama as reflecting life, but rather as *operating on* it, though in a complex manner" (17,
emphasis added). In this latter claim, Hornby is influenced by the work of
twentieth-century linguists who "stressed the *operative* nature of language,"
seeing words as "not merely reflect[ing] what is 'out there,'" but instead, as
"device[s] for categorizing and measuring the enormous range of phenomena that are actually perceived" (26). Applying a similar framework to drama,
Hornby argues that "rather than mirroring life passively, drama is instead a
means of thinking about life, a way of organizing and categorizing it" (26).

Building on Hornby, I suggest that a notion of "operative realism" offers
a way to re-examine realism's aesthetic rules, so that we can accommodate
contemporary visual modes that have become part of the way we think about,
understand, and perceive everyday life experiences, even if these modes are
absurdist or expressionist. *The Oxford English Dictionary* yields several definitions of the word "operative," two of which are particularly useful for my
purposes here. As an adjective, it is defined as:

1. Of the nature of or involving a surgical operation; resulting from
   a surgical operation.

As a noun, meanwhile, it is defined as:

2. orig. and chiefly *U.S.* An agent employed by a detective agency, secret service, or similar organization; a private investigator. In later use: an intelligence agent. ("Operative")

If conventional realism is seen as a conservative form in which "realist plots and characters are constructed in accordance with secular empirical rules" and where "events and people in the story are explicable in terms of natural causation without resort to the supernatural or divine intervention" (Morris 3), "operative realism"[4] engages in "surgical acts" that promote disturbances and uses "intelligence" in unfamiliar ways. Artists operate on reality in the sense that they "treat" or even "doctor" our perceptions of encountered phenomena, using theatrical devices or stylized forms (in Yee's case, those of film noir and hard-boiled detective fiction; in Bau and Leung's, those of the popular musical) within realist frameworks in order to provide competing narratives to what might on the surface officially appear as truth. In terms of "intelligence," the playwrights or artists in question might be seen as the agents who covertly utilize dominant or mainstream resources and tools— here, conventional realist devices and their implications of stability—in order to unsettle normative social and political structures.

Neither Yee's *lady in the red dress* nor Bau and Leung's *Red Letters* has been recognized as conventionally "realist." Playwrights Canada Press has described *lady in the red dress* as "a modern-day noir that draws from both Haruki Murakami and Frank Miller." It is a play that is "part didactic narrative about the plight of Chinese Canadian immigrants, part magical realist fantasy, and part violent, hard-boiled noir" (J. Walker). *Red Letters*, on the other hand, is an original "musical telling the tragic story of a family torn apart by unjust government policy and of a son's struggle to understand the parents who were lost to him" ("Synopsis"). It also takes its "inspiration from

---

4   "Operative realism" is not a new term. Scholar George Liska uses it in his study of the complex relationship between world politics and world history. It has also been used in studies on Pragmatism (see A. Moore), and in relation to Idealism (see Morgenbesser's collection on John Dewey).

the musical *Les Miz* [*Les Misérables*] for the theme of love kept apart by social injustice" (Schaefer). What is it, then, that propels me to analyze these
works as examples of "operative realism"?

While press materials do not represent these works as "realist," the creative
compulsion behind them clearly stems from a desire to seek truth excavated
from lived reality. Yee writes:

> I don't actually consider *lady in the red dress* to be an "angry play"
> or a "vengeance play." I prefer to think of it as a play that refuses to
> forget. It (loudly) considers the effect this shit has *really* had on all
> of us Asian Canadians. Or just Canadians. (viii, emphasis added)

Similarly, as Joyce Lam, the artistic producer of Vancouver Asian Canadian
Theatre (VACT), explains in the *Red Letters* program:

> This musical is not about knowing the specific facts and dates of the
> Chinese head tax and Exclusion Act, but *feeling* the hardship en-
> dured by those who were affected by restrictive immigration laws at
> that time. This play is *truly* about the disruption of family, the sev-
> ering of relationships and of father-son bonds. (emphasis added)

In using synonymic indexes such as "really" and "truly" to point to collective
emotional experiences as well as to the documented social repercussions of
this historical event, Yee and Lam reveal the underlying aims of these shows.
Both stress the crucial role affect played in the creation of both works: each
is underpinned by a longing to "re-live" and even "re-feel" the central events
of the Chinese Canadian Head Tax and its redress. Yee, Bau, and Leung have
thus created works designed as acts of remembrance both to express "real"
Canadian histor(ies) from a Chinese Canadian viewpoint and to counter
or coexist with official narratives on the Chinese Canadian experience for a
community that has now been officially redressed—but which may or may
not have experienced "closure."

RED LETTERS

Bau and Leung's *Red Letters* engages the model of operative realism by deploying the Broadway musical form for its power to elicit strong feeling. As Lam's message in the program reveals, the production was mainly geared toward retracing the hardships common to victims of the time, especially with regards to the breaking up of families, the enforced separation of lovers, and, with a patriarchal bias arguably familiar in traditional Chinese culture, the disruptions to the male line of a family. As such, the musical sets off to provide catharsis for audiences who are part of the redressed community, but also allows access to audiences outside of that group through its formal adoption of the popular genre. This English-language musical also meets the Vancouver Asian Canadian Theatre company's mandate to showcase Asian Canadian theatre content, "provide opportunities for Asian Canadians in artistically significant roles," and to encourage and facilitate communication across different bodies and groups on the "significant contributions of Asian Canadians in theatre and the theatrical industry" ("About VACT"). Beginning with a ten-page, two-song idea in 2006, Bau and Leung developed *Red Letters* with VACT using a $62,000 grant from the community historical recognition program that was established as part of the 2006 official redress (Chamberlain 1).

The musical opens with an old man, Ping, watching the live telecast of the prime minister's apology speech. Switching off the television, Ping launches into a song about his memories of his parents, who spectators later learn were victims of the Head Tax and Exclusion Act. He reads the letters his parents wrote to each other years before, and the scene shifts to an earlier time in which the tragic love story between Shen and Mei unfolds. Though they are young and in love, Shen leaves his pregnant wife Mei in China, amid famine and poverty, to journey to Vancouver in order to earn a living at his uncle's laundry shop.[5] Despite Shen's industriousness and good nature, the immigration measures prevent him from bringing Mei and young Ping over to join him; Mei subsequently dies before they can be reunited. Shen encounters the

---

5   The character of Shen's uncle is credited as Boss in the program book.

"white" Joseph who blames immigrants like Shen for "stealing" his job. When Joseph robs him, Shen attempts to get his money back but accidentally kills Joseph when the latter attacks him with a knife. Despairing of a judicial system prejudiced against Chinese immigrants, Shen hangs himself. To ensure that Shen's death was not in vain, his uncle uses his own funds, and at tremendous risk finally brings Ping over. The musical ends with an ensemble song with this main refrain:[6] "Tomorrow is a better place, it's achieved, because our hearts believed. We need to understand our past, share the wrongs, we will all join again, as one again, some day." Ping sings about how "we can stand tall and free today" but the "battle is not yet won till all wrongs are undone." Shen and Mei sing from their "place beyond," noting that they have "witnessed their son's fate," which is "blessed with love and choice." The character of Joseph, though deceased, sings the lines, "I see the growth through all the years; we came a long, long way to where we are today." Ping also sings, "I must learn from my troubled past; it's not too late to see, the better father I can be," implying that he has become estranged from his son due to unresolved issues from this past trauma.

The production in Vancouver and in neighbouring community venues utilized several strategies that heightened historical atmosphere, contributing to the feel of authenticity surrounding the work. These included extensive background research, the mining of factual information carried out by Leung (Schaefer), and the display of historical artifacts such as real Head Tax certificates (Lyon). Recognizable signs of realism also featured in the production design, just as they did in *Les Misérables*, whose performances include period costumes ranging from the ornate to the destitute and an elaborate, revolving barricade set. All the characters wore costumes appropriate to their time and place: Mei and Shen appeared in "silk brocade" clothes in scenes set in China, but in Canada Shen changed into a simple white T-shirt and black trouser combination similar to that of his uncle. Another Chinese character in the

---

6   VACT sold a compact-disc recording of songs and music from the musical during the intermission and after the show. I transcribed the following lyric quotations from this recording.

Vancouver scenes appeared wearing a homburg hat and brown three-piece suit, referencing the styles of the era. Most of the Vancouver scenes took place at the laundry shop—a cleverly constructed space consisting of two adjacent dull-coloured walls to indicate a small room, a table for ironing, what looked to be an old Hotpoint electric iron, piles of white cloths, and Uncle's narrow bed cramped behind the table. The shop was set at an angle against a background of slanted flats covered with enlarged, grainy, old sepia photographs of crowds, so that it appeared nestled amongst other, unseen shops. On top of the regular, non-musical dialogue, the production also used a recording of the prime minister's 2006 apology speech, broadcast from a television set as if it were live. The combination of illusionistic scenic and design elements created an absorbing and reassuring atmosphere that felt "time-locked" and distant from the present—realist staging at work. Still, the show could not be classified as strictly realist; no musical can be. Even if the plot, setting, and moments of prosaic dialogue follow some of the stylistic tenets of modern realism, stressing "a conflict between internal psychological motives and external economic or social pressures" (Worthen 15), the songs function centrally to move the action forward and to reveal character motivations through the specific medium of aural pleasure. And, even amid seemingly pristine illusionistic stage conventions, other kinds of "operative realism" were at work in *Red Letters* too.

Chief among the elements used to disrupt conventional realism in the show was casting. While visually accurate "Asian-looking" actors played all the Chinese characters,[7] the casting of the "white" character of Joseph created a jarring effect that was almost Brechtian in its incongruity. During the initial stage reading at the Performing Arts Lodge Theatre, Andrew Cohen played Joseph.[8] For the full production, however, Isaac Kwok, who looks

7   See Natalie Alvarez's paper in this volume for an in-depth discussion on realism and casting issues for ethnic minority actors.

8   Cohen is an acting graduate of the University of British Columbia. Whatever his genetic makeup, he appears clearly "white" onstage.

mixed race, yet "Asian," and who had previously played the male lead, Wang
Ta, in VACT's *Flower Drum Song*, was cast as Joseph. Given the overt racist
attitude expressed and embodied in the character of Joseph, Kwok's casting
in the role was not only visually surprising, but created a range of conflicting meanings. As the antagonist to the sympathetic Shen, Joseph is, on the
surface, a villainous role. Even though he defends his right to Shen's money,
claiming that he has lost job opportunities to immigrants and has his own
family to provide for, his position is still a negative one, as musically expressed
in the sinister tone of his songs where he schemes to "take what is mine" as
well as in his criminal actions against Shen. Although Kwok's casting could
be linked to VACT's mandate to provide performance opportunities for Asian
Canadian actors, Joseph's racism and Cohen's earlier stage reading—for audiences that had attended both versions—created the expectation that this
character would be played by a white actor. Kwok's "mixed" features unsettled
the image of the "white" character as racist, breaking the illusion of historical veracity. Instead, his presence on stage served to remind audiences about
the current demographic of Asian Canadian theatre-makers and the complex
range of identities within this community, and moved the musical away from
directing blame for racist attitudes toward "white" audience members reductively and exclusively. In this way, Kwok's casting agitated the realist illusion
of the piece, complicating absolute racial binaries and creating a disturbance
that raised uncomfortable questions even as the show at large sought the performance of reconciliation.

   Red Letters also achieved similar effects through songs and characters
that moved the musical beyond simple pleasure and comfort. While the main
narrative revolves around Shen, Mei, and Ping (who, as a baby, represented
hope and familial continuity and, as an old man, stands as a sign of post-re-
dress purgation and the beginnings of reconciliation), the character of Boss,
played by the charismatic Jimmy Yi, managed to steal the show at various
points. Amidst the psychologically revealing solo pieces, expository love du-
ets, and rousing ensemble pieces, one of Boss's songs, "Keep Your Head Low,"
ruptured the neatly packaged illusion of staged history. Played as a comedic
interlude, including a hat-and-cane tap dance, the upbeat ditty appeared to

lighten the serious atmosphere; however, the lyrics revealed darker issues. Referring to himself as "Mr. Chinatown," Boss sings that his "luck [has rolled] right to the top" because he owns a laundry shop. His chorus reads: "Just a little Chinese man, who has his own survival plan; keep your head low, do what they say. No matter what anyone thinks, the law's for whites; yes, it stinks, unwelcome guests, every single day." The jauntiness of the song, along with Yi's dancing, could easily have lulled audiences into a false sense of security and even encouraged them to sway to the music. However, because this pleasurable piece shed light on the very real violence and hostility early migrants faced, enjoyment brought with it a sense of discomfort, especially for non-Chinese audience members. Boss's song disrupted the realist veneer of the staged history, creating a moment of tension between pleasure and unease.

In her article on the Brechtian aspects of the musical *Urinetown*, Anne Beggs argues that musicals "can be simultaneously commercial, middlebrow, and subversive" and that "commercial success and radical political critique are not necessarily contradictory" (41). *Red Letters* is not radically political or explicitly "Brechtian" in construction; it engages the familiar trope of "star-crossed lovers caught in moments of social rebellion" (Beggs 45) and includes an ending that is relatively hopeful, heteronormative, and male-centred. Even so, Bau and Leung's musical embodies one form of operative realism as it creatively engages with Chinese Canadian history, the official act of redress, and the repercussions of both from an artistic position committed to serving the Asian Canadian community both economically and affectively. In utilizing the musical form, *Red Letters* opens up these experiences to Canadian audiences through a conventionally "safe" genre, but its inclusion of disturbances encourages question and discussion to penetrate the "closure" marketed by official narratives.

LADY IN THE RED DRESS

David Yee's *lady in the red dress* offers quite a different example of operative realism via a playful mix of recognizable, conventional realist tropes and "agitating" elements such as fantasy, magic, the supernatural, and the televisual.

Developed under the auspices of several playwriting programs in Toronto and Vancouver, it premiered at the Young Centre for the Performing Arts in Toronto in 2009. A founding member of fu-GEN, an Asian Canadian theatre company in the city, Yee worked in a manner that aligns crucially with aspects of the company's mandate. Besides "explor[ing] and address[ing] issues of Asian North American's [sic] societal roles, responsibilities and identity in the past, present and future," *lady in the red dress* fulfills the "vision" criterion of "diversity of practice: using non-traditional space, time, methodology & philosophy" ("About Us: Mandate"). Set in 2006 in Toronto but flashing through other time frames, the play revolves around protagonist Max Lochran, a department of justice negotiator who, in the middle of arguing with a CCNC representative regarding the terms of the redress settlement over the phone, finds himself facing several crises. His autistic son, Danny, is bothering him at work, he has looming deadlines and meetings, and his CCNC interlocutor is threatening to quote him, racist opinions and all. He faints, but then wakes to an encounter with Sylvia, a mysterious and violent half-Chinese figure clad in a red brocade dress who sends him on a mission to find someone named Tommy Jade. Through several inexplicable, non-linear, and empirically impossible episodes, the audience, along with Max, finds out four important things: 1) that Tommy was Sylvia's father and a victim of the Exclusion Act, which resulted in his failure to bring his Chinese wife to Canada; 2) that Tommy was seduced by Max's grandmother, Muriel, with whom he fathered Sylvia; 3) that Max's grandfather was an exploitative immigration official who cheated Tommy of his money and became his murderer when he learned of the affair; and 4) that the baby Sylvia was shot at, but appears to have survived and now exists in an ageless, youthful, vengeful form, killing villainous immigration and law-enforcement officials. These discoveries, gleaned only through torture, investigation, and deprivation, cause Max to reconnect with his son as well as to rethink his stance on the ethics of redress.

With its absurd elements and fragmentation of time and place, Yee's work echoes Dolan's comments about the need to update and reinvigorate established realist approaches for a new century. Like *Red Letters, lady in the red dress* is fundamentally about family reconciliation, a core theme of classical realism. Both the musical and the play end with the compulsion of a father to reconcile with his son (the mothers are conspicuously absent and, indeed, deceased); in both, the historical background of the Head Tax and its contemporary resolution infuse this conventional trope with the traditional Chinese cultural bias towards the patrilineal. Yee's play, however, offers an important revision: he not only adds to the mix a woman, Sylvia, who is driven to track down her father, but she is also mixed race and mythic, a spirit or trickster figure. According to Yee, the character of Sylvia embodies "the voice [he] wish[es] for Chinese Canadians, a mix of Bruce Lee and Confucius and all the ghost stories about the vengeful bride with the white hair. She's the voice of struggle, fighting for Chinese Canadians throughout history" (qtd. in Kaplan, "Yee"). Sylvia is the agent of disruption in Max's contemporary Toronto, upsetting time, place, and even his sense of reality. While Yee's engagement with cultural icons such as Bruce Lee, Confucius, and the vengeful bride brings to mind the assimilation of aspects of Chinese martial arts, philosophy, and folk legends into mainstream Western culture, Sylvia's construction goes beyond that, disrupting not only common perceptions of "Chineseness" but also common realist conventions. She is a central device for Yee's "operation" on Chinese Canadian history and the contemporary events leading up to the redress: her presence upsets the realist framework that contains Max and his problems, creating in the process a unique perspective that competes with official narratives of redress.

At first glance, Sylvia appears to embody what Dolan has deemed one of realism's main conservative elements: the "installation of the enigma that requires purging" ("Feminist Performance" 455). Max's encounter with her throws his life into chaos—he wakes up in odd places, often with injuries, and can suddenly understand Chinese script. He is forced to seek out strange characters in Chinatown for help, even though they are either physically or verbally abusive toward him. Through them and through his own research, his sense of the historical "truth" changes dramatically, altering his perspective on his role as a redress negotiator, which he had previously taken flippantly. His change in attitude—now more sympathetic to Chinese Canadians—draws the ire of his superior, Thomas Hatch, a racist mouthpiece who believes that "white people are the minority" and that immigrants should not complain when they are given jobs, land, and opportunity (Yee, *lady* 88). Toward the end, Max threatens to kill Hatch, thinking he has lost his son, Danny, forever. However, Sylvia, who has kidnapped Danny, unexpectedly bonds with him over their shared mixed-race identities. This allows her to reconcile with her own past even as she relieves Max of his burden. We might argue, then, that she is not so much an enigma that needs purging within the realist structure as an "operative" element used to doctor perceptions and shift perspectives—even, crucially, her own.

As the antagonist that confronts the insouciant Max, Sylvia represents not only the anger and sadness directly experienced by victims of the Head Tax, but also the corrective force driven by a Chinese Canadian community that has inherited this injustice. She serves as a vocal and cathartic weapon against past and present bodies that refuse to understand the wrongs that have been meted out through unjust governmental policies. At the same time, however, Sylvia's provenance gives her a mixed-race identity, so that she is more exemplary of the pluralities of contemporary Asian Canadian identity formation than she is a representative of a unified "Chineseness" (like, say, Ping in *Red Letters*). This "mixed" dimension allows Yee, who is himself of Chinese and Scottish descent, to express not only the social stigma and racism that many Asians in Canada have faced and do face, but the specific suffering of people with dual or multiple ethnic backgrounds.[9] In a dramaturgical sense, too, Sylvia's identity is radically plural. As a female character who does not fit comfortably either into the empirical realm of reality or into the mould of the passive woman, she follows, symbolically, a long line of "new women" and "bad girls" in modern realism, from Ibsen's Nora to Shaw's Vivie. At the same time, as she unsettles and then drives the plot, manipulating its "reality" along the way, she also resembles a trickster figure, familiar to Canadian audiences principally from First Nations theatre. Sylvia often recites Yeats's poetry while contemplating a murderous act:

---

9   In a touching scene between Sylvia and Danny, Yee presents two opposing views of what it means to be of *Hapa*, or hybrid, descent. While Sylvia has internalized racist perceptions of herself as a "mongrel," "filthy mutt," and "half-breed" (39–40), Danny offers her Max's description of Hapa as being "twice-blessed" (84).

we might thus see her on one hand as representing the Western educational background of playwrights like Yee and the Western canon that steers it,[10] and on the other as embodying the agent of anarchy and transformation familiar from Yeats's poem "The Second Coming."

The denouement, in which Max's experience is revealed as a dream, seems quite conventional in that it ends with the "restoration of the status quo" (Dolan, "Feminist Performance" 455), but that is not really the case. Sylvia's "lesson" is evident in Max's changed mentality, in his physical injuries, and in Danny's new-found ability to address his father as "Dad" and not "Max." The play ends on a decisive cusp: Max's secretary informs him that Hatch and CCNC's Linda are on separate lines and need to speak to him urgently. The audience sees Max press a line and open his mouth, but we do not get to know his choice. Although the redress had already occurred when Yee's play premiered in 2009, Yee's *lack* of resolution raises compelling questions where the official redress would impose closure, forcing audiences to think about what Max *could* do, and what his choices might mean. If he answers Linda, will he now be more earnest about the negotiation and the terms of the redress? If he answers Hatch, will he challenge his superior? Will he be forced to resign? Will he have the power to change the system?

Where Bau and Leung deploy the easily accessible and traditionally entertaining Broadway musical form for their work in order to open up their show to mainstream audiences, Yee utilizes not only film noir aesthetics but also self-referential devices to create moments of operative realism. In *lady in the red dress*, Max's investigations into the story and whereabouts of Tommy Jade require him to seek out some help in Toronto's Chinatown. On three different occasions, he meets Willy, Biff, and Happy Chan. This "citation" of Arthur Miller's iconic American realist trio, Willy, Biff, and Happy Loman, operates as a Brechtian element that reminds audiences of the theatrical frame of the show. A key text of modern American drama, *Death of a Salesman* is itself an early example of operative realism: a realist play featuring expressionistic

---

10   See Knowles, *Theatre of Form*, for a discussion of dramaturgical inheritance in Canadian universities' theatre syllabi. This is arguably still true today.

elements that seek to represent the protagonist's state of mind in order to critique the logic behind the "American Dream." In *lady in the red dress*, Yee's citation of this very familiar text works both as a device for exploring Max's psychological unravelling and his re-evaluation of personal principles, and as a disruptive (per)version of stereotypical Chinese family dynamics.

Whereas Miller's play revolves around the deterioration of a family built upon a father's highly idealized yet misplaced and naive "dream," Yee uses the characters of Willy, Happy, and Biff Chan to destabilize familiar images of Chinese immigrant families and Chinese attitudes toward work. In 2008, echoing a common, racist stereotype, Toronto mayor Rob Ford (still a city councillor at the time) declared that, "those Oriental people work like dogs. They work their hearts out. They are workers non-stop. They sleep beside their machines. That's why they're successful in life" (Yoon, "Reflections" 84). Similarly, early in the play Max says that the Chinese are "taking over. They study harder in school, they work harder, and then they bring each other up the ladder because who knows, right?" (Yee 23). Yee's Chans move beyond the restaurant and laundry trades that early Chinese immigrants were typically known for, but they also occupy unexpected, somewhat outrageous roles that agitate the familiar view of Asian immigrant groups as a hard-working model minority. Willy Chan is the owner of the Golden Pearl, a strip club in Chinatown. Unlike Willy Loman, Chan seems to be a successful purveyor of vices such as liquor, girls, and "lovely illicit narcotics" (Yee 36). He also owns a peep show booth that works as a portal into the past where Max first gets a glimpse of Sylvia and one of her victims in 1943. His offspring, Happy and Biff, both seem successful. They are completely unconnected or answerable to their father (unlike in Miller's play or in the familiar trope of Chinese filial piety). They too—much like Sylvia—resist clear definition. Happy, for example, is a "one-man radio station" who plays Chinese pop music, reports on traffic in Toronto, and claims he is "1/5 Chinese, 1/7 Japanese, 3/8 Korean, 1/10 Filipino, 2/5 Taiwanese, 1/9 Laotian, 5/16 Mongolian and 3/4 Vietnamese" (Yee 44). Happy also serves as a portal for Max: to let Max "speak" to Tommy, Happy "becomes" the latter by channelling his spirit through his own body. Biff, on the other hand, is a "one-man TV station" who interacts with "invisible cameras" that apparently follow him and Max in their interactions. Another portal figure, his power is grounded in the medium of acting: Biff conflates time, space, past, and present (just as television can do), and interacts with Max both as an actor who can "snap out of a scene," and as a telecast showing a story. Both Happy and Biff are layered embodiments of electronic media, but also act as signifieds (or ideographs) for the word "mediums," meaning in this case "spirit-channellers." Their multiple personae have a clear metatheatrical dimension: if Sylvia is a trickster, Willy, Happy, and Biff Chan seem to echo other literary figures, such as Charles Dickens's three ghosts in *A Christmas Carol* or the three witches in *Macbeth*. At once familiar and wildly uncanny, the Chan/Miller trio acts as a reference to another reality: the education of Asian Canadian playwrights in Canadian institutions that tend to centre on a syllabus built on a Euro-American dramatic canon. The "operative" disturbances of Yee's play not only stage scenes of historical reality via the conventions of psychological, emotion-driven realism, but also effectively remind us of the contemporary lived experiences of Chinese Canadians whose identities are always torn between a foreign origin visibly marked on their bodies and a vulnerable, precarious "Canadianness."

THE POLITICS OF RECEPTION

Rather than embracing the complexities of "operative realism," many reviews of these productions disparaged them for not being conventionally realist. At stake in the critical reception of these shows appears to be the "truthfulness" local reviewers expected of representations of the Chinese Canadian redress experience, given its emotional, ethical, and political implications. Behind their criticisms lurks a clash over the "real truth" about Chinese Canadian experience. The reviewers of and the artists behind these shows all clearly wanted something "real," but their versions of this realness and ideas about how it might best be accessed by audiences differed. Reviewing *Red Letters* in the *Vancouver Courier*, Jo Ledingham noted that "somewhat surprisingly, the music is quite Western—in spite of [the] occasiona[l] playing [of] the *erhu* (a two-stringed Chinese instrument)." She continues, "Considering the seriousness of the subject, it does sometimes feel awkward" when "songs of love and longing [are] interspersed with lighter, even amusing tunes." Colin Thomas in the *Georgia Straight* pointed out that "despite the inclusion of the two-stringed *erhu* in the instrumentation, Bau's music is mostly standard Broadway-style fare, complete with a patter song and many ballads. It's an odd filter through which to hear a period story about immigration from China."

These reviewers' concerns arise, I believe, out of their desire (even anxiety) to corroborate what they intuitively already know about "Chinese" culture from the general wealth of material popularly available around them. Faced with the destabilizing strategies of Bau and Leung, they wish, instead, for a conventional realist approach wherein a mimicking of several historical episodes around the official redress and an inclusion of recognizable "Chinese signifiers" could provide reassuring points of reference, allowing them to discuss both the plays and the redress with authority. Of course, this is the very type of realism Belsey and Dolan have deemed conservative, in which familiar tropes or props (such as the *erhu*, in this case) "confirm the patterns of the world we seem to know" (Belsey, *Critical* 47).

In the case of David Yee's *lady in the red dress*, too, mainstream theatre reviewers tended to reveal inexperience in processing and understanding the nuances of Asian Canadian identity politics, again finding the play's form incongruous and accusing it of disservice to the Chinese Canadian redress. Here, again, there appears to be an anxiety about approaching the "real" event in a dignified and appropriate way, a goal that, the reviewers' comments imply, can only be achieved through a conventionally realist form. Robert Crew of the *Toronto Star* declared: "The subject deserves better. This mishmash of a play has all the depth—and some of the gore—of a video game" ("Play has the depth"). Paula Citron, reviewing the play for radio listeners, stated categorically that "playwright David Yee, unfortunately, has approached his subject from a supernatural viewpoint" and that ". . . some very good acting gets lost in the unreality of the vengeful lady as metaphor." Toronto playwright and actor Johnnie Walker suggested in his review for the *Torontoist* that the "larger problem with the play" is that "it doesn't quite know how far down the rabbit hole it's gone; how much of what happens is dark fantasy and how much we're supposed to relate to on a realistic level." These reviews point to a general longing for a secular, empirical, and therefore conventionally "realist" approach to the play. Respondents, meanwhile, combatted these criticisms. Four out of five people who commented online to Crew's review of Yee's play disagreed with his views: for Internet handle "mattw," Yee had presented something more than a "boring history lesson" and for Jean Yoon, he had "created a play for ACs [Asian Canadians] who know the history but not how to respond." For her, "revelling in a revenge fantasy, hip to pop culture [and] outgrown stereotypes" is "way more fun" than the sober realist history Crew had sought ("Great Show").

These responses raise the issue of ownership: whose stories are these, and who gets to tell them? How should these stories be presented? Who are these productions for? Further, what do the reviewers' and artists' underlying dialogical tensions tell us about the discourses at stake when "(re)organizing" historical "reality"? By utilizing aspects of realism only to disrupt its illusions with discomfiting elements, Brechtian devices, imaginative fantasy, and intertextual references, Bau, Leung, and Yee offer compelling ways for countering the "closure" expected in and through official narratives of suffering and redress. By taking ownership of the representation of a "real" historical event, these artists deprive reviewers of the right to talk conclusively about their productions and also about their communities' experiences. They show that, from their point of view, this history is at once for and *not* for all Canadians. Through surgical interventions and playful deployments of realist strategies, *Red Letters* and *lady in the red dress* create space for new forms that provoke engaged reflection and, perhaps, even the beginnings of collective transformation.

FEMINIST REALISM IN CANADA: THEN AND NOW

SUSAN BENNETT AND KIM SOLGA

Despite the substantial progress achieved by feminist activists over the past several decades in North America, in many ways the difficulties faced by women are not radically different today than they were in the 1960s and 1970s. Women still struggle for income parity with men, especially in the private sphere. Women are far less likely to run large corporations, or to wield power within them, than men are; single mothers, women of colour, and women with disabilities are at even greater disadvantage. Women remain far more likely than men to be injured or killed at the hands of a domestic partner.

To add to this injury, "feminism" as a political performative has, over the last fifty years, lost a tremendous amount of its cultural currency. The term has been productively fractured by internal debates about which women are best served by a "unified" feminist movement (typically, white middle-class women), and which are left out; it has also, however, been riven by fierce fights pitting those among the so-called "third wave" against those dedicated to the broader-scale women's justice movement typically associated with "second wave" feminism. As both Dorothy Chansky and Jill Dolan have recently argued, under this model (which is only one of several, arguably quite imperfect, methods of feminist categorization) the third-wave feminist believes that "feminism is accounted for and 'spent'—a force that has done its work and can now be both assumed as normative and implicitly dismissed" (Dolan, "Feminist Performance" 434; see also Chansky 352).[1] Political and

---

1   The differences between third- and second-wave feminism are a matter of debate. Some critics argue that the third wave marks a resurgence in feminist activism that has

media voices contribute significantly to this persistent myth of feminism's "ending." As Chansky writes, popular media "have been heralding the death and trumpeting the triviality of feminism since its inception," but the term has also been subject to a severe and concerted backlash in the US since at least the 1990s, fuelled by globalization-era capitalism's arguments that women's full equality has been achieved and that success or failure for individuals is more a matter of independent effort than available community support or systemic, institutionalized discrimination (353). In other words, at the same time that women continue to fight for their basic material rights in the US and Canada, the traditional language of feminism with which they might wish to politicize their actions has become a liability.

Female artists in Canada struggle daily with this paradox: an ongoing need for feminist force—sometimes simply in order to get noticed or taken seriously—coupled with very real anxiety that identifying with the term "feminist" will negate the gains of their labour. For Canada's performing women, the legacy of stage realism plays an especially tricky role in this story. Feminist artists and scholars have been told for decades that realism is ideologically perilous, but at the same time the route to artistic success has, for women writers and performers, more often than not been paved with realist dramas and psychological realist praxis. Does this mean that women artists who "choose" realism are politically suspect? Have they "sold out"? Or does it mean that feminist performance theory's engagement with realism needs to be revised in order to better account for the paradoxes of late feminism and the complexities of women's engagements with realism, both historically and today?

This essay begins with the emergence of feminist theatres in Canada through the late 1960s and 1970s, spurred by the energies of second-wave feminism and its vigorous rejection of what was seen as a hegemonic realist practice on the country's main stages. We follow this discussion with four

---

more in common than not with its predecessor, and that it is "post-feminism" rather than third-wave feminism that suffers from the perils of an individualistic agenda. For a helpful overview of this argument, see S. Scott 220.

case studies examining Canadian women's realism—one historical and three contemporary—in order to revisit some of the core precepts of that foundational feminist theatre labour. We aim to measure, first, the value of earlier dramatic work by women whose stage realism was ignored, if not outright rejected, by second-wave feminist performance, and then to consider more recent practices that can reanimate both feminism and realism for the contemporary stage. In all cases we temper the theoretical struggle between feminism and realism by paying careful attention to the material: labour, costs, and outcomes. What does realism *do* for working women artists in Canada? What are the limits of its power? When is realism genuinely perilous—and when is it, in fact, quite the opposite?

THEN: THE SECOND WAVE AND BEFORE

Canada's first feminist theatres (Nellie McClung Theatre in Winnipeg [1968], Redlight Theatre in Toronto [1974], and Théâtre Expérimental des Femmes in Montreal [1979]) ushered in strategies of production that differed widely from the dominant ones of their time. Their creators assumed that new methodologies, innovative styles, and an invigorated politic were crucial in educating their target audiences. Developing practices alternative to, and outside, Canada's mainstream theatres was not simply a matter of choice, however; it was plainly a necessity, as Rina Fraticelli's landmark report *The Status of Women in Canadian Theatre* (1982) would show. Commissioned by the federal government, Fraticelli's publication demonstrated the woeful under-representation of women in Canada's theatres, especially in the field of playwriting (only 10% of plays produced were authored by women). With very limited opportunity to participate in Canada's signal theatres, feminist theatre artists not surprisingly looked to other performance spaces, different audiences, and new practices—agitprop, worker's theatre, and collective creation from other English-language theatres; *l'écriture feminine*, cabaret, and more imagistic styles from continental Europe, among them—that would stage their social, political, and aesthetic aims (see S. Bennett).

Not long after the Fraticelli report appeared, an incipient feminist theatre criticism emerged to champion the various innovations that feminist theatres were crafting to challenge mainstream realist practices. As Elin Diamond succinctly put it: "Setting out to offer truthful versions of experience, realism universalizes but one point of view, ignoring the force-field of human-social contradiction. In the process of exploring social (especially gender) relations, realism ends by confirming their inevitability" (*Unmaking Mimesis* xiii). Realism was vigorously critiqued by feminist scholars for passing off as "universal" the monolithic perspective of educated, white, heterosexual men. As a counter action, Diamond argued, women performers should "put their feminist thinking and their dangerous bodies into spaces of representation precisely to challenge reigning notions of mimetic doing, to imagine differently the dominant cultural norms of representation, embodiment, and pleasure" (181). The Fraticelli report left no doubt that women were very much restricted in their participation in Canada's mainstream theatres; at the same time, in academic settings, feminist scholars had an onerous task in challenging the almost exclusively male canon of dramatic literature. An assault on realism symbolized, at that time, a revolt against the very many ways that women had been and continued to be outsiders, whether that was in the theatre or in the theatre department. Thus, as Jill Dolan has more recently concluded, in the 1980s feminist theorists put theatrical realism "under the microscope, examining its operations and diagnosing that the form itself was 'lethal' for women" ("Feminist Performance" 437).

By 2006, little seemed to have changed. The national campaign Equity in Canadian Theatre: The Women's Initiative (produced by Nightwood Theatre, the Playwrights Guild of Canada Women's Caucus, and the Professional Association of Canadian Theatres [PACT]) released damning statistics demonstrating that barely any progress had been made since Fraticelli; the percentage of produced women playwrights had risen, but only to 29% (S. Scott 21–23; see also Posner). Still, notwithstanding the tenacity of the status quo in mainstream theatres, the last thirty years have seen an emphatic recognition of feminist theatres and performers in the pages of Canada's foremost English-language field publications (*Theatre Research in Canada, Canadian Theatre Review*) as well as in book-length studies and anthologies. This extended attention to feminist performance has unquestionably changed the terms of engagement for contemporary drama generally and brought new perspectives to the classroom.

In many ways, ideas of "feminist theatre" have become a yardstick by which to measure women's theatrical activity in the late twentieth- and early twenty-first centuries. But it is just as important, as scholars are now realizing, to consider how this rubric has effectively erased earlier women's work—and especially the work of women who chose *not* to reject realism—from theatre history. Realist plays authored by women were easily dismissed by the proponents of second-wave criticism as not political enough, not experimental enough, and, particularly, not feminist enough; revisionist feminist scholarship has only recently begun to re-emphasize the long history of women writing for the stage and to suggest the many ways that some of these dramatists worked *with* realist practice to raise issues directly relevant to their own lives and to (female) audiences. As historians such as Katherine E. Kelly note, realisms explored by women writers in the early twentieth century were highly attuned to the material conditions of production in which their "gender norms" were experienced (8). As an illustration of how women in the theatre *before* second-wave feminism defied what we have come to see as the constraints of realist practices, we turn now to Gwen Pharis Ringwood's well-known *Still Stands the House* (1938), a play that Geraldine Anthony described in 1981 (just before the arrival of feminist criticism) as "performed more often than possibly any other one-act Canadian play in English" (n.pag.).

GWEN PHARIS RINGWOOD: LISTENING TO REALISM

Still Stands the House offers a snapshot of the grim hardships of rural life in Alberta before the second world war, constructed through the kind of mimetic detail we expect and recognize from Ibsen's equally harsh settings somewhere along a Norwegian fjord. Like *A Doll's House*, *Still Stands* features a long opening stage direction that leaves little doubt about the play's environment:

SCENE: Western Canada. The living-room of the Warren farmhouse in Alberta.

TIME: The present. Seven o'clock on a January night. (27)

Ringwood elaborates information about the weather (we should hear the howling of an "icy wind of a northern blizzard"), the decor ("a faded austerity, a decayed elegance that is as remote and cheerless as a hearth in which no fire is ever laid"), and the layout of the stage space (the usual cluster of furniture punctuated by doors to both outside and elsewhere in the house) (27). Ringwood's stage direction also guides the appearance and character of the two actors we find onstage in the opening sequence: Ruth, wife of farm owner Bruce Warren, and Arthur Manning, a real estate agent whom Ruth wishes to contract to sell the farm. Ruth is "small, fair-haired, and pretty" (28) in contrast to her sister-in-law Hester, described on her entrance shortly afterward as "tall, dark, and unsmiling" (29). These two women are the heart of the play and embody what Ringwood evidently saw as binarized options for rural women: Ruth, at "twenty-five or twenty-six years of age," is married and pregnant with her first child, anxious to move on from a farm that can barely support them, while Hester, at forty, has lived a spinster's life of devotion—to the farm, to her father, and to the Bible (choices that have rendered her "stern" and "bitter") (29). The younger woman is still optimistic that they can build a life closer to a nearby town where there will be employment, neighbours, and schools. Hester is resigned, trapped in the past, creating a sense that her father's death foreclosed the possibilities of her own life—a condition Ringwood realizes with Ibsenesque undertones of misplaced sexual longing.

Like many realist plays, *Still Stands the House* reveals a debt to its predecessor genre, the melodrama, and Hester's role resembles that of the characteristic villainess: by the end of the short one act she has engineered events to ensure Ruth and her husband are likely lost in the blizzard conditions, certain to die from hypothermia. A final sequence has Hester act out a familiar routine, as if her father were still alive, setting out his slippers and reading to him from the Bible. This is a realist play that is literally "lethal" for

Ruth—certainly the more forward-looking of the two rural women. Equally, though, Ringwood's taut drama stresses that expectations for Hester—that as the only daughter in the family she would care for her ailing father—killed off her own chance at making a life. As Margaret Laurence comments in a foreword to Ringwood's collected plays, "Remember that for Gwen Pharis Ringwood, it must have been initially difficult—as it was for all women writers at the time—to portray women as she *knew* they were, not as they had been presented by generations of male writers" (xii, emphasis in original).

Still Stands the House more than put Gwen Pharis Ringwood on the map of Canadian dramatists of her era. In 1939—the year of her graduation from the University of North Carolina, where she won the Ronald Holt Cup for outstanding work in drama (G. Anthony 25)—*Still Stands* was staged at the Medicine Hat Little Theatre, took first prize at the Dominion Drama Festival, and was produced by CBC Radio. This was also the year that Ringwood returned to Canada to start an appointment as "Director of Dramatics" at the University of Alberta—a position previously held by Elizabeth Sterling Haynes. Living in Edmonton, Ringwood continued to write plays, prepare community pageants, and teach. She also collaborated with Elsie Park Gowan to write twelve "Alberta folk plays" commissioned for broadcast on CKUA Radio (see G. Anthony 32). In 1941 (only three years after writing *Still Stands the House*), Ringwood received a Governor General's Gold Medal for Outstanding Service to Canadian Drama.

Clearly, not all realism was "lethal" for women; for Gwen Pharis Ringwood, it was the foundation of a long career in the theatre. As it reflected the starker features of western Canadian rural living, *Still Stands* provided a mimetic match for the experiences of the women who must have heard this play on the CBC in their own farmhouses, or seen it produced at local drama festivals. It is clearly not a feminist play in the ways this category has come to be constructed in later twentieth-century theatre histories, but as Ringwood insists on speaking to other women (whether in the theatre or at home) and deploying realist methods for this distribution, *Still Stands* offers an urgent proto-feminism for those unable to conceive a life outside of rural patriarchy. Throughout her career, Ringwood fostered strong collaborations with other women who were equally inventing a new Canadian theatre in the West—Elizabeth Sterling Haynes, her mentor, and Elsie Park Gowan, her more "feminist" fellow playwright. Like the second-wave feminist theatres that would follow, each of these women created performances in alternative spaces (festivals, community gatherings, on radio) outside mainstream cultural institutions and directed them at particular local audiences.

The determination of second-wave feminist scholarship to unravel the grip of male-authored realism on main stages and in school curricula has overlooked the work of "amateur" or "community" theatres, such as those that supported Ringwood's work. These theatres frequently employed realism but also tested, in their own times, other conventional conditions of production and reception. On the flip side of the twentieth century, that same feminist determination risks eliding women artists' continued pragmatic engagements with realist form, the conditions that determine those engagements, and the political potential that, nevertheless, resides within them.

NOW: THREE CONTEMPORARY CASE STUDIES

Whether they identify openly as feminist or not, for women performing artists in Canada during the first decade of the twenty-first century, day-to-day labour remains the same as it might have been forty or seventy years ago: supporting and mentoring one another in an effort to gain recognition and, hopefully, legitimacy; figuring out ways to take up more space in a restrictive, male-dominated theatre culture; strategizing about how to obtain control over, and freedom of political speech within, the existing means of artistic production. Many women artists have come to use the language of feminism *strategically* in this work, deploying it only after gauging audience expectations and possible reactions against their own needs (see, for example, S. Scott 164–65). This may seem like an absolute failure of feminist progress to some, but it can also be understood positively: as a case of professional female wordsmiths trying to reclaim control over a language that has fallen prey to the manipulations of North American neo-conservatism.

Similarly, for many women playwrights and performers in the contemporary moment, "realism" has become a strategic tool—one that increases the likelihood of mainstream success while also allowing for a thorough, often quite complex, stage representation of women's lives. If prevailing academic opinion has maligned the European tradition of stage realism and its North American inheritors, popular theatre culture remains committed to realist dramaturgies, and professional theatre critics almost universally prefer them. Today, even academic critics long opposed to the hegemonic potential of realist dramaturgy have begun to realize the genre's strategic value; as Jill Dolan wrote in a 2009 essay: "The fact remains that visibility in commercial, mainstream, popular forums like Broadway matters for women playwrights and performers, so it is important for feminist critics and scholars to dissect what their presence there means and what it accomplishes" ("Feminist Performance" 442). For women artists seeking not just visibility but long-term viability, the strategic redeployment, manipulation, and reinvention of realist tropes and conventions can be a useful—even political—act of cultural takeover.

TARA BEAGAN: SHIFTING THE BORDERS OF THE "REAL"

Born and raised in southern Alberta by a mother from the Ntlaka'pamux/ Thompson River Salish nation and an Irish father, Tara Beagan is something of a theatrical rarity: a loud, proud, activist feminist. The current artistic director of Native Earth Performing Arts (NEPA) describes herself as "Feminist. [C]apital 'F'. . . . I remember being called a dyke in high school for insisting on being proud of being a Feminist" (Beagan, Message). Beagan's work, however, never considers feminist themes in isolation: they are always bound up with her investments as a First Nations writer, performer, and activist. As she told Ian MacKenzie in 2007, while preparing the script for *The Fort at York* in Toronto: "Any play built around the events that shaped this city must deal with the absent ones—First Nations people *and* female people. So little is said about these cats in history and it makes me boil." All of Beagan's labour—her writing, her work as a performer and director, her work as a mentor at numerous organizations (see Beagan, "Elder Up!"), and her work as an artistic director—revolves around this very plainly stated political goal: "Art can affect change, and voicing those who have been silenced is a part of that" (MacKenzie).

It may seem surprising that someone so vociferously feminist and openly polemical would frequently choose "traditional" stage realism as the dramaturgical structure for her plays. Beagan, however, never simply imitates European technique, even in her most conventionally realist work (such as *Dreary and Izzy* [2005] and *Miss Julie: Sheh'mah* [2008]). Always attentive to the political power of language, and especially of words spoken publicly, Beagan deploys the logic of First Nations oral histories alongside realist tropes and frameworks. This marriage of European and Indigenous forms of knowing has become increasingly important in two of her most recent plays (the magic-realist *The Woods* [2010] and the poetic *free as injuns* [2011], an adaptation of Eugene O'Neill's *Desire Under the Elms*), but it is tangible everywhere she works. She makes a concerted effort to expand her audience's understanding of who in our culture gets to count as "real": as a grievable body, as a human being whose story is worth telling in all of its complexity, its anger, and its desire on the stage.

This challenge of expanding the borders of our "real" marks especially *Miss Julie: Sheh'mah*, which was nominated for five Dora Mavor Moore awards and granted Beagan serious currency in the Toronto theatre market. *Sheh'mah* is a rewrite of August Strindberg's *Miss Julie* (1888), one of the most (in)famous plays in the European naturalist canon and a frequent subject of study in English literature and theatre history classrooms. Commissioned by two women—Melee Hutton and Christine Horne of KICK Theatre—Beagan's adaptation sets Strindberg's action in the British Columbia interior in 1929 and transforms Julie's two servants into First Nations peoples Jonny (Secwepemc/Shuswap) and Christie Ann (Ntlaka'pamux/Thompson River Salish). Beagan roughs up Strindberg's language throughout, modernizing it in a way that allows the original's own linguistic directness (a cause of controversy in its time) to translate for a contemporary audience. She also includes Shuswap phrases in the text during moments when Jonny and Christie Ann choose to communicate privately, references to Canada's "Indian" laws of the time (266, 305), and allusions to both Jonny and Christie Ann's abusive experiences in residential school—the latter's likely one of rape (270). These references, importantly, become part of the characters' psychological-realist "backstories," as does Julie's revelation that her mother had carried on an affair with a First Nations man in the hopes of revealing to her husband that "Indians are people, too" (306). In the world Beagan draws, sexual desire experienced across rigidly demarcated racial boundaries becomes as real as the sexual abuse experienced by generations of First Nations men and women at the hands of their colonial overlords.

Beagan's most significant departure from Strindberg's script is also the one that caught the most critical attention: her choice to stage Julie and Jonny's sex (it takes place offstage, amidst musical innuendo, in the 1888 original) openly and at length. Beagan's sex sequence is extensive; it is designed to be as true-to-life an encounter as possible given the limitations of live public performance, and in production it lasted close to ten minutes, generating substantial audience squirming along the way. Although both Robert Cushman at the *National Post* and the reviewer at the *Globe and Mail* ("Strindberg's pressure cooker") suggested this material was included to shock, and Cushman argued it "makes sense of a lot of things" ("A Midsummer's Night" AL4) in the second half of the script, Beagan's motivation in creating the extended scene was less to shock or clarify than to push. She wished to press her actors to discover their characters' genuine passion for one another, despite the race-based laws policing the colour line between them; she also wanted her audiences to recognize—visibly, audibly, and in some cases sensorily (as props and sweat flew around the tight performance space)—what this desire *could have* meant for both of these characters in a world less racist. Beagan seeks the moment when sex between a wealthy white man's daughter and an angry Native servant in 1929 encounters the borders between "us" and "them," expected and unimaginable, "realistic" and "real," and invites her audiences to think about what those borders mean for us right now.

ALISA PALMER: FEMINIST PRAGMATISM AT WORK

Alisa Palmer is no less an "out" feminist than Tara Beagan—as the co-artistic director of Nightwood Theatre from 1994 to 2000, her bona fides are not in question—but as a high-profile director who shuttles regularly between the "alt" and "mainstream" theatre worlds she tends to be more pragmatic about how she deploys feminism's terminology and endorses its claims. Long recognized as both extremely talented and "politically-astute" (Ouzounian, "*The Women*"), Palmer brings real economic and social power to every organization—and all of the women artists—with whom she works. As Shelley Scott notes of Palmer's achievement at Nightwood, "Because she had been associated with companies other than Nightwood, and because she maintained a strong profile within the theatre community as an award-winning playwright, director, and actor, she was most successful in finally establishing Nightwood as a 'legitimate' theatre company—one with an artistic vision, not just a political mandate" (160). As they worked on fundraising, long-range planning, and pursuing Nightwood's goal to develop women artists over the long term, Palmer and her co-A.D. Leslie Lester made "a conscious choice" to "downplay" the word "feminism" (163), at least to external observers and potential funders (165). As current artistic director Kelly Thornton told Scott in a recent interview, "we just need to take up more space" (184); for Palmer and Lester, that meant asserting the company's feminism forcefully—but through the back door.

Palmer's canny ability to take feminism "mainstream" was most recently evident at Soulpepper Theatre, where she directed an all-star cast in Caryl Churchill's *Top Girls* in 2007 and 2008, and at the Panasonic Theatre on Toronto's Broadway-style strip, where she directed Churchill's *Cloud 9* for Mirvish Productions in 2010. Churchill is recognized as one of England's most important political playwrights, and also as an inheritor of Bertolt Brecht, the modernist German playwright and director most famous for espousing a Marx-inflected "epic" theatre that runs, in his theoretical writings, directly counter to what he calls the "culinary" tendencies of European naturalism. Yet Brecht considered himself a realist, too, albeit within a politicized dramaturgical framework that emphasized alternatives to the social and economic status quos he staged (something he felt fourth-wall naturalism was unable to sustain). As Fiona Shaw argued during a recent discussion about her work as Mother Courage at the Royal National Theatre in 2009, Brecht's dramaturgy is actually similar to that at "the heart of all emotion theatre: . . . there's something unbearable in the very centre of the play." The "unbearable" emerges, in Brecht, from the contrast *between* the contradictory ideals characters must represent as they attempt to navigate their dilemmas. For Shaw, the actor's job is to play each scene, each choice, each dilemma as realistically as possible, and then let the audience come to terms with the questions those choices pose in the grander scheme of the story.

Palmer's approach to *Top Girls* matches Shaw's description neatly. Her actors developed their characters using psychological-realist techniques; Churchill's socialist feminism became the framework constraining them and governing their interactions with one another, rendering the play's feminist politics plainly visible *as a direct effect* of well-wrought realist performance.[2] Casting some of the most celebrated actors in Canadian theatre and television—including Ann-Marie MacDonald, Megan Follows, and Kelli Fox—Palmer ensured that Churchill's sometimes dated language and briefly sketched characters would be made to appear as naturalistic as possible, while attention was drawn away from the script's perceived imperfections by the actors' strong performances and aura of celebrity. The result: near-universal rave reviews, focused principally on the outstanding acting on offer *but also* recognizing the play's continued relevance for contemporary audiences (see especially Kaplan, "*Top Girls*"). Reviewers loved the show because it chose

---

2   In a chat with Jon Kaplan of *NOW Magazine*, Ann-Marie MacDonald described *Top Girls* thus: "After that fantastical and highly theatrical start [a dinner party scene starring a smorgasbord of women from history], Churchill pulls us into a *naturalistic close-up* of Marlene, with no fanfare, *exposing the grit* of what her life is really like. *Churchill trusts the audience* to keep in their psyches, their hearts, their minds what's discussed in the first scene, for it all comes up later with shocking force. . . . Even in rehearsals we find ourselves crying by the end of the play, because the characters' struggles are so hard and so many limbs are lopped off along the way" (qtd. in Kaplan, "*Top Girls*," emphasis added).

realist dramaturgy over "straight" Brecht, and thus offered political force without polemic. Kamal Al-Solaylee praised Palmer for "placing the emphasis on performance as a unifying element" and eschewing a "grand concept," thus avoiding the play's heavy-handed anti-Thatcher tone ("Sisterhood's Past"); John Coulbourn congratulated the cast for managing Churchill's "highly episodic and often seemingly disjointed script" by "sketch[ing] in Marlene's backstory" and allowing audiences to understand her "journey" as one marked "by often cruel choices" ("*Top Girls*"). Robert Cushman wrote: "*Top Girls* is hardly a detailed naturalistic play, but these scenes, with their echoes of past conflicts, serve notice that Churchill could write an excellent one if she felt like it" ("Sisters").

Arguably, as they play up virtuosity and emotion and downplay politics, these reviews reveal Palmer's *Top Girls* as something of a "sellout." So what did Palmer gain by "selling" Churchill in this way? In a blunt 2009 email to principal *Globe and Mail* reviewer J. Kelly Nestruck, reproduced on his popular blog,[3] Palmer made her gains plain. She recounted the difficulties she experienced in getting anyone to consider programming *Top Girls* at all; for years, she was told repeatedly the play was dated—despite the fact that similarly time-and-place specific works by male modern playwrights such as Mamet, Pinter, or Stoppard were already considered classics. She also noted that, after ten years of producing such "classics" in Toronto, Soulpepper had, by 2007, still not produced a single play by a woman. Palmer felt this was an injustice perpetrated not only against women artists, but also against audiences:

> During my time at Nightwood, I had enjoyed some success—I found there was a growing and largely untapped audience of women and men, many of them young, others 35 and beyond, who were not limiting themselves to the traditional theatrical canon. I also knew that not only were the issues in *Top Girls* far from dated, *but women, children, and work were not "issues."* (emphasis added)

---

3   Many of Palmer's comments in this email appear elsewhere in print. See especially G. Scott and also Posner.

The unabashed success of *Top Girls* in both the original 2007 production and the 2008 revival proved Palmer right. "One of the most valuable things about having *Top Girls* produced by Soulpepper, and one of the reasons I proposed the play to them initially, was that a Soulpepper production would re-position *Top Girls* as a 'classic,'" Palmer told Nestruck. Further: "*Top Girls* turned out to be, according to Leslie [Lester], Soulpepper's most successful production [ever]" and has opened the door to further work by women appearing at the theatre, and to further Churchill productions (including Palmer's *Cloud 9*) being mounted to critical acclaim in Toronto and across Canada.

REBECCA NORTHAN: DOING IT FOR HERSELF

Rebecca Northan differs markedly from both Beagan and Palmer: she is an improv performer, she is not a "loud and proud" feminist, and her engagements with stage realism are less obvious and far more eclectic than theirs. Nevertheless, Northan's most popular work offers a snapshot of how the tropes and techniques of European realism can be effectively manipulated by women artists working across performance genres in order to smooth the way toward substantial material gains.

Trained at Loose Moose Theatre's improv troupe in Calgary, Alberta, Northan has been a star in the improv community for some time; she broke into the mainstream in 2007 with *Blind Date*, a ten-minute piece she created for *The Spiegel Show* at Toronto's inaugural Luminato Festival in conjunction with Harbourfront World Stage. *Blind Date* went on to become a roughly ninety-minute "one-plus" woman show, in which Northan, dressed as Mimi the clown, cruises her cabaret-style audience for a suitable young man to invite up on stage. Northan works from a predetermined structure for the show, but varies it on the fly according to the offers made by her (totally untrained) improv partner each night. The work is light, a comedy with "heart," and Northan's oft-stated goal is to help each man on her stage to come out of his shell and have fun, while encouraging her audiences to "fall in love" with him (see Clevett; Mooney; Northan, "Professional"; and Northan, "Northan talks *Blind Date*").

Clearly this is not a "feminist" work of art. But it is also an undeniable hit for this self-proclaimed "self-employed artist" (Boettcher), one that has taken her to New York and on a North American tour. The show was originated with the encouragement of World Stage head programmer Tina Rasmussen, championed by New York impresario Kevin McCollum, and since its transformation into a touring piece has created high-profile employment for two more female artists: Northan's colleagues Julie Orton and Renee Amber Hunt, both of whom play Mimi in repertory with Northan. In short, *Blind Date* has turned Rebecca Northan from a minor, local star into a substantial theatrical celebrity, has allowed her to create meaningful, well-paying work for other women artists, and has allowed her to claim a great deal more economic control over her craft than most women in performance can imagine.

At first blush *Blind Date* does not sound much like realism: an improvised show built for laughs, it seems the furthest thing imaginable from fourth-wall social drama. And yet, the obvious "real"-ness of improv work aside, Northan's show trades, both hilariously and somewhat subversively, in the tropes of Ibsen- and Strindbergesque naturalism. For one thing, the settings of her performance are largely domestic: a cozy restaurant, a car, her living room, and bedroom. *New York Press* critic Deb Sperling remarked upon the financial savvy behind this choice: "The crowd is captivated, frequently breaching the paper-thin fourth wall to issue instructions [to the date]. Music and sound effects are carefully incorporated to produce maximum realism (and comic effect) with minimal set design. Around the half-way mark, you start thinking about buying tickets to a second or third showing." For another, the main thrust of Northan's very basic plot is driven by classic psychological realism: her goal is to examine her partner, Freud-like, to figure out his romantic (and sometimes even sexual) problems. *Blind Date* thus effects a clever role reversal: Northan, via the harmless-seeming Mimi, becomes a version of Judge Brack, the endlessly seductive father figure at the heart of Ibsen's *Hedda Gabler*, while her date becomes the object of her audience's clinical scrutiny—a role naturalism almost always casts as female. She remains in control, the puppet master, throughout the show's affair; her date earns her audience's love and affection (as she notes repeatedly in the press), but it's Northan who earns the prestige, the media attention, the money, and the artistic independence that come with them.

The question, however, is at what price—and this is where *Blind Date*'s economic and celebrity potential, despite its covert political engagement with European realism's gendered legacy, becomes a salutary caution. *Blind Date* is an astonishing amount of work for Northan: "It is the hardest piece of theatre I've ever done, and takes 120 per cent of my energy," she told Stephen Hunt of the *Calgary Herald* in August 2011. Northan's labour is emotionally and physically draining, but for the most part that labour must go unrecognized, both on stage and in the press, in order for Northan to keep the show's light-hearted focus on her "date," his pleasure, and his self-discoveries. Moreover, Northan's labour—managing, supporting, and guiding her "date"—is un-abashedly "women's work." As Sam Mooney astutely sees, "At first, it seems like the success of the evening depends on the date, but the truth is, the suc-cess depends on Mimi. She has to gauge who might be a good choice and then she has to make them comfortable enough to 'perform' on a stage in front of a bunch of strangers." As she seeks out the "right" man, flirts and flatters, encourages him to open up, and eventually brings him home to a five-years-later scenario, Northan's Mimi enacts, night after night, a very 1950s version of the heterosexual contract. Which leaves a feminist spectator wondering: does *Blind Date* suggest that non-celebrity women working in theatre (as Northan was), who have extraordinary skill, talent, and want to be indepen-dent producers (as Northan does), need to *disguise* the real nature and scope of their work in order to get where they want to go?

Northan's work in *Blind Date* is a kind of *in extremis* snapshot of the potential endgame of Palmer's feminist strategizing: she deploys well-worn realist tropes that have historically skewered female characters on stage and uses them to her and her colleagues' financial and creative advantage. Even so, as *Blind Date* improves Northan's lot, it also perpetuates a grotesque and persistent stereotype of female power, in which charming Mimi is regarded as both harmless and "manipulative" (and even more funny and charming for it: see Genzlinger). Who does Northan's strategic use of female stereotype and naturalist trope benefit? And whom might it harm? The same question needs to be asked of all artists who choose to deploy their feminism (and their realism) strategically, regardless of the apparent activism of their work's outcomes. Getting women artists working is essential, but that advantage cannot come at the expense of women beyond the boards if we are to make *all* of our labour relevant, proud, and powerful for a new generation of female voices.

NOT AN ENDING

After two generations of *agon* between feminism and realism, we are now at a moment when women artists, scholars, and audiences can—in fact *must*—come to more nuanced terms with the complicated interplay between these two frameworks. The stakes are high, because the fight is not over. In 2011, Stuart Jeffries published a provocative entry on *The Gurdian Theatre Blog* in which he justified walking out of a London revival of *Top Girls*. He complained: "We were back . . . in the pseudo-feminist milieu of Judy Chicago's near-contemporaneous installation *The Dinner Party*, in which any woman was worth eulogising in virtue of having sucked on the fuzzy end of patriarchy's lollipop. Which is not enough: any artistic engagement with women's oppression surely has to go beyond hymning women for being women." Whatever the motives behind his review, Jeffries's dismissal of a play whose "classic" status, as Alisa Palmer's recent experience demonstrates, is by no means a given, suggests that "feminist" may have become just as "lethal" to women's theatrical production as "realism" was once understood to be. Can a reinvigorated women's realism help to combat the ongoing denials and demonizations of feminism as we push further into the twenty-first century? Or will it simply aid and abet them? A better grasp of the material power embedded in both "realism" and "feminism" is crucial if either is to retain value, strategic or otherwise, in the fights to come.

SCRIPTING REALITY IN THE SUBJUNCTIVE MOOD: EVERYDAY LIFE PERFORMANCE AT THE 2010 TORONTO G20 PROTEST AND POLICE KETTLE

SUSANNE SHAWYER

In June of 2010, thousands of demonstrators converged on downtown Toronto to protest the G20 summit. As the leaders of the world's economic powers met to discuss international economic co-operation and development, protesters marched through the city. Dressed in costumes, waving placards, and chanting slogans, the activists hoped to influence the global policy-makers by drawing attention to a variety of political and social debates. Diverse demonstrators called for the G20 to support Palestine and Tibet and to end the wars in Iraq and Afghanistan, while others critiqued large corporations like Hewlett-Packard and Chapters Indigo. Some protesters, intent on breaching the security perimeter around the summit site, resorted to vandalism, smashing glass storefronts and burning police cars near the convention centre. Armed with pepper spray, batons, and riot shields, the police responded to the demonstrations by taking hundreds into custody, setting records for the largest mass arrest in Canadian history (Mahoney and Hui). With the downtown core surrounding the convention centre in a security lockdown, disparate demonstrators disagreeing on tactics, the police on high alert, and a tense Toronto anticipating more violence, the last day of the summit saw the most extreme police response to mass protest when several hundred people were caught inside a police kettle.

The kettle happened in the late afternoon of 27 June. Organized demonstrations had disintegrated by then into scattered groups. A small crowd of activists marched at the intersection of Queen Street West and Spadina Avenue, surrounded by journalists, curious onlookers, and a watchful band of police officers in riot gear. The police surprised the crowd with a flanking manoeuvre, forcing several hundred people at the intersection into a makeshift holding pen constructed solely from the bodies of the police. For four hours, the police kept the marchers, journalists, and onlookers trapped inside this improvised cordon. Unable to move from the intersection, those penned inside the kettle shouted their anger at the police, broadcast their experiences on social media, and waited long hours to be released. Darkness fell as rain showered both the cops and the corralled. One by one the demonstrators were allowed to exit the kettle, though some were detained for questioning and arrest (Morrow et al.). Reading about the incident in newspapers and on blogs the next day, Canadians from coast to coast learned a new word: *kettling*, the containment of large numbers of people in a makeshift cordon for long periods of time.

Also known as containment, or corralling, kettling has been used several times at recent mass demonstrations against capitalism and globalization. The point is to forestall violence. The practice is controversial, for it is indiscriminate: large portions of a crowd may be kettled even though only a few individuals may threaten the peace. Kettling is also controversial because it depends upon the anticipation, not the actualization, of violence: the threat of imminent hostile behaviour alone is enough to warrant a kettle. This anticipation in turn relies on a historical knowledge of past mass protests, and an understanding of the many different roles a participant might play in a demonstration: a peaceful parader, an impassioned arguer, an aggressive anarchist. This anticipation also depends on an understanding of the myriad protest scripts in play in modern demonstrations: protest as anarchy, protest as utopian vision, protest as civil right. The act of kettling at a mass protest is therefore a complicated negotiation among the media, security forces, protesters, and their performance scripts.

During mass protest, activists, security forces, and the media compete to dominate public discourse—in other words, to control the script. The prevailing aesthetic of mass protest performance is realist. Participants respond to contemporary issues and reflect lived experience as they mirror their preferred vision of reality: the media generates fear and excitement with images of violent demonstrators looting and burning; the police reinforce their authority with imposing representations of riot shields, batons, and phalanxes of orderly officers; and the activists exploit their right to protest with passionate arguments for a better world. Although the realist aesthetic that dominates most protests glosses over the highly constructed nature of protest scripts, the fierce contest for discursive dominance at mass protests exposes the contrivance of each script. As competing scripts clash, so do the multiple notions of reality at play. Certainty collapses as mass protest performance demonstrates the fluid and contingent nature of the real.

MASS PROTEST AS EVERYDAY LIFE PERFORMANCE

As expressive human activity, mass protest contains many elements of performance: choreographed movement such as marching; props and costumes such as placards, bullhorns, masks, or message T-shirts; and symbolic representations such as effigies or demonstrators lying down to represent the death of an ideal. Some demonstrators simply rely on their massed presence to send a message of dissent; others use theatre to communicate opposition. Oxfam Canada, for example, protested the 2010 G8 summit with dancers dressed as bankers and oil-spill victims (K. Allen). Organization president Robert Fox explained that theatrical protest was chosen because it "gets people talking, creates some buzz . . . you need a hook to get people's attention" (K. Allen). In the past half-century, coinciding with the rise of performance studies as a field of inquiry, both scholarship and the popular media have embraced the concept of mass protest as performance. Performance scholar Baz Kershaw, arguing for a "dramaturgy of protest as performance," demands an "alertness to the aesthetic assumptions informing radical action for sociopolitical change" (91). The popular media responds to the aesthetics of mass protests, using the theatrical metaphor to describe and comment on public demonstrations. For example, *The New York Times* sent theatre critic Clive Barnes to review the demonstrations at the 1968 Chicago Democratic National Convention, while in 2001 Canada's *Globe and Mail* newspaper sent theatre critic Kate Taylor to report on mass protest at the Organization of American States (OAS) summit in Québec City. In 2001 CBC television commentator Reg Whitaker wryly described the Summit of the Americas demonstrations as a "theatrical performance," adding that protesters were "all acting according to a script" (Boag). The theatrical metaphor positions global justice demonstrators as actors, performing representations of their ideologies for an audience of media and policy makers.

But beyond the theatrical metaphor, mass protest exemplifies everyday life performance. Sociologist and performance theorist Erving Goffman argues that everyday life is a series of performances, behaviours meant to convince others of a particular viewpoint. Goffman defines these performances as "all the activity of a given participant on a given occasion which serves to influence in any way any of the other participants" (15). In daily life, humans construct identities and perform behaviours for the benefit of observers; for example, communicating a gender identity, demonstrating affinity with a social group, or advocating for a political ideology. Complex and multi-faceted, humans daily participate in a number of everyday life performances for a variety of audiences. A businesswoman may present herself as a dedicated and serious professional in a sober suit at work, but may wear paint-splattered overalls to communicate her artistic side on the weekends. An advocate for animal rights might choose a vegan diet and wardrobe, or might also march in a demonstration. Both actions communicate her concern for animal welfare. Global justice advocates—also known as antiglobalization demonstrators—may feel that governments and policy-makers ignore the issues most important to them. By demonstrating, they publically perform the principles, values, politics, and desires by which they define themselves. By demonstrating, they also try to convince others of the worth of their positions, advocating for their particular point of view. Resist Toronto, a group organized specifically to protest at the Toronto G20 summit, argued on its Facebook page that, through mass protest, "people will manifest liberating social conflict" ("Resist

Toronto"). Mass protests, like the Toronto G20 demonstrations, are everyday life performances of social and political debate.

For many people in Western democracies, mass protest also forms part of the lived experience. Even if we do not participate in demonstrations ourselves, we consume news media reports of protests: tuition fee protests in the United Kingdom, anti-nuclear rallies in Japan, strikes against economic austerity in Greece, the uprisings of the Arab Spring, and the Occupy Wall Street movement, to name a few examples from the past year (2010–2011) alone. Hardly a week goes by without a news headline about a protest or a strike, or a Facebook call to support a cause. Thanks to the news and social media, we are surrounded by protest performance even if we are not marching. We may be familiar with onscreen scenes of shouting protesters, police in riot gear, or fires in the street. We may even engage in everyday life performance of our own political positions through debate or discussion of issues with family, friends, or colleagues. Thus, protest performance forms part of the script of our everyday life as the performance of a position, as engaged debate, or as background scenery to the quotidian.

Through social media, blogs, twenty-four-hour television news channels, and all the communications technology that now surrounds us, we are wired into demonstration and debate. Television programs like CBC's *The Lang and O'Leary Exchange* or MSNBC's *Hardball with Chris Matthews* encourage contentious discussions of economic, social, and political issues. Major news outlets have followed the lead of blogs by enabling comments sections where consumers can opine about the day's stories. Even the simple "like button" on Facebook allows a user to perform an opinion by expressing a "like" of a photo, status update, person, or organization. By consuming media we learn the tropes and traditions of protest performance. Advertising teaches us that a pink ribbon symbolizes support for breast cancer research and the Susan G. Komen for the Cure organization. We might learn to engage politically by copying and pasting a Facebook status, or re-tweeting a political message on Twitter. By many means, we learn the "script" of protest.

If protest is part of our lived experience, and protest can be considered everyday life performance, is mass protest a kind of realist performance? By framing everyday actions as performance, Goffman and performance theory aestheticize daily life. Actions that seem natural, and occur as part of normal life, are instead recognized as crafted and deliberate when framed as performance. During the Realist movement of the nineteenth century, artists and playwrights also aestheticized daily life. Émile Zola in works like *Thérèse Raquin* and Rosa Bonheur in paintings like *Labourage nivernais* used art to represent everyday lived experience. Through their artwork, these Realist artists argued that the quotidian was worthy of consideration. The Realist artists sought scientific objectivity, and Realist playwrights aimed to present Jean Jullien's famous "slice of life" on stage; however, it cannot be denied that their plays, novels, and paintings were consciously crafted creations. This is one of the principal contradictions that animates Realism: although Realist performances work hard to look natural and uncontrived, they are in fact carefully scripted by means of specific viewpoints, character choices, and selected settings.[1] Everyday life performance contains a similar, albeit opposite, contradiction: aestheticizing everyday actions frames them as contrived and perhaps unnatural, supporting a post-Modern reading of human activity and behaviours as fluid and contingent, rather than fixed and natural. Aiming for the natural, the Realists aestheticized lived experience through contrivance, whereas Goffman and the performance theorists aestheticized lived experience to demonstrate the contrivance of seemingly natural behaviours. Mass protest, then, is an everyday life performance that reveals the contradiction of its own realism: seemingly natural due to its familiar ubiquity, yet demonstrably crafted and scripted, it emphasizes its contrivance as it suggests alternatives to behaviours naturalized in the social and political status quo.

---

1   For more background information on the nineteenth-century Realist movement, and especially its internal contradictions, see the editors' introduction to this volume.

SCRIPTING PROTEST PERFORMANCE

Although antiglobalization protests can seem scripted, the antiglobalization movement is so diverse and disparate that there is little agreement among participants about exactly how to perform a protest, or about exactly what the protest script might be. For example, participants posting to the Resist Toronto Facebook page vigorously debated the efficacy of hunger strikes and non-violent action before the summit began ("Resist Toronto"). Global justice demonstrators represent a wide range of political and social viewpoints in part due to the broad scope of political and economic institutions like the G8, the World Bank, the International Monetary Fund (IMF), the European Union, the OAS, or the Asia-Pacific Economic Cooperation (APEC). The multiple agendas of the global justice movement include opposition to free trade, deforestation, genetically modified foods, and World Bank loans to developing nations, as well as support for women's rights, Indigenous people's rights, micro-loans, and animal welfare. In Toronto, one portion of the crowd included demonstrators arguing for an independent Palestine, animal rights, and tuition reform, while others marched against poverty and NATO-led airstrikes on Iran (Intini et al.). Because lived experiences and therefore everyday life performances differ according to each individual, antiglobalization demonstrations fail as a coherent performance: this is a movement with many methods and various purposes, and ultimately no single protest script.

Without a clearly defined protest script, mass protest in the name of global justice has long struggled with the balance between peaceful assembly and violent unrest. At the November 1999 demonstrations against the World Trade Organization in Seattle, a minority of violent demonstrators stole the spotlight from thousands of peaceful protesters. In the decade since, anarchist factions have consistently taken media attention away from non-violent antiglobalization demonstrators; for example, at Québec City in 2001, or the London May Day protests in 2009. The absence of a coherent message means that the antiglobalization movement is prey to anarchist groups, such as the mask-wearing Black Bloc, who disrupt non-violent protest actions with violence and vandalism.

At the same time, because antiglobalization is such a varied movement with a wide range of goals and political agendas, the most spectacular and theatrical scripts dominate media coverage of the movement. While earnest demonstrators may use costumes or props to send a message, ultimately it is vandalism and violence that garners the most media attention. For example, a report from the *Globe and Mail* depicted non-violent protest at the first major street demonstration of the Toronto G20 summit weekend, but began with an account of "tense confrontations" with police (Morrow). Images of police dressed in riot gear accompanied descriptions of marchers playing guitars and vuvuzelas, and carrying a coffin filled with coat hangers to protest cuts in abortion funding (Morrow). The report's headline, "Police Don Riot Gear to Contain First Major Protest of G20 Weekend," emphasized the potential for violence over peaceful protest. The media helped shape a protest script that focused less on the issues the demonstrators hoped to highlight, and more on their interactions with the police. This is not surprising. Because demonstrators' access to economic policy-makers and diplomats at international economic summits is severely restricted, it is now normal for some protesters to engage the police in skirmishes, and to hope that water cannon or tear-gas attacks can generate media attention. Despite the peaceful demonstrators also participating in antiglobalization events, the media typically presents the global justice movement as a familiar and repeated battle between authoritative power and radical dissent.

The repeated conflict between demonstrators and security forces, eagerly reported by the mainstream media, sets up expectations of behaviour—the anticipation of a specific protest script. Although thousands of peaceful demonstrators offer alternate visions of what protest can look like, the media fascination with violent protest emphasizes an agonistic script, creating fearful expectations of vandalism and chaos in the streets. In a short video made for *CBC News* the week before the G20 summit, veteran reporter Ian Hanomansing described increased police presence in downtown Toronto. He referred to Toronto's new "police state," and tested the strength of a security fence (Hanomansing). By pushing on the fence to check its stability, he insinuated that others might soon attempt to topple it in an act of vandalism. A report detailing the use of Québec police for Toronto summit security noted that the Québec officers have "extensive experience in dealing with large, possibly riotous events, including the 2001 Summit of the Americas in Quebec City and recent riots in Montreal during the NHL playoffs" (CBC News, "G8/G20"). By mentioning previous urban unrest, the report implied that it might be repeated at the upcoming summit.

The expectation of a script of hostile behaviour at the 2010 Toronto G20 demonstrations was accentuated by the historical memory of the protests at the 2001 Summit of the Americas meeting in Québec City.[2] The 3.8 kilometre concrete and metal fence around the Québec City summit site, popularly known as "the wall of shame," became the target of demonstrators as a symbol of non-democratic practices dictating global economic policy (Peritz A1; Dabrowski A7). On 20 April 2001, several thousand protesters broke off from a peaceful march to attack the fence with chunks of concrete, bottles, cans, rocks, snowballs, paint balloons, hockey sticks, and golf balls (Freeze A2; Sallot et al. A1). Some then used a portion of the fence as a battering ram, and charged the police line, even as riot police responded with batons, tear gas, and rubber bullets (Brown A16). The day before the 2010 Toronto summit, *CBC News* reminded readers that "The Summit of the Americas was notorious for its images of riot police with shields and gas masks, thick clouds of tear gas and masses of protesters clashing with police and yanking down a three-metre tall concrete and wire fence" (CBC News, "G8/G20"). Not only did the report prompt memories of the Québec City violence, but it also suggested that similar violence was about to occur in Toronto: "Along with the tear gas, police used water cannons and rubber bullets to disperse the demonstrators, some of the same techniques that police will employ, if necessary, in

---

2   This meeting of the Organization of American States negotiated the Free Trade Agreement of the Americas (FTAA), and was the last large urban summit meeting in Canada prior to the Toronto G20. In addition to the 2010 G8 summit in Huntsville, Ontario, and the 2010 Toronto G20, Canada has hosted several international meetings: the 1981 G7 summit in Montebello, Québec; the 1988 G7 summit in Toronto, Ontario; the 1995 G7 summit in Halifax, Nova Scotia; the 2001 OAS Summit of the Americas in Québec City, Québec; and the 2002 G8 summit in Kananaskis, Alberta.

Huntsville and Toronto" (CBC News, "G8/G20"). There were plenty of peaceful demonstrators in Québec City in 2001, but the media in 2010 focused on the rioting to create a fearful expectation of future violence in Toronto. With this script of violence already established even before the Toronto summit began, it is no wonder that news of cheerful vuvuzela-playing demonstrators and activists offering free hugs were drowned out by images of police in riot gear (Morrow). By emphasizing civil unrest, national mainstream media like *CBC News* and the *Globe and Mail* constructed a script of protest for the G20 as violent confrontation. By continually repeating this script, which was based on the actions (or anticipated actions) of only a small part of all the demonstrators, the media used aggressive activism to represent mass protest by the entire diverse global justice movement. Consumers of media, in turn, thus become accustomed to the repeated link between antiglobalization and violence, and interpellated into the contrived script of mass protest as hostile conflict with police.

This scripting of protest as aggression had real consequences. In Toronto, the security forces allowed the media-scripted fear of violence to control demonstrators' movements during the protest, especially around the convention centre. As in Québec City, the police constructed a concrete and metal fence around the summit site. They created a restricted access "high security zone" in downtown Toronto to limit both vehicle and pedestrian traffic (Vu). The security zone was extensive: many streets were blocked off, and of the $930 million federal government dollars allocated to the Integrated Security Unit for summit security, $122 million went to the Toronto Police for summit perimeter security (Gee and Freeze). Unconfirmed rumours spread among demonstrators and the media that police had the power to "stop and search anyone coming within five metres of the G20 fences in Toronto for a one-week period" (Canadian Press). The rumour seemed plausible given the expectations of conflict with the police and the memory of the attack on the fence in Québec City. In fact, the Toronto police had no special power to stop people automatically from approaching the fence; however, they purposely did nothing to correct the misinformation until after the summit weekend (Canadian Press). The ghost of the Québec City violence, along with the media-scripted fear of violence, proved sufficient, as many peaceful Toronto demonstrators stayed away from the high-security zone and consequently away from the world leaders and summit delegates.

The script of mass protest as civil unrest also influenced the police decision to kettle the protesters on the last day of the summit demonstrations. Because the kettling technique is used to prevent potential violence and to cool down the heightened, and possibly dangerous, affect of an unruly crowd, it depends on an expectation that mass protest will turn to violence. The police had already seen this script enacted earlier in the weekend by self-proclaimed members of the Black Bloc, an amorphous group of anarchists who take their name from the dark clothing that obscures their identities: hooded black sweatshirts, black hats, and dark bandanas or face masks. When these anarchists smashed storefronts and set police cars on fire on 26 June, the Toronto police were unable "to effectively prevent, mitigate and respond to Black Bloc tactics employed within the broader theatre when mass disorder was taking place" (qtd. in CBC News, "G20"). Determined to prevent further vandalism, the police cracked down on any demonstrator suspected of Black Bloc activity. The kettle on 27 June was a response to a perceived Black Bloc threat: the police told reporters that some people in the crowd were about to put on masks and "wreak havoc similar to the damage done to storefronts and property" the day before (Paperny). In response, the police corralled the demonstrators, even though many of those kettled maintained the demonstration was peaceful (Jutras, "Caught").

Although the script of violence dominated the Toronto G20 media coverage and police response to the demonstrations, it was not the only script at play that weekend. The kettle itself had its own script to follow, one that negotiated competing performance agendas: the need for security forces to maintain the peace, the script of peaceful mass protest, and the script of civil unrest. In performance terms, kettling is used to keep performers to a specific and approved script—a script without challenge to authority or threat of security breach—and to prevent improvisers from writing a different script, a script of violence. Kettling is often employed in the United Kingdom, for example, to separate rival football fans after games (Campbell). In legal terms, the kettle has a strict script it must follow. If the kettle goes "off-script," it can violate laws concerning free speech and the right to public assembly. Law courts in the United Kingdom have ruled on kettling as a result of recent high-profile cases, such as the 2001 anti-capitalism May Day demonstrations in London (Fenwick 743), and the 2009 London G20 demonstrations, when thousands found themselves kettled for up to eight hours (Laville and Campbell). The courts have argued that kettling does not infringe on the right to peaceful protest if the police believe in good faith that a violent situation or breach of the peace is imminent (Scorer). Thus the police must have good reason to believe that the performance of social and political debate is about to go awry and become a performance of anarchy. The police must negotiate multiple scripts: the Black Bloc's readiness to create havoc, the other marchers' determination to demonstrate peacefully, the police's powers to maintain the peace, and the parameters of kettling provided by the law.

These competing scripts make visible the inherent contradiction of realist everyday life performance. On the one hand, protest scripts of violence seem like a familiar part of the everyday, due to the repetition of hostile behaviour by the Black Bloc at international summit events, and also due to the media preoccupation with civil unrest. Performance theorist Richard Schechner writes that performance "means: never for the first time. It means: for the second to the nth time. Performance is 'twice-behaved behaviour'" (*Between Theater* 36). In other words, performance refers to behaviours that are repeated, recognizable, and familiar. The media continually tells us that mass protest must equal civil unrest; therefore instances of violence at mass protest seem to represent the reality of lived experience. On the other hand, the competing scripts in the kettle demonstrate the contrived and contingent nature of this reality. The Toronto police claimed there were Black Bloc members in the crowd; those trapped inside the kettle denied there were any anarchists among them (Jutras, "Caught"). The police argued that kettling was required to prevent mischief and to keep the peace (CBC News, "G20"); the Canadian Civil Liberties Association, however, claimed that the police denied to demonstrators the right to peaceful protest (3, 12). Different participants in the protest read the situation differently based on their own agendas and realities. There was no one scenario that truthfully represented the performance of mass protest in Toronto; rather, there were multiple, contingent scripts, each one representing a slightly different reality.

THE KETTLE'S COMPETING REALITIES

In the kettle, competing protest scripts clashed. Each side physically performed its preferred script through costume and choreography. Dressed in riot gear, the police hemmed in the crowd with four solid walls, forming a dark rectangle that stretched across the intersection of Queen Street West and Spadina Avenue (Naimark). Officers stood with grounded weight, feet firmly planted, the body balanced, and the core solid and strong. Protective shields pushed back at the unarmed demonstrators. Dozens of plastic restraints hung from belts, promising arrests to come. In a strange parallel to the ghostly Black Bloc, some police wore black masks—gas masks (Van Paassen). Faceless and uniformed, arrayed in rows, the police performed strength and authority. Bulky in riot gear, they hulked over kettled marchers clad in thin rain jackets and T-shirts (Hallett). The neat array and straight lines of the police contrasted with the brightly coloured crowd, who scattered and bunched, clearly disorganized. A large group of kettled demonstrators clumped in the northeast corner of the intersection by the CIBC Bank building, while a smaller faction grouped in the northwest corner by the McDonald's restaurant. In the disordered middle, the corralled milled about above the black asphalt and criss-crossing streetcar tracks (Naimark). With no place to sit, those kettled had an uncomfortable wait, their boredom quickly turning to misery as thunder rumbled and cold rain fell. They turned to a choreography of co-operation and support, grouping under shared umbrellas and passing food to the most hungry (Jutras, "Boxed"). Two performances of teamwork manifested during the kettle: the uniform precision of the police, and the improvised collaboration of the corralled.

The improvised co-operation of those inside the kettle demonstrated an insistent rebuttal to the familiar police and media script of protest as violent.

Writer Lisan Jutras joined the march as a journalist and described a "relaxed" and "curious" crowd of marchers and onlookers surprised and intimidated by the sudden "crushy manoeuvre [sic]" by police in riot gear ("Caught"). In addition to the protesters, Jutras noted others trapped in the kettle: photographers looking for shots of the demonstrations, a "corporate lawyer walking home with a friend," "a woman who had six bags of food from Chinese grocers," and a "destitute man" ("Boxed"). The threatening Black Bloc anarchists were either absent from the kettle or concealed within the crowd. They did not materialize to challenge the security forces. The kettled crowd "stayed very, very calm. Very respectful of each other" ("Boxed"). This one description from a participant challenged the police claims of imminent violence and the media anticipation of an unruly mob. It offered an alternate version of the reality of the kettle, and a different understanding of the lived experience of that day. Although Jutras and police both participated in the kettling incident, their distinct perceptions of the reality of the moment mean that each took part in a slightly different performance of protest.

The competing performance realities inside the kettle demonstrate performance in "the subjunctive mood," or, in other words, performance that challenges the vision of reality as fixed and unchanging while simultaneously offering alternate possibilities *of* or *in* the real. Brazilian director and performance theorist Augusto Boal uses the notion of the subjunctive to refer to performances that contain within them critiques of the status quo and alternate models for action (39). In Boal's Forum theatre, participants can change scripts by offering suggestions to the actors and rewriting character choices. Boal writes that his subjunctive method is "the comparison, discovery and counterposition of possibilities[,] . . . the construction of diverse models of future action for a particular given situation, enabling their evaluation and study" (40). Although it does not present alternatives as explicitly as Boal's method, Realist everyday performance of mass protest nevertheless also works in the subjunctive. It must do so: mass protest is created by crowds of people, each with a distinct lived experience. The kettle at the G20 illustrates performance in the subjunctive because of the various versions of protest script involved. Each script—from the mainstream media, the police, the protesters, and the onlookers caught up in the action—suggests a different way of look-ing at the reality of both the protest and the kettle.

It is not just the different versions of reality at play that highlight the subjunctive mood of performance at the G20 protest, however, but also the performances of the demonstrators themselves, especially those caught up in the kettle. Dance and performance scholar Susan Leigh Foster argues that the labour of participating in and creating "political interference calls forth a perceptive and responsive physicality that . . . deciphers the social and then choreographs an imagined alternative" (412). Writing of her own experience marching in the 1999 Seattle demonstrations, Foster argues that protesters' physicality—literally, their bodies in space—calls into being alternate social possibilities. Protesters gathered in a park, for example, physicalize their trust in public space and its possibility as a place of action. Affinity groups walking together not only represent symbolic unity of purpose but also actualize that unity in space. The people at the intersection of Queen and Spadina marching down the street in a haphazard fashion, or loitering on the corner, or navigat-ing the crowd on their way home from shopping, created an alternative to the orderly and precise police formation generated by the kettle. Their colourful clothing and improvised teamwork performed a different social reality than that of the uniformed, forceful police. As each side struggled to impose their script and version of reality on the other, multiple notions of real, lived ex-perience converged. At stake: possible future realities and lived experiences. Would the police script prevent civil unrest or push an angry mob into aggres-sive action? Would the corralled crowd work together to stay calm or become the very thing the police and media feared? Would the media consider the ket-tling event worthy of notice amid a day of demonstrations throughout the city? Would Canadians care enough about G20 security to debate the police actions for months following? Whose script and subsequent performance would domi-nate? Performance in the subjunctive mood, as it offers alternate visions of what is and what could be, activates these kinds of questions, and highlights the fact that reality—social and political norms—is fluid rather than fixed.

Another way that the kettled crowd put forward alternatives to the script offered by the police and mainstream media was through the use of social media. Even before the summit began, the Resist Toronto Facebook page included posts advocating non-violent protest ("Resist Toronto"). The Toronto Community Solidarity Network blogged updates about the demonstrations and called for official inquiries into police actions. On 26 June they posted a notice of a planned peaceful demonstration for the next day, a "low-risk solidarity rally to demonstrate" in support of jailed activists ("June 27"). These blog posts and Facebook status updates directly challenged the mainstream media's script of protest violence; from inside the kettle, Twitter updates continued this subjunctive performance of alternatives. Journalist Jutras tweeted often throughout the ordeal, using mobile telecommunications to keep friends and the *Globe and Mail* editors updated on the action ("Caught"). At first confused about why the police were surrounding the crowd, she researched their actions on the Internet. Her growing understanding of the situation appeared in her Twitter feed: "Wikipedia says we could be detained here several hours. God I hope not" ("Caught"). As time passed, Jutras defended her fellow detainees and argued against police claims of imminent violence. She tweeted that those inside the kettle included shoppers, passersby, and peaceful demonstrators, not anarchists seeking to erupt into violence. Social media allowed her to keep challenging the script being forced upon the protesters by the kettle.

The protesters' turn to mobile media, such as tweeting, making calls, and sending texts from inside the kettle, were breaches of the authoritative reality imposed by the police. But the calls, texts, and tweets sent from inside the kettle also demonstrated that the physical space of containment—that stretch of asphalt between Queen and Spadina—did not in fact contain the reality of the kettle. The reality of the protest performance extended out into the virtual world and, consequently, through time into the future. Only time travellers could return to that rainy evening to experience the crush of the confused crowd, the static strength of the police line. But Internet users can experience Jutras's confusion, frustration, and boredom in the kettle by reading her Twitter feed (that still exists at the writing of this essay). Performance scholar Rebecca Schneider notes that "Bodies engaged in repetition are boisterous articulants of a liveness that just won't quit" (38–39). Schneider is writing of

the live body in performance that continually animates historical (re-enact-
ment) scripts, but her idea of the insistent "liveness" of performers rings true
in a protest context. Social media extends the live body in space and time,
and, if archived, ensures that competing protest realities "just won't quit."
Saved texts and tweets keep the performance alive even when the participating bodies have fled the scene. The result is an insistent reality that remains
even when other, more physically bounded, realities have ended. The kettle
is no more. The Toronto G20 demonstrations are over. Yet the participants in
the protest performance—their lived experience, their political viewpoints—
transcended the physical location and temporal specificity of the kettle. The
persistent "liveness" of their social-media archive retains the political force
of their "imagined alternative"—at least, as long as consumers can still access that archive.

During the kettle, the forceful script imposed by the police seemed to
dominate the physical action; however, the bodies of the corralled, extended
through mobile communications, were nevertheless able to offer alternative versions of the protest script, and to extend those versions into time and
space beyond the kettle. Even today, those alternative versions remain in the
virtual archive, still repeating the performance of mass protest for curious,
or politically compelled, onlookers. The archived scripts offer consumers of
protest performance a choice: they can take for granted the mainstream media's emphasis on fear and violence, they can accept the narrative of imminent
anarchy offered by the police, or they can trust the teamwork and peaceful
nature of the Toronto demonstrators. They can also recognize that perhaps
no single script can fully express the numerous realities at play. Clearly the
choices between scripts are always present, but an archive helps keep these
choices visible after the heightened emotional moment of the event passes.
Which competing script will dominate the performance? Perhaps it will not
be the most forceful script in the physical moment, but rather the best archived script, the script that is still accessible in the years to come.

While the aesthetic of realism demonstrates the contrivance of seemingly
fixed behaviours, the realist performance of the mass protest at the Toronto
G20 summit suggests something more: realist performance today, although

rooted in the present, also offers multiple futures. The nineteenth-century aesthetic of Realism informs the twentieth-century theory of everyday life performance and invigorates the subjunctive mood of twenty-first century mass protest performances. In a globalized modern world, rival media compete for consumers, offering many scripted versions of reality. While the forceful and spectacular narratives of civil unrest may dominate in the present, the tranquil and restrained plots of peaceful protest can also linger in media archives. These competing scripts remind the consumer of the contingency of human activity, and suggest other possible outcomes. These different realities exist beyond the physical in a virtual subjunctive mood, offering visions of futures as diverse as the demonstrators of the antiglobalization movement. The everyday life performance of mass protest thus demonstrates realism's activist potential—played out in city streets today and inspiring new visions of reality in the virtual worlds of tomorrow.

IN PLAIN SIGHT: INSCRIPTED EARTH AND INVISIBLE REALITIES

MONIQUE MOJICA[1]

Across the thirteen moons on Turtle's back, across multiples of centuries, the Mother Mounds are calling to their children: "Come home. . . ." They call, sing, coo, echo, hum. They infiltrate our sleeping and our waking dreams with whispers of thoughts they make as if our very own: "Come home . . . it's time. Come home to rest your hearts in the layered folds of Mother's skirts." They send out a call.

We who think these thoughts as if they were our very own search for the source of the song, the Mother voice, and then gently lay down each boney vertebra of our spines one by one on the ancient, textured soil. Then, vibrating, we align our frequencies to the constellations and join a dialogue begun long ago, mirrored from the Upper World onto nodes and nerve centres on Turtle's back, creating the World Between through earthworks imagined, crafted, and mounded, basket by fifty-pound basket, by minds, hands, thighs, and muscled backs, through Earth itself.

We are in conversation. This is real.

This is a journey. It tracks an ancestral imprint that holds for us the ancestors' profound understanding of architecture, astronomy, ceremonial space, and the human relationship and responsibility to them all. This journey begins

---

1   Research for this paper was funded in part by a Research/Creation grant from the Social Sciences and Humanities Research Council of Canada.

in the urban landscape along Lake Ontario; it moves to the northern head-waters of the Mississippi River and traces that writhing great serpent into the Mississippi River Valley; it then moves deeper south still to the southern grasslands and to the region between the grasslands and the swamplands that opens up to the delta and the Gulf of Mexico. Then east to the Rappahannock River Valley, Cat Point Creek, the tidal rivers on the Atlantic coast, to the land of the Rappahannock, Pamunkey, and Potomac before resuming on the Great Hopewell Road.

This is my journey captured in words legible in the "enemy's language" (see Harjo and Bird).

THIS IS REAL.

How do I talk about realisms when definitions of realism (and what is perceived and presumed to be real) depend on my continued erasure, my vanishing out-line against the "preservation of archaeological remains/collection of data/confirmation of evidence," of language and signage that declares our cultures "abandoned" as they "fell into decline"? Effigy mounds and earthworks are among the extraordinary structures built by Indigenous peoples long before European contact. Their encoded visual language, cosmo visions, and percep-tions of realities still define Indigenous peoples today. It is the double helix of our DNA and we are its embodiment. (*We are still here, still here, still here . . .*)

I am engaged in artistic research (field, archival, and studio), into Indigenous aesthetics and performance principles in theory, process, and practice, and in the practical application of these investigations and principles as the structural base from which to construct a performance, design a set, or dramaturge a script. Through these investigations I practice an Indigenous ar-tistic research methodology that speaks to the embodiment of place. The land *is* our archive and our embodied relationship to the land defines Indigenous identities, history, science, cosmology, literature—and our performance.

My current project—on embodied research into the literary structure of effigy mounds and earthworks as a dramaturgical framework for a new play,

Side Show Freaks and Circus Injuns—ignites new growth in my long-term artistic pursuit of developing Indigenous dramaturgies, and it solidifies the location of Indigenous performance principles at the centre of my artistic practice. It regenerates my creative source by placing me on the life-giving land in an embodied research process that requires me to walk on, touch, feel, smell, and absorb the stories, forms, and structures of effigy mounds and earthworks, to connect to the ancestors who built them and to the peoples who still inhabit the region. Simultaneous to this sacred work, I am challenged to "talk back" to colonial erasure, to peel away that veil, to refocus my lens. Once we were not victims. Once we had our own sciences, medicine, literary, and performing arts.

I feel a deep sense of responsibility as I imagine how I might transpose the still-legible story narratives and literary structures of these amazing ancient earthworks and apply them to serve scriptwriting and performance purposes. As an Indigenous artist-scholar I challenge myself to encounter "hyper-visible intangibles" and "tangible invisibilities" by means of a creative process that seeks to repair my self and my culture(s) through artistic practice and sacred art.

Others accompany me on this journey, most closely my two mentors, two brilliant scholars from mound-building Muskogean cultures. Nations among those ripped away from their Mother Mounds and forcibly "removed" to Indian Territory—Oklahoma, a word that means "the Red People." They are poet, novelist, and performer LeAnne Howe (Choctaw), my co-writer of the script *Side Show Freaks and Circus Injuns*, and literary scholar Chadwick Allen (Chickasaw), whose work on Allison Adelle Hedge Coke's *Blood Run* inspired me to undertake this investigation—this "research as ceremony" (see S. Wilson). This quote from Allen propelled me and gave me permission:

> Readers are guided toward perception of messages still encoded within Indigenous earthworks extant and destroyed, toward recognition of a still readable form of Indigenous writing—not simply *on* the land but literally *through the medium of* the land itself—toward nothing less than the imagination of possible renewal. (808, emphasis in original)

And this quote sustains me:

> [T]he seemingly lost figure of the sacred snake at Blood Run reasserts its celestially aligned body of mounded earth as an active Indigenous presence in the layered landscape of Hedge Coke's poems, an impetus to an activist present seeking Indigenous futures. (809)

I seek those Indigenous futures. I have a responsibility to do so.

It is a responsibility that inspires me to excavate deep within my body to connect myself through time and place to the vast Indigenous Knowledges from which effigy mounds, earthworks, and other sacred sites are inscribed. They are still legible on the land. It is a responsibility that propels me to privilege these Indigenous ways of knowing and to make visible that which has been made invisible. It is a responsibility that compels me to remember things I never knew and restore them to consciousness.

These structures were built with deliberate creative intent, requiring precise knowledge of physics, engineering, astronomy, and architecture. They have been lovingly mounded to carve out ceremonial spaces conscious of their theatrical impact in order to prepare the human body to be aligned in body, mind, spirit, and heart within the cosmos.

This is real.

MOUND CRAWL—THE JOURNALS

I never have been good at journaling. It's as if the act of "writing it down" interferes, gets in the way of my *feeling* a place, a situation. I often find this is so with the camera lens too—that it separates me from what I really want to record. I record and document with my body—that is my methodology—so circumstances that distract from that process result in material that is much less "usable" for my purposes. I suspect that this is a part of an Indigenous epistemology that I'm becoming more familiar with identifying. Nevertheless,

I did keep a journal on this Mound Crawl (though there are some holes in what I wrote down that, luckily, are recorded in my body memory).

This journey began and ended in urban landscapes, though less by design than by instinctively following its unfolding. It began in densely populated Southern Ontario and Toronto's sprawling High Park in the rain and concluded in a quiet, affluent residential area of Columbus, Ohio, again in the rain.

LeAnne Howe at the Southwold Earthworks National Historic Site, St. Thomas, Ontario. Photo by M. Mojica.

JUNE 21, 2011—SOUTHWOLD EARTHWORKS NATIONAL HISTORIC SITE, ST. THOMAS, ONTARIO

My collaborators, co-writer and mentor LeAnne Howe, dramaturg Ric Knowles, co-investigator Dr. Brenda Farnell, and I set off on an early summer road trip to visit one of the few protected earthworks in Southern Ontario. Here there is signage, but it's disturbing. Archaeology is an interpretive art after all—not an exact science. And "evidence" is interpreted to follow a certain script. The word "prehistoric" jumps out at us.

There was a village here. Inhabited by Neutrals, the sign says. The sign says that Mohawk and Seneca raids caused their "demise." How do they know that? A double-walled embankment encircles the site, reminds us of the serpent twins, the double helix. Birds scold us for disturbing their sanctuary and curious bees hover, wondering who has come to visit. Even the spirits of this village are long, long gone. Fled suddenly, and neither they nor the wind are giving up their secrets.

JUNE 22, 2011—HIGH PARK, TORONTO, ONTARIO

We approach the Snake Mound site with caution. Traffic noise from cars and streetcars on Lake Shore is constant. The last time Brenda and I visited had been painful. The mound had been bald, wounded, pitifully sad. There had been an encampment of Native people protecting the mounds from BMX bikers who had been using them as jumps. There had been controversy. Archaeologists saying there were no mounds there. Others disputing to which nation the mounds belonged. On this day there is no one. There had been ceremony, and some healing of the land, it seems to us. The city agreed to protect the Snake Mound. The land is pushing up green. There is now a brand new orange fence around the area that reads:

Forest Regeneration Zone. Area Closed.

Help us protect this area by keeping out.

No signs mentioning Indian mounds. We of course enter through a break in the fence and make our offerings of tobacco and prayers. There are fifty-seven mounds in High Park. We go in search of them with a map on my iPhone. Costume designer Erika Iserhoff joins us and together we try to locate them through the palms of our hands, soles of our feet, our heartbeats straining to detect a shift in energy or a rise in the ground. And we do feel . . . something . . . but without signage acknowledging their presence I am about to cut myself a dowsing wand! There are signage and plaques for every tree, bench, flower bed, and statue in the park—but none for Indian mounds. Only the names of the streets in the neighbourhood lend a hint: Indian Grove, Indian Road Crescent, Indian Trail. It is raining and my feet are soaked.

We continue to Magwood Park in Etobicoke in search of the Thunderbird Mound. Here there is signage acknowledging the Seneca village site on the promontory above us. Now smothered by wealthy homes. We tromp the trails but cannot identify the Thunderbird Mound. It is frustrating knowing it has to be close. The Humber River rushes by. The mounds are always near water. Dramaturg Ric Knowles makes two critical observations: that the mound we located was identifiable *because* of its desecration and that in the play we are creating, *Side Show Freaks and Circus Injuns*, there is a tense relationship between Indigenous hyper-visibility, "Indians" marked as exotics, and our invisibility: a deliberate concealment and erasure of the evidence that marks our sustained presence on the landscape and in societal consciousness.

Indian Mounds Park, St. Paul, Minnesota. Photo by M. Mojica.

AUGUST 24, 2011—INDIAN MOUNDS PARK, ST. PAUL, MINNESOTA

Proud and defiant mounds of light and shadow rise in this city park. Contained by a wrought-iron fence, announced with signage:

Please Respect

Indian Burial Sites

Keep Off

Thank You

The earth ripples fluid like waves beneath my feet, rises and falls before me. I am dizzy, a bit seasick on this bluff overlooking the majestic Mississippi River.

A black butterfly with yellow markings leads me, fluttering, hovering over a mound. A yellow butterfly with black markings passes me. I follow these messengers of transformation, of light and shadow, mirror images: positive and negative.

A white squirrel appears right behind me on my right side; a true albino, with pink eyes. It circles, disappears into the bush, later returns. A black squirrel is the next to greet me. Light and shadow. The resplendent Mississippi polluted by industrial noise, railroad tracks, an airport on one side; a strong, peaceful feat of ancient architecture and engineering, ancestral remains on the other. I stand on the meridian between the mounds and vibrate like a tuning fork. My arms buzz and tingle, and then I get a low-grade headache.

AUGUST 25, 2011—RED WING ARCHAEOLOGICAL PRESERVE, ENERGY PARK SITE, RED WING, MINNESOTA

My brother's partner and I set out from the Twin Cities to search out the Red Wing Archaeological Preserve. It is accessible from the Cannon Valley Trail. We get lost and go too far. At the end of a long rural road we stop for directions at an ice cream parlour. There we meet the trail manager for the Cannon Valley Trail when he overhears us asking for directions. He is very helpful but warns us, "There's nothing there to see—just an open field"—but then adds, "The mounds around here are connected to the ones in Cahokia, you know."

We find the access road and set off down the trail. A small spotted frog greets us, another being of transformation and of the underworld. It is a long way and we are accompanied by finches, red-wing blackbirds, and pass an entire roost of brilliant red cardinals. We arrive at the site; the signage tells us so and that the village above the trail is a younger site: just over eight hundred years old. We start to climb earthen stairs cut into the side of the hill thick with ferocious mosquitoes. At the top the bush opens out into a meadow. We walk its perimeter, drop our tobacco, tell the ancestors that we came to visit. We stand looking out over the valley. That's where the mounds are. Back along the trail, closer to where we parked the car, there's another village site called Silvernale. The mounds here are not visible to the naked eye either, but they are there. I am reminded of what a Mattaponi man told me when I first visited the Powhatan territory of Virginia in the mid 1990s. He said, "You want to know what saved us? We hid in plain sight. We hid in the marshes and in the backwoods and in that Baptist church out at the crossroads. We hid in plain sight."

The majestic Mississippi River—Effigy Mounds National Monument, McGregor, Iowa. Photo by M. Mojica.

AUGUST 27, 2011—EFFIGY MOUNDS NATIONAL MONUMENT, MCGREGOR, IOWA

I am travelling on this road trip with my brother and his partner. We have followed the Mississippi River to the sleepy little tourist town of McGregor, Iowa, where cigar store Indians still line the streets, frozen in awkward poses. It is an idyllic late summer day here, but we are worried about our elders in New York City who are battening down for Hurricane Irene to hit. Lower Manhattan is being evacuated, we hear.

At breakfast in the B&B we learn that Indian mounds are so numerous in Iowa that the state has a "Stewardship Covenant" that describes the distance from a mound that any structure or septic system may be built. Some Iowans have bought prime land overlooking the Mississippi only to find they could not, by law, build on it. Stewardship Covenant. We need more of those.

On arrival at the Effigy Mounds National Monument we are in deep woods. It is good to read this signage:

> We ask that as you walk over this land to please remember this is sacred ground to those of the mound building culture The descendants of this culture are not a lost people but rather living, thriving American Indian cultures that today reside in what is called the Midwest These native descendants continue to honor their ancestors buried here in religious ceremonies on these sacred sites Please enjoy and respect your time among the "old ones" as their spirits will watch over you while you are here—Clorys Lowe, Ho-chunk, 2005

> Welcome to your outdoor museum Please enjoy everything that is here, but remember there is no collecting of anything within effigy mounds national monument Everything at this sacred site today was left by those who were here before us, so please leave it as you found it for the enjoyment of those who come after us (National Parks Service sign at Effigy Mounds National Monument, Harpers Ferry, Iowa)

It is quite a climb up a steep winding path along cliff faces to the sites of Little Bear Mound Group, Great Bear Mound Group, Fire Point, and Eagle Rock—the Northern Unit. The climb challenges the power of our legs and lungs. Here there are clusters of mounds close to the ground. Some are burial mounds in different shapes and sizes. They are magnificent, old and patient. Then come the bear effigies, their shapes hard to discern when right next to them; they have been outlined in white to make them easier to see. Again the butterflies are guiding, leading us from mound to mound, hovering.

I sit on the ground by Little Bear Mound to feel the earth beneath me. I begin to hear a rising chorus of song. Many voices. My body feels the heaviness of bear movements dancing. Rhythmic. It is a bear song I am hearing. The ancient ones danced to honour the bears here among layers of earth, layers of worlds. This is real.

We quickly grab a cellphone so I can sing the song into an answering machine before it retreats back into time.

By the Great Bear Mound two white-tailed deer step out of the woods and stand looking at me before leaping off. The vista opens up before me to reveal the full power of the mighty Mississippi. Two men, a woman, and a child are buried in the mound overlooking the river. The woman was buried face up, arms folded, with her bundle of sewing needles made of bird bone tucked under her right arm. I know because the sign says so. I tell her I am so sorry she was disturbed.

I speak with some tourists at the point who are here with their dog. They are white Americans. When I tell them that I live in Canada, they welcome me to their country. "Welcome to *you*," I reply, "Welcome to Indian Country." Unwilling to acknowledge the irony of our exchange they quip, "Oh well, we are all citizens of the planet, after all!!" (Really . . . ?)

The Marching Bear Group is in the Southern Unit, and I am sad that I am not able to visit them on this trip. It is a distance of six kilometres to walk from the road to the Marching Bear site and back and we must reach Illinois by tonight. I guess that means I'll be coming back.

The view across the plaza from the top of Monks Mound, Cahokia Mounds National Historic Site, Collinsville, Illinois. Photo by M. Mojica.

AUGUST 28, 2011—CAHOKIA MOUNDS NATIONAL HISTORICAL SITE, COLLINSVILLE, ILLINOIS

Cahokia, the mound city, city of the sun; the largest pre-contact community north of Mexico. One hundred and twenty mounds over six square miles. It feels a lot like the pyramids in Mexico but built from earth instead of stone. It is huge, martial, show-offish, with a plaza and the imposing Monks Mound— so named because in 1809 a group of Trappist monks had built their monastery on the site and had their orchards on the terraces of the mound itself. Even earlier, in 1735, French priests had come along and plunked their chapel down right on top of it. The present day city of St. Louis, Missouri, across the river, whose skyline we can see from the top of the mound, was also plunked right down on top of an existing mound city, obliterating one reality and superimposing another. Many mounds were deliberately destroyed to make way. I meet LeAnne Howe here at the top of this one hundred foot mound. We are greeted once again by butterflies, joined now by dragonflies and the cicadas' song.

We sit on the ground near the plaza, close to the Twin Mounds. I lie back to rest and to feel the length of my spinal column against the earth. The earth beneath me begins to vibrate as it synchronizes my frequency to this place. zap! zing! ka-chung! click! An electric current sends its voltage coursing into my sacrum—interface! I am plugged in like an old-style switchboard whose wires carry conversations. A thousand tributaries radiate from my spine into my limbs and connect to the satellites and constellations of mounds in conversation—a dialogue from below the earth to the sun, stars, planets, like beacons, lighthouses, signal switches, watchtowers. Eye in the hand! The stars have eyes! Hawk Man, Star Panther Woman, Underwater Panther, the Double Headed Serpent. Mounds of light and shadow. I am aligned.

I am annoyed by the word "demise." It is everywhere, on all the signage and in the state-of-the-art museum and interpretive centre: "The demise of Cahokia." (*We are still here, still here, still here . . .*)

SEPTEMBER 1 AND 2, 2011—POVERTY POINT STATE HISTORIC SITE, PIONEER, LOUISIANA

LeAnne and I set off from her home in Ada, Oklahoma, along the Chickasaw Turnpike, through the heart of the Choctaw Nation and on through Texas (lunch in Paris), then across Louisiana toward the border of the state of Mississippi. This is the Deep South now, a region I have never visited. Along the route we are escorted by two great blue herons, white-tailed deer, and Coyote himself.

It is late and very dark when we arrive in the tiny town of Delhi, Louisiana, where we've booked a room in a popular hotel chain. But we can't find the hotel. We drive on through the town armed only with our MapQuest printout. Its directions take us farther and farther away from any town or lights as it lists turnoff after turnoff. The roads keep getting smaller and smaller and darker and darker. We start to feel afraid. Because we are two unarmed Indian women on the back roads of rural Louisiana and this can't be the right way because LeAnne smells the river. We use the last of the battery on LeAnne's cellphone to try to locate the hotel. We are only able to find out that there is no such hotel in Delhi. We criss-cross a triangle of roads until we are back on the road into Delhi, where we discover that the name of the hotel has indeed been changed.

In the morning we head out to the Poverty Point site. Upon entering the interpretive centre the first thing we see is a display about the Jesse James/Cole Younger Gang having had a hideout on the site. It went from behind the largest mound into a tunnel that led to a cabin from which no one ever saw them enter or exit. The gang came here because they had relatives in the area, in Epps. And then, there it was: a map showing the triangle where we had been so hopelessly and eerily lost the night before between Delhi, Epps, Floyd, and Lake Providence. For over one hundred years people have dug up the ground around the mounds looking for Jesse James's gold. Instead they found us: flints, arrowheads, pottery shards, pot-bellied owls, and effigies of pregnant women.

We are the only people in the park. There is no one else here but the staff. We get a personal tour of the site in a golf cart and then we go back to the impressive Bird Mound on our own. It is now about seventy feet high but it used to be a hundred. It had been built in three months. Bird Mound is oriented east-west. The head is mostly eroded (from people digging for Jesse James's gold, I'm thinking). Since we are the only ones here we are able to do some embodied improvisation on the Bird Mound while the cicadas sing, surging and fading: she is a nurturing maternal energy, a female bird flying west, leading her children to safety, looking back over her wing calm and serene. She tells me so and she gifts LeAnne with a song.

Inside Mound B petrified baskets filled with earth were found. They were used to stabilize the structure of the mound. This mound feels wounded. There is much erosion from the days of the Poverty Point Plantation. Mound C is the only mound inside the plaza. A wagon track, the old Floyd Trace, cuts through the middle of the mound. It had been used to take cotton to market in Floyd. Silver galena and yellow ochre are layered inside, colours and textures that changed every twenty to thirty years. LeAnne says the layers, textures, and colours are a text written within the soil, an adornment in homage to and in relationship with the spirit-beings inside the earth. And I wonder: how do we begin to decode the text layered between the strata of soil?

SEPTEMBER 5, 2011—SPIRO MOUNDS STATE PARK, SPIRO, OKLAHOMA

There are wildfires along the highway on the way to Spiro. We pass through Seminole, Choctaw, Cherokee, Caddo, Wichita territories. When we arrive at the site it is closed, shut up tight, closed in on itself. I will not write about Spiro Mounds except to say that some things that have been buried were meant to stay buried. This site has been severely looted. There are many more burials here than at other sites we visited. Here there is no sound. No cicadas, no butterflies, no dragonflies, no animals—a dead zone. We do not stay.

SEPTEMBER 28, 2011—BELLE MOUNT VINEYARDS, RICHMOND COUNTY, VIRGINIA

First attempt: In Virginia, where my great-grandmother was born, we hid so well we became invisible. Dancing Point is the historical village of the Rappahannock werowance (the head chief or Powhatan). Nevertheless it took three attempts to locate the burial mounds that my Rappahannock hosts remembered visiting thirty-six years ago. The elder who is with us is sure there were three burial mounds side-by-side and visible from the road. It is now Belle Mount Vineyards and Heritage Park Resort. We approach the building, which is still a working vineyard, and ask about Indian burial mounds. "What? Who? Oh, you mean the Indians? The Rappahannock Indians? Well, we had the Rappahannock Indians out here for a powwow. You can go ahead and look around." What we find is decay: the grounds fallen into disrepair, neglected, rotting picnic tables, mouldy campers, abandoned cabins on this land that was once our village. A field of rusted-out junked cars, a flock of wild turkeys, two leaping deer. Invisible. (*We are still here, still here, still here . . .*) I can feel the ancestors out at the point, Dancing Point on Cat Point Creek.

SEPTEMBER 29, 2011—NAYLORS BEACH, RICHMOND COUNTY, VIRGINIA

Second attempt: At Naylors Beach landing I greet the graceful and dignified Rappahannock River. We are drawn to explore upriver and then continue warily down a private road by the waterfront. Something sad and suffering took place on this land—disease, removal, a confusion of disoriented spirits in a land of amnesiacs.

We turn into a wildlife preserve. Nature conservancy protects the frogs, reptiles, birds, watershed—but what about the original people of this land? Invisible.

At Wilna Pond we talk to a friendly and helpful "Smokey the Bear"-type ranger. "Who? Oh, you mean the Rappahannock Indians? Burial mounds? Archaeological sites? I don't know. I should know that, but I don't know anything about your pottery shards, arrow points, postholes, and bones . . . I don't know."

We return to Belle Mount. This time we turn left at the fork in the drive and pass a grand old house fallen to ruin. Here there are some cabins that almost look inhabitable. We are drawn to a corner near the grapevines; then the energy pulls us down the embankment. There are big trees pulled up by the roots—hurricane damage, but no burial mounds.

SEPTEMBER 30, 2011—PAMUNKEY INDIAN RESERVATION, KING WILLIAM COUNTY, VIRGINIA

My new Rappahannock family and I travel from Rappahannock territory, crossing the Mattaponi River to the Pamunkey Indian Reservation on the banks of the Pamunkey River. We pull up to the home of a Pamunkey elder and renowned potter. She shows us some of the pots in her workshop and then we pile in the car again to go down by the river to the spot where the women dig clay in the spring. "The river's been rising," she tells us. "We have to stand in the water now. It's getting harder and harder to get to the clay." We go on to another place by the river where there is a burial mound that I've visited before. The large burial mound is bisected by railroad tracks. It is widely believed (and the sign says) that this is Powhatan's gravesite. Pamunkey oral history says that the bones of Wahensonacook (Pocahontas's father) were moved to this mound and buried by his brother, Opechancanough. No one knows for sure. Our Pamunkey hosts feel that the mound is actually much larger than what we can see and that there are many more back in the bush. We stand in the middle of the burial mound and our attention is drawn across the river to the non-reservation side. There, directly aligned with where we are standing, is a house built on a rise that has a very familiar form—is that a mound? Could it be a sister mound to this one we are standing on? The magnetic pull between them is strong. For the nations of the Powhatan, so much of our history was deliberately obliterated as part of the land grab. We were legislated into invisibility.

OCTOBER 3, 2011—MENOKIN AND BELLE MOUNT VINEYARDS, RICHMOND COUNTY, NORTHERN NECK, VIRGINIA

Third attempt: On this day there is a sweet Virginia breeze, the kind that is a caress on the cheek. A gentle touch from the ancestors—they were there, I tell you, running alongside the van, there at Cat Point Creek. All along the tributaries of the powerful, sustaining Rappahannock River, they lived—they are there still. We are here!

The plan was to go back to Belle Mount Vineyards, to search once more for the mounds and then to continue upriver to Leedstown, stopping at a landing or two to get close to the river within Westmoreland County where my great-grandma was born. A stop at the Northern Neck Department of Tourism in Tappahannock yields a detailed map of the Northern Neck and a recommendation to visit Menokin just down the road because it was built on the site of a Rappahannock village and many artifacts have been found there. Menokin is the name of the original village, but now Menokin is also the ruins of the home of Francis Lightfoot Lee, a plantation (and slave) owner and a signer of the Declaration of Independence.

The executive director of the Menokin site greets us. She is really glad to see a group of Virginia Indians asking questions. She takes us down a wooded trail to Cat Point Creek in her four-wheel drive. We are directly across from Dancing Point. She stands back and respectfully gives us space to make our offerings. The tidal river offers up saltwater clamshells.

We walk the perimeter of the big collapsing house made from sandstone hewn from nearby quarries. My ancestors smile—hover on the edges of the exposed guts of a house cleaved open by time and the elements. A murmur, a name, a sigh, a melody fragment caught in the leaves: pine, cedar, oak, willow. The Old Ones peek around the crumbling chimney to catch a glimpse of this faraway granddaughter come looking for them.

We approach Belle Mount again, resolved to search the area in front of the derelict house. Decay and neglect greet us. The door is wide open and there are curtains still on the windows. It once was grand.

We tromp through the high grass looking carefully for any trace of a rise, a bump in the earth. There is a moment of dread when we speculate that the mounds may have been covered over by the swimming pool. The elder is determined. She keeps walking over uneven ground, steadied by her grandson. At the top of the hill we look toward the road. The field below us is not hung with grapes but it has been plowed. We head toward the road, toward the trees. When we get to the bottom of the hill we realize that the three burial mounds are right there—hidden in plain sight. The largest one has the campsite sign on it; the other two are barely visible. We make our offerings on the largest mound at the foot of the sign. We walk onto the plowed and mowed field and locate the other two mounds.

I sing an ancestor's song to let the Grandmothers and Grandfathers know we remember them. We stand, hold hands, give thanks, and pray. We pray to heal the past, we pray to heal the future, we pray for the land, we pray for each other, we pray for ourselves: generations standing together, refusing to remain invisible; a rent in the veil of amnesia.

OCTOBER 5, 2011—PISCATAWAY OSSUARY AND BURIAL GROUNDS, TAYAC TERRITORY, MARYLAND

On the train between Richmond, Virginia, and Washington, DC, two bald eagles fly over the car I am riding in and pass right past my window. The iconic architecture and monuments of the US capital strike me as ironic on this sun-drenched morning. My Piscataway friend meets me at Union Station and we set off across the Potomac to Accokeek, Maryland—Tayac Territory. I am on the lands of close allies of my Rappahannock ancestors. Within the Accokeek Creek site is the Piscataway ossuary. Up until about forty years ago the outline of its mound was still visible; now a red cedar tree holds its place. We walk the boardwalk along the revitalized shoreline. We are directly across the river from Mount Vernon, the estate of George Washington. More mounds over there. A great blue heron, a bald eagle, and several ospreys bless us with their company.

OCTOBER 9, 2011—OCTAGON EARTHWORKS, MOUNDBUILDERS COUNTRY CLUB, AND NEWARK EARTH WORKS GREAT CIRCLE, NEWARK, OHIO

A group of about forty Indigenous scholars and our allies arrive by chartered bus and private vehicle at the Octagon Earthworks, this sacred site–turned–golf course. One of my mentors, Chadwick Allen, brought us together to attend a symposium commemorating the centennial of the founding of the Society of American Indians that took place in Columbus, Ohio, on Columbus Day weekend in 1911. We all rose way earlier than we are accustomed to do and travelled forty-five minutes from Columbus to visit these remarkable ancient geometric forms. We represent many diverse Indigenous nations from across Turtle Island and even Aotearoa. We are aware that our presence is unwanted here, that on a usual day we would not be allowed on this site. It is leased to the Moundbuilders Country Club until 2075. There is a narrow window of time allotted us. We must be off the green by 9:30 a.m. when the golfers arrive.

Approaching, we take in the bizarre juxtaposition of rows of parked golf carts, the clubhouse, the putter's green with its flag piercing the centre of an earthen circle. There is a soft mist and the grass is heavy with dew as we set out toward the earthwork dubbed "the observatory" because it is higher than the embankment walls around the octagon. Once these embankment walls lined a road that directed the ancestors between here and the Mound City Group in Chillicothe. Walking the Great Hopewell Road has recently been revived. This is a night place: its gateways align with lunar risings throughout the year.

We do our best to walk with gentle feet, make our offerings, and climb the mound. One hundred years ago a group of Native scholars stood at this spot and sang "America the Beautiful." We know we will not sing that song but we sing others: a harvest song from Santo Domingo Pueblo, a song from *Chocolate Woman Dreams the Milky Way*, a Maori song, ones in Anishnaabe, Creek, Choctaw, and a prayer song in Dakota as they start to herd us off the green. Golf carts whizz past us as we stand on soaking feet.

By the time we arrive down the road at the Newark Earth Works Great Circle site I cannot take in any more information telling me what I should think about these structures. It is all I am able to manage to sit on the ground next to the borrow pit with some others who are also on overload. We sit and feel the earth beneath us.

Monique on the lookout at Great Serpent Mound National Historical
Landmark, Peebles, Ohio. Photo by Chadwick Allen.

OCTOBER 11, 2011—ALONG THE GREAT HOPEWELL ROAD: GREAT SERPENT MOUND NATIONAL HISTORIC LANDMARK, PEEBLES, OHIO; SEIP MOUND STATE MEMORIAL, BAINBRIDGE, OHIO; MOUND CITY GROUP NATIONAL MONUMENT, CHILLICOTHE, OHIO

As I perch atop the outlook the Great Serpent Mound uncoils below me, reaching toward the point of land above the escarpment, reaching toward water. A meteor hit this place millennia ago; the ancestors knew this and here they built this exquisite effigy honouring the Great Serpent. Three coils of its tail, seven undulations of its body, a release of energy at the mouth, and a circle; it is the largest serpent effigy in the world.

A sob catches in my throat and escapes. I weep to see this place! We are weeping. Bones ground to dust by time and the unbearable weight of a world that cannot or will not see them. Add tears and stir: we reconstitute our bodies from the pulverized bones of the ancestors mixed with tears.

We lie bellies down upon the Great Serpent Mound, hearts heaving. The serpent writhes and undulates beneath us. A song begins. Thank you for leaving this behind for us to cling to when all is almost gone. All but our blood and bones and memory.

"People coming!" We stand and "act normal." Blend in with the tourists, camouflage ourselves in the tangible and visible world. We hide in plain sight.

Monique at Seip Mound State Memorial, Bainbridge, Ohio. Photo by Chadwick Allen.

A bit farther down the Great Hopewell Road we come to Seip Mound. It can be seen from the road: proud and impressive. It is thirty feet high, 240 feet long, and 130 feet wide. There is a half-naked man in a lawn chair sunning himself while his boom box plays country western or gospel music, we can't quite tell which. Why would anyone sunbathe at a burial site? There are many buried here. We are struck by how different the mound looks from its various sides. This was also once a complex of geometric shapes carved out and defined by earthen embankments. Only the burial mound remains, posholes and part of the embankment wall remains. The rest went under the farmer's plow.

The Mound City Group sits directly behind the Chillicothe Correctional Institution, another odd juxtaposition in our view. The mounds here are well manicured but it's much harder to feel their energy. Maybe that's because during World War I the site was occupied by Camp Sherman and barracks were built on top of the mounds as the military prepared for war. Those are gone now too. We walk the perimeter; it is a large grouping, immaculately kept, but the extensive wartime excavations have distanced the ancestors' presence.

OCTOBER 12, 2011—NEWARK EARTH WORKS GREAT CIRCLE, NEWARK, OHIO, AND JEFFERS MOUND, WORTHINGTON, OHIO

It is raining as Chad Allen and I return to the Great Circle at Newark Earth Works. But that is auspicious: because it is raining, we are the only ones there. We walk within the Great Circle, imagining the ring of water that would have run along the inner wall. Seasonally, peepers would have created a soundscape on the site and the embankments and mounds would have been covered in a layer of yellow clay. At one point in the early twentieth century the site had been turned into an amusement park. Today it is empty, and I am able to do some embodied improvisation on its central mound—Eagle Mound. I open my arms and allow my body to take on the shape and rhythm of the Eagle. I look up to see dancers entering the Great Circle by clan, family, nation. Shells and pearls hang swaying from their ceremonial clothes as they dance in intersecting geometric patterns. Interlocking and falling away like shapes through a kaleidoscope, like light through a prism. I hear their song as the procession continues.

My last mound visit in Ohio is to a quiet residential street in the near suburbs of Columbus. These are affluent homes tucked away from the main drag and nestled along a circular drive. There in the centre of the circle is Jeffers Mound. It is thirty feet high and ungroomed, covered with trees and brush. There is signage here identifying it as a prehistoric mound used for rituals. There are also three stone flagstones in the earth with the words: approach. with. respect. Marti Chaatsmith, the Comanche program director of the Ohio State University Newark Earth Works program, comes to meet us. We "Approach. With. Respect." and make our offerings before walking around the mound to get another view. Chad photographs me framed by an American flag with the mound in the background. We wonder about the people in the houses . . . what do they think of this sacred burial site at their front doorsteps? What do they dream? Marti would like to knock on doors and interview them.

***

This embodied engagement with effigy mounds and earthworks, the effort required to connect my body to the inscriptions made on the land through the extraordinary knowledge of my ancestors, is my "realism." This hyperreal invisibility made visible by privileging ancestral knowledge: feats of astronomy, engineering, architecture, physics, and social organization that manipulate the landscape to evoke a heart-spirit response that can impact and align the human body in relationship to the earth and stars . . . across all these centuries.

WORKS CITED

"About." *Scotiabank Caribbean Carnival Toronto 2011*. Festival Management Committee, 2011. Web. 31 Dec. 2011.

"About Us: Mandate." *fu-GEN Asian Canadian Theatre Company*. fu-GEN Asian Canadian Theatre Company, n.d. Web. 31 Dec. 2011.

"About VACT." *Vancouver Asian Canadian Theatre*. Vancouver Asian Canadian Theatre, 24 Oct. 2010. Web. 31 Dec. 2011.

Adams, Rachel. *Sideshow U.S.A.: Freaks and the American Cultural Imagination*. Chicago: U of Chicago P, 2001. Print.

"Address by the Prime Minister on the Chinese Head Tax Redress." Prime Minister of Canada Stephen Harper. N.p., 22 June 2006. Web. 29 Jul. 2011.

Aguirre, Carmen. *The Refugee Hotel*. Dir. Carmen Aguirre. Perf. Beatriz Pizano, Juan Carlos Velis, Cheri Maracle, Salvatore Antonio, Leanna Brodie, and Terrence Bryant. Alameda Theatre. Theatre Passe Muraille, Toronto. 17 Sept.–4 Oct. 2009. Performance.

---. *The Refugee Hotel*. Vancouver: Talonbooks, 2010. Print.

Alarcón, Norma, Caren Kaplan, and Minoo Moallem. "Between Woman and Nation." Introduction. *Between Woman and Nation: Nationalisms, Transnational Feminisms, and the State*. Ed. Kaplan, Alarcón, and Moallem. Durham: Duke UP, 1999. 1–16. Print.

Alford, C. Fred. "Levinas and Violence." *Journal of Power and Ethics* 2.3 (2001): 243–58. Print.

Allen, Chadwick. "Serpentine Figures, Sinuous Relations: Thematic Geometry in Allison Hedge Coke's *Blood Run*." *American Literature* 82.4 (2010): 807–34. *EBSCOhos*t. Web. 30 Dec. 2011.

Allen, Kate. "At Global Summit, All the World's a Stage." *Globe and Mail*. The Globe and Mail Inc., 25 June 2010. Web. 1 Sept. 2010.

Al-Solaylee, Kamal. "Identity Crisis Mars Powerful Performance." *Globe and Mail* 19 Jan. 2005: A12. Print.

---. "Sisterhood's Past Still Relevant Today." Rev. of *Top Girls*, dir. Alisa Palmer. Soulpepper Theatre Company, Young Centre, Toronto. *Globe and Mail* 6 July 2007: R5. *Canadian Periodicals Index Quarterly*. Web. 10 Oct. 2011.

Ambros, Veronika. "Prague's Experimental Stage: Laboratory of Theatre and Semiotics." *Semiotica* 168.1 (2008): 45–65. Print.

Ambush, Benny. "Pluralism to the Bone." *American Theatre* 6.1 (1989): 5. Print.

Anderson, Benedict. *Imagined Communities: Reflections on the Origin and Spread of Nationalism*. London: Verso, 1991. Print.

Ansen, David. "Life is a Cabernet." *Newsweek*. The Newsweek/Daily Beast Company LLC, 24 Oct. 2004. Web. 28 Sept. 2011.

Anthony, Geraldine. *Gwen Pharis Ringwood*. Boston: Twayne, 1981. Print.

Anthony, Trey. *'da Kink in my hair: voices of black womyn*. Toronto: Playwrights Canada, 2005. Print.

---. "The History of *'da Kink*." Introduction. Trey Anthony, *'da Kink* v–vi.

Aquino, Nina Lee, and Ric Knowles. Introduction. *Asian Canadian Theatre*. Ed. Aquino and Knowles. Toronto: Playwrights Canada, 2011. vii–xvi. Print. New Essays on Canadian Theatre 1.

Archambault, François. "Le jeu de la vérité." *Jeu* 85 (1997): 73–75. Print.

Armstrong, Jennifer. "Dr. Oh." *Entertainment Weekly*. Entertainment Weekly Inc., 28 March 2005. Web. 2 Aug. 2011.

Arrizón, Alicia. *Latina Performance: Traversing the Stage*. Bloomington: Indiana UP, 1999. Print.

Auerbach, Erich. *Mimesis: The Representation of Reality in Western Literature*. Trans. Willard Trask. Princeton: Princeton UP, 1953. Print.

Auslander, Philip. "'Just Be Your Self': Logocentrism and Difference in Performance Theory." *Acting (Re)considered: Theories and Practices*. Ed. Phillip Zarrilli. London: Routledge, 1995. 59–68. Print.

Auster, Paul. *La musique du hasard*. Paris: Actes Sud, 1991. Print.

Austin, J.L. *How To Do Things With Words*. New York: Oxford UP, 1962. Print.

Barber, John. "We Know Something the Fearmongers Don't." *Globe and Mail* 13 March 2004: M2. Print.

Barnes, Clive. "Drama: 'Mac the Knifed' Presented as a Convention Sequel." *New York Times* 27 Aug. 1968: 29. Microfilm.

Barthes, Roland. "The Reality Effect." *French Literary Theory Today: A Reader*. Ed. Tzvetan Todorov. Trans. R. Carter. Cambridge: Cambridge UP, 1982. 11–17. Print.

---. *S/Z*. Trans. Richard Miller. Oxford: Blackwell, 1990. Print.

Barton, Bruce. "Devising the Creative Body." Introduction. *Collective Creation, Collaboration and Devising*. Ed. Barton. Toronto: Playwrights Canada, 2008. vii–xxvii. Print. Critical Perspectives on Canadian Theatre in English 12.

Batt, Noëlle. "Que peut la science pour l'art." *L'art et l'Hybride*. Ed. Christian Doumet, Michèle Lagny, Marie-Claire Ropars-Wuilleumier, and Pierre Sorlin. Paris: P U de Vincennes, 2001. 73–82. Print.

Bau, Alan, and Kathy Leung. *Red Letters*. Dir. Andy Maton. Perf. Alan Wong. Vancouver Asian Canadian Theatre. Roundhouse Performance Centre, Vancouver. 28 Nov. 2010. Performance.

---. *Vancouver Asian Canadian Theatre Presents Red Letters: Songs and Music from the Original Theatrical Production*. Perf. Isaac Kwok, Rosie Simon, Alan Wong, Jimmy Yi, Yawen Wang, and Ge Li. Don Mann Sound, 2010. CD.

Beagan, Tara. *Dreary and Izzy*. Toronto: Playwrights Canada, 2007. Print.

---. "'Elder up!': A Mentor/Mentee Memoir." *Canadian Theatre Review* 147 (2011): 68–73. Print.

---. Message to Kim Solga. 12 Sept. 2011. Email.

---. *Miss Julie: Sheh'mah*. *New Canadian Realisms: Eight Plays*. Ed. Roberta Barker and Kim Solga. Toronto: Playwrights Canada, 2012. 237–328. Print.

Beauregard, Guy. "After Redress: A Conversation with Roy Miki." *Canadian Literature* 201 (2009): 71–86. Web. 20 Oct. 2011.

Beck, Dennis C. "The Paradox of the Method Actor: Rethinking the Stanislavsky Legacy." Krasner, *Method* 261–81. Print.

Beggs, Anne. "'For Urinetown Is Your Town . . .': The Fringes of Broadway." *Theatre Journal* 62.1 (2010): 41–56. Web. 29 Dec. 2011.

Belsey, Catherine. "Constructing the Subject: Deconstructing the Text." *Feminist Criticism and Social Change: Sex, Class, and Race in Literature and Culture*. Ed. Judith Newton and Deborah Rosenfelt. New York: Methuen, 1985. 45–64. Print.

---. *Critical Practice*. 2nd ed. New York: Routledge, 2002. Print.

Ben-Ari, Raikin. *Habima*. Trans. A.H. Gross and I. Soref. New York: T. Yoseloff, 1957. Print.

Benedetti, Jean, ed. *The Moscow Art Theatre Letters*. London: Methuen, 2006. Print.

---. Translator's Foreword. *An Actor's Work: A Student Diary*. By Constantin Stanislavsky. Ed. and trans. Benedetti. London: Routledge, 2008. xv–xxii. Print.

Bennett, Melanie, Hartley Jafine, and Aaron Collier. *Garden//Suburbia: Mapping the Non-Aristocratic in Lawrence Park*. 2010. TS.

---. *Garden//Suburbia: Mapping the Non-Aristocratic in Lawrence Park*. Dir. and perf. Bennett and Jafine. Presented as part of Performance Studies International (PSi) 16. Lawrence Park, Toronto. June 2010. Performance.

Bennett, Susan. Introduction. *Feminist Theatre and Performance*. Ed. Bennett. Toronto: Playwrights Canada, 2006. vii–xvii. Print. Critical Perspectives on Canadian Theatre in English 4.

Berland, Jody. "Writing on the Border." *CR: The New Centennial Review* 1.2 (2001): 139–69. Print.

Bissoondath, Neil. "Multiculturalism." *New Internationalist Magazine* 305 (Sept. 1998): n. pag. Web. 1 Oct. 2011.

Blair, Rhonda. Introduction. *Acting: The First Six Lessons, Documents from the American Laboratory Theatre*. By Richard Boleslavsky. Ed. Blair. London: Routledge, 2010. ix–xxvi. Print.

Boag, Keith. "Outside the Fence." *The National*. CBC. St. John's, 20 Apr. 2001. Television.

Boal, Augusto. *The Aesthetics of the Oppressed*. Trans. Adrian Jackson. New York: Routledge, 2006. Print.

Boettcher, Shelley. "Rebecca, I Think." Interview With Rebecca Northan. *UMagazine*. University of Calgary, Spring 2006. Web. 21 Sept. 2011.

Bordwell, David, Janet Staiger, and Kristin Thompson. *The Classical Hollywood Cinema: Film Style and Mode of Production to 1960*. New York: Columbia UP, 1985. Print.

Bourriaud, Nicolas. *Esthétique relationnelle*. Dijon: Presses du réel, 2001. Print.

Bouthillier, Guy, and Édouard Cloutier, eds. *Trudeau's Darkest Hour: War Measures in Time of Peace, October 1970*. Montreal: Baraka, 2010. Print.

Braxton, Greg. "The Hot Button of a Casual Embrace." *Los Angeles Times*. Tribune Co., 11 Feb. 2007. Web. 10 Feb. 2012.

Brecht, Bertolt. "The Street Scene." *Brecht On Theatre*. Ed. John Willett. New York: Hill and Wang, 1964. 121–29. Print.

Brown, DeNeen L. "Demonstrators Turn Anger on Trade Meeting's 'Wall.'" *Washington Post* 21 Apr. 2001: A16. Microfilm.

Brunette, Candace Brandy. *Returning Home Through Stories: A Decolonizing Approach to Omushkego Cree Theatre Through the Methodological Practices of Native Performance Culture (NPC)*. M.A. thesis, U of Toronto, 2010. Print.

Burke, Edmund. *A Philosophical Enquiry Into the Origin of Our Ideas of the Sublime and Beautiful*. London: R. and J. Dodsley, 1759. Print.

Butler, Judith. *Bodies That Matter: On the Discursive Limits of Sex*. New York: Routledge, 1993. Print.

---. *Giving an Account of Oneself*. New York: Fordham UP, 2005. Print.

---. "Performative Acts and Gender Constitution: An Essay in Phenomenology and Feminist Theory." *Performing Feminisms: Feminist Critical Theory and Theatre*. Ed. Sue Ellen Case. Baltimore: Johns Hopkins UP, 1990: 270–82. Print.

Cameron, James E., and John W. Berry. "True Patriot Love: Structure and Predictors of Canadian Pride." *Canadian Ethnic Studies/Études ethniques au Canada* 40.3 (2008): 17–41. Print.

Campbell, Duncan. "Did the Handling of the G20 Protests Reveal the Future of Policing?" *Guardian*. Guardian News and Media Ltd., 2 Apr. 2009. Web. 1 Sept. 2010.

Canadian Civil Liberties Association. "A Breach of the Peace: A Preliminary Report of Observations during the 2010 G20 Summit." *Canadian Civil Liberties Association*. CCLA, 29 June 2010. Web. 1 Oct. 2011.

Canadian Press. "Chief Admits 5-meter G20 Security Rule Didn't Exist." *CBC News*. CBC/Radio Canada, 29 June 2010. Web. 1 Sept. 2010.

Carlson, Marla. "Acting and Answerability." Krasner, *Method* 81–95. Print.

Carlson, Marvin. *The Haunted Stage: The Theatre as Memory Machine*. Ann Arbor: U of Michigan P, 2001. Print.

Carnicke, Sharon M. *Stanislavsky in Focus*. London: Routledge, 1998. Print.

Case, Sue-Ellen. *Feminism and Theatre*. New York: Methuen, 1988. Print.

CBC News. "G8/G20 Summits Get Help from Quebec Police." *CBC News*. CBC/Radio Canada, 25 June 2010. Web. 1 Sept. 2010.

---. "G20 Report Highlights Policing Problems." *CBC News*. CBC/Radio Canada, 23 June 2011. Web. 1 Oct. 2011.

Chai, Camyar. "Which Box Should I Tick?" in "All White All Right?: Vancouver Theatre Artists Talk about Vancouver's Monochrome Stages." By Jerry Wasserman. *alt.theatre* 7.1 (2009): 14. Print.

Chamberlain, Adrian. "Red Letter Day for Head Tax Payers: Play Highlights Plight of Chinese Who Paid for Entry into Canada." *Times Colonist*. Postmedia Network Canada Corp., 6 Jan. 2011: 1–2. Web. 8 Jan. 2011.

Chansky, Dorothy. "Usable Performance Feminism for Our Time: Reconsidering Betty Friedan." *Theatre Journal* 60.3 (2008): 341–64. Print.

Chartrand, Michel, et al. *Le procès des Cinq*. Montreal: Lux, 2010. Print.

"Chinese Head Tax and Exclusion Act." Chinese Canadian National Council (CCNC). N.p., n.d. Web. 29 Jul. 2011.

Chocolate Woman Dreams the Milky Way. By Monique Mojica. Dir. José A. Colman. Chocolate Woman Collective. Helen Gardiner Phelan Playhouse, Toronto. 2–19 June 2011. Performance.

Cieslar, Patrick. "Colour-blind Casting and The Shaw." *Share the Stage*. Facebook, n.d. Web. 28 July 2010.

Citron, Paula. "fu-GEN Asian-Canadian Theatre Company/Young Centre—David Yee's *lady in the red dress*." Rev. of *lady in the red dress*, dir. Nina Lee Aquino. fu-GEN Asian Canadian Theatre Company, Young Centre, Toronto. *The New Classical 96.3fm*. Classical 96.3fm, n.d. Web. 8 Jan. 2011.

Clarke, George Elliott. "'Symposia' in the Drama of Trey Anthony and Louise Delisle." *Theatre Research in Canada/Recherches Théâtrales au Canada* 30.1–2 (2009): 1–16. Print.

Clevett, Jason. "Blinded by Brilliance: Rebecca Northan Brings Back *Blind Date* as Fundraiser." *Gay Calgary and Edmonton Magazine*. Gay Calgary, Sept. 2010. Web. 21 Sept. 2011.

Clurman, Harold. *The Fervent Years: The Story of the Group Theatre and the Thirties*. New York: Hill and Wang, 1957. Print.

Colonna, Vincent. *Autofiction et autres mythomanies littéraires*. Auch: Tristram, 2004. Print.

Coulbourn, John. "*da Kink* Da-Lightful; Minor Flaws Don't Dampen Spirit of Fringe Fest Original." Rev. of *da Kink in my hair*, dir. Weyni Mengesha. Plaitform Entertainment, Theatre Passe Muraille, Toronto. *Toronto Sun* 14 June 2003: 36. Print.

---. "'Top Girls' is Top Notch." Rev. of *Top Girls*, dir. Alisa Palmer. Soulpepper Theatre Company, Young Centre, Toronto. *Jam! Canoe.ca*. Canoe Inc., 5 July 2007. Web. 12 Oct. 2011.

Crew, Robert. "Factory Theatre." *The Canadian Encyclopedia*. The Canadian Encyclopedia, n.d. Web. 20 Jan. 2011.

---. "Mirvishes Draw on Fringe, London, Broadway." *Toronto Star* 23 March 2004: C5. Print.

---. "Play Has the Depth of Gory Video Game." Rev. of *lady in the red dress*, dir. Nina Lee Aquino. fu-GEN Asian Canadian Theatre Company, Young Centre, Toronto. *Toronto Star*. Torstar Corporation, 30 Jan. 2009. Web. 26 Aug. 2010.

Croce, Arlene. "Discussing the Undiscussable." *New Yorker* 26 Dec. 1994: 54–60. Print.

Cushman, Robert. "A Midsummer's Night Sex Theatre." Rev. of *Miss Julie: Sheh'mah*, dir. Melee Hutton. KICK Theatre, Theatre Centre, Toronto. *National Post* 20 Nov. 2008: AL4. *ProQuest Canadian Newsstand*. Web. 14 Oct. 2011.

---. "Sisters Are Doing it for Themselves: An Improved *Top Girls* Showcases Incredible Talent." Rev. of *Top Girls*, dir. Alisa Palmer. Soulpepper Theatre Company, Young Centre, Toronto. *National Post* 8 Nov. 2008: TO7. *ProQuest Canadian Newsstand*. Web. 14 Oct. 2011.

Cyr, Catherine. "Représentation et olfaction: le spectateur au parfum." *Jeu* 125 (2007): 127–33. Print.

---. "Ronfard et la méthode expérimentale: une symbiose de la théorie et de la pratique à travers l'appropriation interdisciplinaire." *L'Annuaire théâtral* 35 (2004) : 24–42. Print.

---. "Le 'solo performatif': rencontres éphémères." *Jeu* 127 (2008): 135–39. Print.

Dabrowski, Wojtek. "Artists Launch Plea to Tear Down Quebec City's 'Wall of Shame.'" *Evening Telegram* [St. John's] 14 Apr. 2001: A7. Print.

Dargis, Manohla. "Plenty of Perky, Even This Early." *New York Times*. The New York Times Co., 9 Nov. 2010. Web. 21 Jan. 2011.

De Jongh, Nicholas. "Critic's Choice: Top Five Plays." *The Evening Standard* [London] 21 Nov. 2006: 44. Print.

De Lauretis, Teresa. *Alice Doesn't: Feminism, Semiotics, Cinema*. Bloomington: Indiana UP, 1984. Print.

DeMara, Bruce. "When Door Closed, She Hired Herself." *Toronto Star* 4 Dec. 2007: L8. Print.

De Villier, Gunther. *Les Laboratoires Crête, en collaboration avec Stéphane Crête*. Montreal: Les 400 coups, 2008. Print.

De Vries, Hilary. "All That Korean Rage, Unbottled." *New York Times*. The New York Times Co., 17 Oct. 2004. Web. 10 Feb. 2012.

Denison, Merrill. "Hart House Theatre." *Canadian Bookman* 5 (1923): 61–63. Print.

---. "Nationalism and Drama." *Yearbook of the Arts in Canada*. Ed. Bertram Brooker. Toronto: Macmillan, 1929. 51–55. Print.

Derrida, Jacques. "The Theater of Cruelty and the Closure of Representation." *Writing and Difference*. Chicago: U of Chicago P, 1978. 232–50. Print.

Destroyer. "Beggars Might Ride." *Streethawk: A Seduction*. Merge, 2010. CD.

Deziel, Shanda. "Rachel's All the Rage." *Maclean's* 18 Jul 2005: 45–48. Print.

Diamond, Elin. "Brechtian Theory/Feminist Theory: Toward a Gestic Feminist Criticism." *TDR* 32.1 (1988): 82–94. Print.

---. "Mimesis, Mimicry, and the 'True-Real.'" *Modern Drama* 32.1 (1989): 58–72. Print.

---. "Modern Drama/Modernity's Drama." *Modern Drama* 44.1 (2001): 3–15. Print.

---. *Performance and Cultural Politics*. New York: Routledge, 1996. Print.

---. "Realism's Hysteria: Disruption in the Theater of Knowledge." Diamond, *Unmaking* 3–39.

---. *Unmaking Mimesis: Essays on Feminism and Theater*. New York: Routledge, 1997. Print.

Dickens, Charles. *Sketches by "Boz," Illustrative of Everyday Life and Every-day People*. London: Chapman and Hall, 1903. *Project Gutenberg*. Web. 1 Oct. 2011.

Dolan, Jill. "Feminist Performance Criticism and the Popular: Reviewing Wendy Wasserstein." *Theatre Journal* 60.3 (2008): 433–57. Print.

---. *The Feminist Spectator as Critic*. Ann Arbor: UMI Research P, 1988. Print.

---. "'Lesbian' Subjectivity in Realism: Dragging at the Margins of Structure and Ideology." Dolan, *Presence* 159–78.

---. *Presence and Desire: Essays on Gender, Sexuality, Performance*. Ann Arbor: U of Michigan P, 1993. Print.

Double Happiness. Dir. Mina Shum. Perf. Sandra Oh, Callum Keith Rennie. Fine Line Features, 1994. Film.

Doubrovsky, Serge. *Autobiographiques: de Corneille à Sartre*. Paris: PU de France, 1988. Print.

Duff, Morris. "Canadian Actors Able . . . But." *Toronto Star* 24 June 1961: n. pag. Print. *Theatre Clippings File*. Toronto: Performing Arts Centre, Toronto Reference Library.

Dupré, Louise. *Tout comme elle*. Montreal: Québec Amérique, 2006. Print.

"Eli Rill Teaches Lane Workshop's Toronto Classes." *Globe and Mail* 3 August 1957: 18. Print.

"Entertainment." *Toronto Star*. Torstar Corporation, 22 Feb. 2001. Web. 31 Dec. 2011.

"Famous Russian Players: Toronto To Be Visited by the Moscow Art Theatre This Season." *Globe and Mail* 10 Nov. 1923: News 17. Print.

Featherstone, Mike, Mike Hepworth, and Bryan S. Turner, eds. *The Body: Social Process and Cultural Theory*. London: Sage, 1991. Print.

Fenwick, Helen. "Marginalising Human Rights: Breach of the Peace, 'Kettling,' the Human Rights Act and Public Protest." *Public Law* 4 (2009): 737–65. Print.

Féral, Josette. "Theatricality: The Specificity of Theatrical Language." *SubStance* 31.2–3 (2002): 94–108. Print.

Fichandler, Zelda. "Casting for a Different Truth." *American Theatre* 5.2 (1988): 18–23. Print.

Fogel, Matthew. "'Grey's Anatomy' Goes Colorblind." *New York Times*. The New York Times Co., 8 May 2005. Web. 2 August 2011.

Forte, Jeanie. "Realism, Narrative, and the Feminist Playwright—A Problem of Reception." *Feminist Theatre and Theory*. Ed. Helene Keyssar. New York: Palgrave, 1996. 19–34. Print.

Foster, Susan Leigh. "Choreographies of Protest." *Theatre Journal* 55.3 (2003): 395–412. Print.

Fraticelli, Rina. "The Invisibility Factor: Status of Women In Canadian Theatre." *Fuse* (Sept. 1982): 112–24. Print.

Freeman, David. *Creeps*. Toronto: U of Toronto P, 1972. Print.

Freeze, Colin. "When the Student Met the Marxist Worker." *Globe and Mail* 21 Apr. 2001: A2. Print.

Gainor, J. Ellen. "Rethinking Feminism, Stanislavsky, and Performance." *Theatre Topics* 12.2 (2002): 163–75. Print.

Gale, Lorena. "Into the Margins." *Canadian Theatre Review* 83 (1995): 16–19. Print.

Garfield, David. *A Player's Place: The Story of the Actors Studio*. New York: Macmillan, 1980. Print.

Gee, Marcus, and Colin Freeze. "Security or Liberty? Toronto Comes to Grips with a Historic Crackdown." *Globe and Mail*. The Globe and Mail Inc., 27 June 2010. Web. 1 Sept. 2010.

Gélinas, Gratien. *Bousille and the Just*. *Major Plays of the Canadian Theatre 1934–1984*. Ed. Richard Perkyns. Richmond Hill: Irwin, 1984. 211–74. Print.

---. *Tit-Coq*. Montreal: Typo, 1994. Print.

Genzlinger, Neil. "It's Date Night, and Lots of Strangers Are Along For the Ride." Rev. of *Blind Date*, by Rebecca Northan. Ars Nova Theater, New York. *New York Times*. The New York Times Co., 14 Dec. 2010. Web. 21 Sept. 2011.

Germain, Jean-Claude. "J'ai eu le coup de foudre." Preface. *Les belles-soeurs*. By Michel Tremblay. Montreal: Holt, Rinehart & Winston, 1968. 3–5. Print.

Gilbert, Helen, and Jacqueline Lo. "Toward a Topography of Cross-Cultural Theatre Praxis." *TDR* 46.3 (2002): 31–53. Print.

Godin, Jean Cléo. "Les avatars du réalisme québécois." *Jeu* 85 (1997): 65–72. Print.

Goffman, Erving. *The Presentation of Self in Everyday Life*. New York: Doubleday, 1959. Print.

Golfman, Noreen. "Double Happiness." *Canadian Forum* Oct. 1995: 25–26. Print.

Grober, Chayele. *Mi-shene tside ha-masakh*. 1952. Trans. Yosef Aḥa'i. Haifa: Pinat ha-sefer, 1973. Print.

---. *Tsu der groyser velt*. Buenos Aires: "Bialistoker Vegn" beym Bialistoker Farband in Argentina, 1952. Print.

Gross, Robert F. "*Fuhrmann Henschel* and the Ruins of Realism." *Theatre Journal* 50.3 (1998): 319–34. Print.

Groys, Boris. "Self-Design and Aesthetic Responsibility." *e-flux* 7 (2009): n. pag. Web. 2 Jan. 2012.

Guilmaine, Anne-Marie. *Au détour de juin, en plein coeur des ambivalences: la pluralité des possibles ou la mise en jeu d'une combinatoire scénique par le biais du performatif*. M.A. diss. UQAM, 1991. Print.

Guilmaine, Anne-Marie, and Claudine Robillard. "Trouver un confetti dans une craque de trottoir et le garder dans sa poche, pour toujours." *Jeu* 129 (2008) : 134–39. Print.

Hallett, Roger. Photograph of Arrests at Queen and Spadina. "In Pictures: G20 Protests." Image 3 of 29. *Globe and Mail*. The Globe and Mail Inc., 27 June 2010. Web. 1 Sept. 2010.

Hanomansing, Ian. "G20 Security Zone Tour." *CBC News*. CBC/Radio Canada, 18 June 2010. Web. 1 Sept. 2010.

Hansen, Pil. "Dramaturgical Strategies: Articulations from Five Toronto-Based Theatre Artists." *Developing Nation*. Ed. Bruce Barton. Toronto: Playwrights Canada, 2009. 169–84. Print.

Hare, John. Rev. of *Bousille and the Just*, by Gratien Gélinas. National Arts Centre, Ottawa. *Ottawa Citizen* 18 Sept. 1976: n. pag. Print.

Harjo, Joy, and Gloria Bird, eds. *Reinventing the Enemy's Language: Contemporary Native American Women's Writing of North America*. New York: W.W. Norton, 1997. Print.

Hayday, Matthew. "Fireworks, Folk-Dancing, and Fostering a National Identity: The Politics of Canada Day." *Canadian Historical Review* 91.2 (2010): 287–314. Print.

Heddon, Deirdre. *Autobiography and Performance*. New York: Macmillan, 2008. Print.

Herbert, John. *Fortune and Men's Eyes. Major Plays of the Canadian Theatre 1934–1984*. Ed. Richard Perkyns. Richmond Hill: Irwin, 1984. 275–327. Print.

Highway, Tomson. *Dry Lips Oughta Move to Kapuskasing*. Saskatoon: Fifth House, 1989. Print.

---. "On Native Mythology." *Theatrum* 6 (1987): 29–31. Print.

---. *The Rez Sisters*. Saskatoon: Fifth House, 1988. Print.

"Historical Walking Tour of Lawrence Park." *Toronto Public Library*. Toronto Public Library, 2007. Web. 1 Oct. 2011.

Hopkins, D.J., Shelley Orr, and Kim Solga, eds. *Performance and the City*. New York: Palgrave, 2009. Print.

Hornby, Richard. *Drama, Metadrama, and Perception*. Cranbury, NJ: Associated University Presses, 1986. Print.

---. "Interracial Casting." *Hudson Review* 42.3 (1989): 459–66. Print.

Hubier, Sébastien. *Littératures intimes: Les expressions du moi, de l'autobiographie à l'autofiction*. Paris: Armand Colin, 2003. Print.

Hunt, Stephen. "Hit Comedy *Blind Date* Making Brief Return to Calgary." *Calgary Herald*. Postmedia Network Canada Corp, 26 Aug. 2011. Web. 21 Sept. 2011.

Hurley, Erin. "Les corps multiples du Cirque du Soleil." Trans. Isabelle Léger. *Globe: revue internationale d'études québécoises* 11.2 (2008): 135–57. Print.

---. *National Performance: Representing Quebec from Expo 67 to Céline Dion.* Toronto: U of Toronto P, 2010. Print.

Ingarden, Roman. *The Literary Work of Art: An Investigation on the Borderlines of Ontology, Logic, and Theory of Literature.* Trans. George G. Grabowicz. Ed. James M. Edie. Evanston: Northwestern UP, 1973. Print. Studies in Phenomenology and Existential Philosophy.

Intini, John, et al. "Showdown in the Streets." *Maclean's* 19 July 2010: 26–29. Print.

Jacques, Hélène, ed. "Animaux en scène." *Jeu* 130 (2009): 40–133. Print.

---, ed. "La tentation autobiographique." *Jeu* 111 (2004): 75–136. Print.

"Janine Manatis Quits as Studio Playwright." *Toronto Star* 23 Dec. 1964: n. pag. Print.

Jeffries, Stuart. "The Joy of Walking Out of *Top Girls*." *Guardian Theatre Blog.* Guardian News and Media Ltd., 4 Oct. 2011. Web. 21 Dec. 2011.

Jennings, Luke. "Spat At by a Naked Dancer: St-Pierre's *Un Peu de Tendresse*." Rev. of *Un peu de tendresse, bordel de merde!*, by Dave St-Pierre. Sadler's Wells, London. *Guardian Theatre Blog.* Guardian News and Media Ltd., 3 June 2011. Web. 4 June 2011.

Johnson, Brian D. "The Double Life of Sandra Oh." *Maclean's* 31 July 1995: 42–43. Print.

---. "Shooting for the Stars: Sandra Oh." *Maclean's* 19 Dec. 1995: 66–67. Print.

---. "The Story of Oh." *Maclean's* 29 Aug. 2005: 54–57. Print.

Johnson, E. Patrick. *Appropriating Blackness: Performance and the Politics of Authenticity.* Durham: Duke UP, 2003. Print.

Jones, Amelia. "Rupture." *Parachute* 123 (2006): 15–37. Print.

"June 27: Jail Solidarity Rally! 10am." *Community Solidarity Network* [Toronto]. N.p., 27 June 2010. Web. 1 Oct. 2011.

Jutras, Lisan. "Boxed in and Arrested on Queen Street West." *Globe and Mail.* The Globe and Mail Inc., 28 June 2010. Web. 1 Sept. 2010.

---. "Caught in the Storm, Penned in at Queen Street." *Globe and Mail.* The Globe and Mail Inc., 28 June 2010. Web. 1 Sept. 2010.

Kaplan, Jon. "*Top Girls* still topical." *NOW Magazine.* NOW Communications, 28 June 2007. Web. 12 Oct. 2011.

---. "Yee is Seeing Red: Playwright David Yee Responds to Racism with a Colourful Look at History." *NOW Magazine*. NOW Communications, 21 Jan. 2009. Web. 22 Jan. 2011.

Kelly, Kate. "Hollywood's New Challenge: Getting Rachel McAdams to Say 'I Do' to a Role." *Wall Street Journal* 18 Aug. 2006: W3. *ProQuest Canadian Newsstand*. Web. 13 March 2011.

Kelly, Katherine E. *Modern Drama by Women 1880s–1930s*. London: Routledge, 1996. Print.

Kershaw, Baz. *The Radical in Performance: Between Brecht and Baudrillard*. London: Routledge, 1999. Print.

King, Barry. "Articulating Stardom." *Star Texts: Image and Performance in Film and Television*. Ed. Jeremy G. Butler. Detroit: Wayne State UP, 1991. 125–54. Print.

---. "Stardom, Celebrity, and the Money Form." *The Velvet Light Trap* 65 (2010): 7–19. Print.

Knowles, Ric. Introduction. *Theatre Research in Canada/Recherches Théâtrales au Canada* 30.1–2 (2009): v–vi. Print.

---. "Multicultural Text, Intercultural Performance: The Performance Ecology of Contemporary Toronto." Hopkins, Orr, and Solga 73–91.

---. *The Theatre of Form and the Production of Meaning: Contemporary Canadian Dramaturgies*. Toronto: ECW, 1999. Print.

Krasner, David. "Empathy and Theater." *Staging Philosophy: Intersections of Theater, Performance, and Philosophy*. Ed. Krasner and David Z. Saltz. Ann Arbor: U of Michigan P, 2006. 255–77. Print.

---. "I Hate Strasberg: Method Bashing in the Academy." Krasner, *Method* 3–39. Print.

---, ed. *Method Acting Reconsidered: Theory, Practice, Future*. New York: St Martin's, 2000. Print.

Kuhn, Sarah. "Dissecting Talent." *Back Stage East* 46.50 (2005): n. pag. Web. 25 July 2011.

"Lady in the Red Dress by David Yee." *Playwrights Canada Press*. Playwrights Canada Press, n.d. Web. 29 Jul. 2011.

Lalonde, Catherine. "Danse—Dave St-Pierre: chercher le trop." *Le Devoir*. Le Devoir, 20 Jan. 2009. Web. 20 Jan. 2011.

Lam, Joyce. "Artistic Producer's Message." *Vancouver Asian Canadian Theatre Presents Red Letters*. Red Letters Program Book, 2010. N. pag. Print.

Larrue, Jean-Marc. *Le théâtre yiddish à Montréal/Yiddish Theatre in Montreal*. Montreal: Jeu, 1996. Print.

Laurence, Margaret. Foreword. Ringwood xi–xiv.

Laville, Sandra, and Duncan Campbell. "Baton Charges and Kettling: Police's G20 Crowd Control Tactics under Fire." *Guardian*. Guardian News and Media Ltd., 2 Apr. 2009. Web. 1 Sept. 2010.

Le Breton, David. *La saveur du monde: Une anthropologie des sens*. Paris: Métailié, 2006. Print.

Ledingham, Jo. "Musical Delivers History Lesson on Chinese Immigration Act." Rev. of *Red Letters*, dir. Andy Maton. Vancouver Asian Canadian Theatre, Gateway Theatre, Vancouver. *Vancouver Courier*. Glacier Media, 7 Jan. 2011. Web. 8 Jan. 2011.

Lehmann, Hans-Thies. *Postdramatic Theatre*. Trans. Karen Jürs-Munby. New York: Routledge, 2006. Print.

Leroux, Louis Patrick. *Le Québec en autoprésentation: le passage d'une dramaturgie de l'identitaire vers celle de l'individu*. Diss. U Sorbonne Nouvelle—Paris 3, 2009. Print.

---. "Tremblay's Impromptus as Process-driven A/B." *Theatre and Autobiography: Writing and Performing Lives in Theory and Practice*. Ed. Sherrill Grace and Jerry Wasserman. Vancouver: Talonbooks, 2006. 107–23. Print.

Leroux, Manon. *Les silences d'octobre: Le discours des acteurs de la crise de 1970*. Montreal: VLB, 2002. Print.

Létourneau, Jocelyn. *Que veulent vraiment les Québécois?: regard sur l'intention nationale au Québec (français) d'hier à aujourd'hui*. Montreal: Boréal, 2006. Print.

Levin, Laura. "Can the City Speak? Site-Specific Art After Poststructuralism." Hopkins, Orr, and Solga 240–57.

Lill, Wendy. *The Glace Bay Miners' Museum*. Vancouver: Talonbooks, 2000. Print.

Liska, George. *Expanding Realism: The Historical Dimension of World Politics*. Lanham, MD: Rowman and Littlefield, 1998. Print.

Loring, Kevin. *Where the Blood Mixes*. Vancouver: Talonbooks, 2009. Print.

Lui, Elaine. "Best Emmy Canadian: Sandra Oh." *Lainey Gossip*. Lainey Gossip Entertainment Inc., 22 Sept. 2008. Web. 5 Aug. 2011.

---. "Hello Kitty at the Grammys." *Lainey Gossip*. Lainey Gossip Entertainment Inc., 10 Feb. 2008. Web. 5 Aug. 2011.

---. "McGosling Glimmer." *Lainey Gossip*. Lainey Gossip Entertainment Inc., 12 Aug. 2009. Web. 13 March 2012.

---. "Most Disappointing: Sandra Oh." *Lainey Gossip*. Lainey Gossip Entertainment Inc., 6 June 2006. Web. 5 Aug. 2011.

---. "People's Choice Best Black: Sandra Oh." *Lainey Gossip*. Lainey Gossip Entertainment Inc., 10 Jan. 2007. Web. 5 Aug. 2011.

---. "Rachel McAdams, Designated Driver." *Lainey Gossip*. Lainey Gossip Entertainment Inc., 25 June 2008. Web. 13 March 2012.

---. "Rachel in Spain." *Lainey Gossip*. Lainey Gossip Entertainment Inc., 13 Jan. 2011. Web. 15 Jan. 2011.

---. "Rachel Rides Rocket and Biel Doesn't Pull the Card." *Lainey Gossip*. Lainey Gossip Entertainment Inc., 27 June 2011. Web. 13 March 2012.

Lutterbie, John. "The Politics of Dramaturgy." *Journal of Dramatic Theory and Criticism* 13.2 (1999): 127–34. Print.

Lyon, Christine. "Musical Aims To Entertain and Educate." *Richmond Review*. Black Press Digital, 21 Dec. 2010. Web. 8 Jan. 2011.

MacKenzie, Ian. "10 Questions: Tara Beagan." Interview. *Theatre is Territory*. Ian MacKenzie, 21 Sept. 2007. Web. 14 Oct. 2011.

Mahoney, Jill, and Ann Hui. "G20-related Mass Arrests Unique in Canadian History." *Globe and Mail*. The Globe and Mail Inc., 28 June 2010. Web. 1 Sept. 2010.

Mann, Laurin. "'Stanislavski' in Toronto." *Theatre Research in Canada/Recherches Théâtrales au Canada* 20.2 (1999): 207–26. Print.

Manning, Erin. "I Am Canadian: Identity, Territory, and the Canadian National Landscape." *Theory and Event* 4.4 (2000): n. pag. *Project Muse*. Web. 28 July 2011.

Margolies, Eleanor. "Smelling Voices: Cooking in the Theatre." *Performance Research* 8.3 (2003): 11–23. Print.

Margolin, Deb. "Mining My Own Business: Paths Between Text and Self." Krasner, *Method* 127–34. Print.

Martin, Carol. "Dramaturgy of the Real." Introduction. *Dramaturgy of the Real on the World Stage*. New York: Palgrave, 2010. 1–14. Print.

Maslin, Janet. "A Delicate Asian Flower in a Motorcycle Jacket." Rev. of *Double Happiness*, dir. Mina Shum. *New York Times*. The New York Times Co., 28 July 1995. Web. 28 July 2011.

mattw. "The Subject Deserves Better? The Play Deserves Better." Comment on Crew, "Play Has the Depth." *Toronto Star*. Torstar Corporation, 30 Jan. 2009. Web. 17 Jan. 2011.

McConachie, Bruce. "Method Acting and the Cold War." *Theatre Survey* 41.1 (2000): 47–68. Print.

McGillivray, Glen. "King/Cate: Stardom, Aura, and the Stage Figure in the Sydney Theatre Company's Production of *Richard II*." *TDR* 54.3 (2010): 158–63. Print.

McQuaid, Peter. "Leaves of Her Portfolio: In Life and in Performance, Sandra Oh, a Canadian of Korean Ancestry, Is a Woman Without Borders." *Los Angeles Times*. Tribune Co., 9 Oct. 2003. Web. 2 Aug. 2011.

Messenger, Ann P. "In Sickness and in Health." *Canadian Literature* 59 (1974): 101–03. Print.

Micallef, Shawn, and Marlena Zuber. *Stroll: Psychogeographic Walking Tours of Toronto*. Toronto: Coach House, 2010. Print.

Michaud, Yves. *L'Art à l'état gazeux. Essai sur le triomphe de l'esthétique*. Paris: Hachette, 2003. Print.

Middleton, J.E. "The Theatre in Canada (1750–1880)." *Canada and its Provinces: A History of the Canadian People and their Institutions by One Hundred Associates*. Ed. Arthur G. Doughty and Adam Shortt. Vol. 12. Toronto: Brook and Company, 1914. 651–61. Print.

Migliarisi, Anna. "Stanislavsky in Canada: A Critical Chronology." Migliarisi, *Stanislavsky and Directing* 239–97. Print.

---, ed. *Stanislavsky and Directing: Theory, Practice and Influence*. New York: Legas, 2008. Print. Studies in Drama and Theatre 7.

Miller, J. Hillis. "The Fiction of Realism: *Sketches by Boz, Oliver Twist*, and Cruikshank's Illustrations." *Victorian Subjects*. Durham: Duke UP, 1990. 119–77. Print.

"Montreal to See Russian Players." *Montreal Gazette* 14 Nov. 1923: 5. Print.

Moodie, Andrew. "Colour-blind Casting and The Shaw." *Share the Stage*. Facebook, n.d. Web. 28 July 2010.

---. "My Open Letter to the Community About Shaw." *Share the Stage*. Share the Stage: Encouraging Diversity in Canadian Theatre, n.d. Web. 28 July 2010.

Mooney, Sam. "Rebecca Northan in *Blind Date*—Harbourfront Centre." Rev. of *Blind Date*, by Rebecca Northan. Harbourfront Centre, Toronto. *Mooney on Theatre*. Mooney on Theatre, 28 Feb. 2010. Web. 21 Sept. 2011.

Moore, Addison Webster. *Pragmatism and its Critics*. Whitefish, MT: Kessinger, 2004. Print.

Moore, Mavor. "A Theatre for Canada." *University of Toronto Quarterly* 26.1 (1956): 1–16. Print.

Morgenbesser, Sidney, ed. *Dewey and His Critics: Essays from the Journal of Philosophy*. Indianapolis, IN: Hackett, 1977. Print.

Morris, Pam. *Realism*. London: Routledge, 2003. Print. The New Critical Idiom.

Morrow, Adrian. "Police Don Riot Gear to Contain First Major Protest of G20 Weekend." *Globe and Mail*. The Globe and Mail Inc., 25 June 2010. Web. 1 Sept. 2010.

Morrow, Adrian, et al. "Police Arrest More than 600 as Toronto G20 Protests Continue." *Globe and Mail*. The Globe and Mail Inc., 27 June 2010. Web. 1 Sept. 2010.

The Moscow Art Theatre. Advertisement. *Montreal Gazette* 24 Nov. 1923: 13. Print.

"The Moscow Art Theatre: Voice of the People." *Globe and Mail* 3 Dec. 1923: 4. Print.

"Moscow Players' Routing Changed: Will Appear in Montreal Early in New Year, Toronto Visit Cancelled." *Montreal Gazette* 28 Nov. 1923: front page. Print.

"Moscow Players To Be Seen Here Week of May 4th: Visit Originally Scheduled for 1923-Tour Rearranged." *Montreal Gazette* 2 Feb. 1924: n. pag. Print.

Müller, Heiner. "The Future is Evil: A Discussion." *A Heiner Müller Reader*. Ed. and trans. Carl Weber. Baltimore: Johns Hopkins UP, 2001. 130–41. Print.

Mulvey, Laura. "Visual Pleasure and Narrative Cinema." *Screen* 16.3 (1975): 6–18. Print.

Naimark, Jonas. Photograph of Kettling at Toronto G20. Jutras, "Boxed."

Naremore, James. *Acting in the Cinema*. Berkeley: U of California P, 1988. Print.

Nestruck, J. Kelly. "Bring in *'da Kink*—Playwright's Therapeutic Writing a Success Story." *National Post* 8 Jan. 2005: TO10. Print.

Newman, Harry. "Holding Back: The Theatre's Resistance to Non-Traditional Casting." *TDR* 33.3 (1989): 22–36.

"No Bolshevist Taint In It, Moscow Theatre Company, Report Circulating in Toronto Brings a Prompt Denial From New York." *Evening Telegram* 26 Nov. 1923: 1. Print.

Nolan, Yvette. *Annie Mae's Movement*. Toronto: Playwrights Canada, 2006. Print.

Northan, Rebecca. "Professional Blind Dater Rebecca Northan Tells Everything She Knows About Men." *Swerve Magazine*. Postmedia Network Canada Corp., 10 Dec. 2010. Web. 21 Sept. 2011.

---. "Rebecca Northan talks *Blind Date*." harbourfrontcentre. *YouTube*. Web. 20 Sept. 2011.

Nuñez, Marilo. Personal Interview With Natalie Alvarez. 28 Oct. 2010. Email.

Oddey, Alison. *Devising Theatre: A Practical and Theoretical Handbook*. New York: Routledge, 1994. Print.

"Operative." *Oxford English Dictionary Online*. Oxford UP, June 2004. Web. 29 July 2011.

Ouzounian, Richard. "*'da Kink* Needs a Trim." *Toronto Star* 19 Jan. 2005: D2. Print.

---. "*The Women*: Director Takes a Wrong Turn with Shaw Play." Rev. of *The Women*, dir. Alisa Palmer. Shaw Festival, Festival Theatre, Niagara-on-the-Lake. *Toronto Star*. Torstar Corporation, 31 May 2010. Web. 12 Oct. 2011.

Over My Dead Body. Dir. Brigitte Poupart. Les films du 3 mars, 2012. Film.

Palmer, Alisa. Email to J. Kelly Nestruck. "Alisa Palmer: Taking the Canadian Curse off Caryl Churchill in the Obama Era." *Nestruck on Theatre*. The Globe and Mail Inc., 21 Apr. 2009. Web. 12 Oct. 2011.

Pao, Angela. *No Safe Spaces: Re-Casting Race, Ethnicity, and Nationality in American Theatre*. Ann Arbor: U of Michigan P, 2010. Print.

Paperny, Anna Mehler. "1,000 Protest G20 Police Tactics." *Globe and Mail*. The Globe and Mail Inc., 29 June 2010. Web. 1 Sept. 2010.

Paskin, Willa. "How Much Better Is Rachel McAdams Than *Morning Glory*?" *New York Magazine*. New York Media LLC, 11 Nov. 2010. Web. 21 Jan. 2011.

Patin, Thomas, and Jennifer McLerran. *Artwords: A Glossary of Contemporary Art Theory*, Westport: Greenwood, 1997. Print.

Pavis, Patrice. *Dictionary of the Theatre: Terms, Concepts, and Analysis*. Toronto: U of Toronto P, 1998. Print.

Peirce, Charles. *Collected Papers*. Ed. Charles Hartshorne and Paul Weiss. Vol. 1 and 2. Cambridge: Harvard UP, 1960. Print.

Peritz, Ingrid. "Concrete Wall Rises in Fortified Quebec." *Globe and Mail* 2 Apr. 2001: A1+. Print.

Petitjean, Léon, and Henri Rollin. *Aurore, l'enfant martyre: Histoire et présentation de la pièce*. Ed. Alonzo LeBlanc. Montreal: VLB, 1982. Print.

Phelan, Peggy. *Unmarked: the Politics of Performance*. New York: Routledge, 1993. Print.

Phillips, Michael. "*Morning Glory*—2 ½ Stars." Rev. of *Morning Glory*, dir. Roger Michell. *Chicago Tribune*. Tribune Co., 9 Nov. 2010. Web. 21 Jan. 2011.

"Planning to Bring the Famous Moscow Art Theatre to Toronto during Christmas Week." *Globe and Mail* 22 Sept. 1923: News 5. Print.

Pollock, Sharon. *Blood Relations and Other Plays*. Edmonton: NeWest, 2002. Print.

---. "The Evolution of an Authentic Voice in Canadian Theatre." *Canadian Culture and Literature: and a Taiwan Perspective*. Ed. Steven Tötösy de Zepetnek and Yiu-nam Leung. Edmonton: Research Institute for Comparative Literature, 1998. 115–24. Print.

Posner, Michael. "In Search of a Little Play Equity." *Globe and Mail* 8 Aug. 2009: R7. *ProQuest Canadian Newsstand*. Web. 14 Oct. 2011.

Probyn, Elspeth. "Bloody Metaphors and Other Allegories of the Ordinary Nation." *Continuum* 11.2 (1997): 113–25. Print.

Pullen, Kirsten. *Like a Natural Woman: Female Spectacular Performance and Classical Hollywood*. New Brunswick, NJ: Rutgers UP, 2012. Print.

Quinn, Michael. "Celebrity and the Semiotics of Acting." *New Theatre Quarterly* 6 (1990): 154–61. Print.

Raboy, Marc. *Missed Opportunities: The Story of Canada's Broadcasting Policy*. Montreal: McGill-Queen's UP, 1990. Print.

Raney, Tracey. "As Canadian as Possible . . . Under What Circumstances? Public Opinion on National Identity in Canada Outside Quebec." *Journal of Canadian Studies/Revue d'études canadiennes* 43.3 (2009): 5–29. Print.

Reinelt, Janelle. "Feminist Theory and the Problem of Performance." *Modern Drama* 32 (1989): 48–57. Print.

Resist Toronto. Facebook, 2010. Web. 1 Sept. 2010.

The Rez Sisters. By Tomson Highway. Dir. Ken Gass. Mainspace Theatre, Factory Theatre. Toronto. 5 Nov.–11 Dec. 2011. Performance.

Richards, Lloyd. Interview. *American Academy of Achievement*. American Academy of Achievement, 15 Feb. 1999: 2. Web. 2 Jan. 2012.

Ringwood, Gwen Pharis. *The Collected Plays of Gwen Pharis Ringwood*. Ed. Enid Delgatty Rutland. Ottawa: Borealis, 1982. Print.

Robert, Lucie. "The Language of Theatre." *Essays on Modern Quebec Theatre*. Ed. Joseph I. Donohoe Jr. and Jonathan M. Weiss. East Lansing: Michigan State UP, 1995. 109–29. Print.

Roman Tragedies. By Toneelgroep Amsterdam. Dir. Ivo van Hove. Festival TransAmériques, Montreal. 29–30 May 2010. Performance.

Romeinse tragedies. Toneelgroep Amsterdam. N.p., n.d. Web. 17 Jan. 2012.

Rozen, Leah. "An Actress on the Brink of a Blockbuster." *New York Times.* The New York Times Co., 31 Oct. 2010. Web. 18 Jan. 2011.

Rubin, Don. "Creeping Toward a Culture: The Theatre in English Canada Since 1945." *Canadian Theatre Review* 1 (1974): 6–21. Print.

"Russian Artists Pledged to Give Share to Soviet." *Globe and Mail* 26 Dec. 1922: News 5. Print.

"Russian's Fault is That He Talks Too Much." *Toronto Telegram* 22 Feb. 1924: n. pag. University of Toronto Archives, ref. A1973–0026/314(42). Newspaper clipping.

"Russian Players Meeting Opposition: Management of Moscow Art Theatre Disturbed by Reports from Toronto, No Soviet Organization." *Globe and Mail* 26 Nov. 1923: 5. Print.

"Russian Plays Off: Local Management Afraid of Financial Failure." *Evening Telegram* [St. John's] 27 Nov. 1923: n. pag. Print.

Ryan, Toby Gordon. *Stage Left: Canadian Theatre in the Thirties: A Memoir.* Toronto: CTR Publications, 1981. Print.

Ryga, George. "Theatre in Canada: A Viewpoint on its Development and Future." *Canadian Theatre Review* 1 (1974): 28–32. Print.

Sallot, Jeff, Rhéal Séguin, and Colin Freeze. "Fortress Quebec is Breached." *Globe and Mail* 21 Apr. 2001: A1+. Print.

Salo, Merja. "Do You Like Me Awake?" Rev. of *Innocence*, by Laura Vuoma. *Pàp—Creative Force from the North* 19 (2006): 92–99. Print.

Sandwell, Bernard K. "The Annexation of Our Stage." *Canadian Magazine* 38.1 (1911): 22–26. Print.

Sarrazac, Jean-Pierre. "L'impersonnage. En relisant 'La crise du personnage.'" *Études théâtrales* 20 (2001): 41–50. Print.

Saunders, Mahogany. "Where Jamaicans Live." *Jamaicans.com.* Jamaicans.com, Aug 2003. Web. 17 Jan. 2012.

"Says Russ Dramatists Without Soviet Bias: Percy Burton States France and United States Investigated Rumor." *Toronto Daily Star* 26 Nov. 1923: 4. Print.

Schaefer, Glen. "Poignant Tale of Lovers Kept Apart." *The Province* [Vancouver]. Postmedia Network Canada Corp., 25 Nov. 2010. Web. 8 Jan. 2011.

Schechner, Richard. *Between Theater and Anthropology.* Philadelphia: U of Pennsylvania P, 1985. Print.

---. "Casting Without Limits." *American Theatre* 27.10 (2010): 26–30. Print.

---. "In Praise of Promiscuity." *American Theatre* 13.10 (1996): 58–60. *EBSCOhost*. Web. 30 Aug. 2011.

---. "Race Free, Gender Free, Body-Type Free, Age Free Casting." *TDR* 33.1 (1989): 4–12. Print.

Schneider, Rebecca. *Performing Remains: Art and War in Times of Theatrical Reenactment.* New York: Routledge, 2011. Print.

Schreiber, Rita, Phyllis Noerager Stern, and Charmaine Wilson. "Being Strong: How Black West-Indian Canadian Women Manage Depression and Its Stigma." *Journal of Nursing Scholarship* 32.1 (2000): 39–45. Print.

Schultz, Roger. "Non-Traditional Casting Update: Multicultural Casting Providing Opportunity for Minority Actors While Stimulating Innovative Productions." *TDR* 35.2 (1991): 7–13. Print.

Schweitzer, Marlis. Editorial. *Canadian Theatre Review* 141 (2010): 3–6. Print.

Scorer, Richard. "Personal Injury: Kettling Matters." *New Law Journal.* New Law Journal, 11 Feb. 2011. Web. 22 June 2011.

Scott, Graham F. "Verbatim: Interview with *Cloud 9* director Alisa Palmer." *This Magazine*. Red Maple Foundation, 18 Feb. 2010. Web. 12 Oct. 2011.

Scott, Shelley. *Nightwood Theatre: A Woman's Work is Always Done.* Edmonton: Athabasca UP, 2010. Print.

Sears, Djanet. Foreword. Trey Anthony, *'da Kink* iii–iv.

---, ed. *Testifyin': Contemporary African Canadian Drama.* Vol. 2. Toronto: Playwrights Canada, 2003. Print.

Sermon, Julie. "Le dialogue aux énonciateurs incertains." *Les nouveaux territoires du dialogue.* Ed. Jean-Pierre Ryngaert. Paris: Actes Sud-Papiers, 2005. 31–35. Print.

Shaw, Bernard. "The Quintessence of Ibsenism." *The Theory of the Modern Stage.* Ed. Eric Bentley. New York: Penguin, 1968. 197–213. Print.

Shaw, Fiona. "Platform Talk with Fiona Shaw and Deborah Warner." Royal National Theatre, London. RNT Digital Archive, 8 Oct. 2009. DVD.

Slotek, Jim. "Laugh 'til You Cry at the Fringe; Trey Anthony Strong in *Da Kink*." *Toronto Sun* 7 July 2001: 37. Print.

Solga, Kim. "Vertical City: Staging Urban Discomfort." *Canadian Theatre Review* 136 (2008): 118–21. Print.

Sperling, Deb. "Taking a Clown Out on the Town." Rev. of *Blind Date*, by Rebecca Northan. Ars Nova Theater, New York. *New York Press*. Manhattan Media, 14 Dec. 2010. Web. 21 Sept. 2011.

St. Bernard, Donna-Michelle. Message To Natalie Alvarez. 1 March 2010. Email.

St-Pierre, Dave. "Désarmer le spectateur." *Jeu* 135 (2010): 110–17. Print.

---. *Over My Dead Body*. Perf. Dave St-Pierre, Éric Robidoux, Julie Perron, and Alexis Lefebvre. Agora de la danse, Montreal. 20–25 Jan. 2009. Performance.

Stanislavsky, Constantin. "Perspective of the Actor and the Role." *An Actor's Work*. Trans. Jean Benedetti. New York: Routledge, 2008. 456–62. Print.

Stanley, Alessandra. "Tales of Sex and Surgery." *New York Times*. The New York Times Co., 25 March 2005. Web. 2 Aug. 2011.

Strasberg, Lee. *Strasberg at the Actors Studio: Tape-Recorded Sessions Edited by Robert H. Hethmon*. New York: Theatre Communications Group, 1965. Print.

Strindberg, August. *A Dream Play*. Adapt. by Ingmar Berman. Trans. Michael Meyer. New York: Dial, 1973. Print.

"Strindberg's Pressure Cooker Delivers Heat." Rev. of *Miss Julie: Sheh'mah*, dir. Melee Hutton. KICK Theatre, Theatre Centre, Toronto. *Globe and Mail* 17 Nov. 2008: R4. *ProQuest Canadian Newsstand*. Web. 14 Oct. 2011.

Stroppel, Elizabeth C. "Reconciling the Past and the Present: Feminist Perspectives on the Method in the Classroom and on the Stage." Krasner, *Method* 111–23. Print.

Swartz, Avery. "Fringe Archives 2001." *The Toronto Fringe*. Toronto Fringe Festival, n.d. Web. 31 Dec. 2011.

Symbiopsychotaxiplasm: Two Takes. Dir. William Greaves. 1968. Criterion Collection, 2006. DVD.

"Synopsis." *Vancouver Asian Canadian Theatre Presents Red Letters. Red Letters* Program Book, 2010. N. pag. Print.

Système Kangourou. *40% de déséquilibre*. Dir. Anne-Marie Guilmaine. Perf. Gregory Flayol, Xavier Malo, Janick Rousseau, Claudine Robillard, Martin Vaillancourt. Théâtre La Chapelle, Montreal. April 2007. Performance.

---. *Bricolages pour femme et ours polaire*. Dir. Anne-Marie Guilmaine. Perf. Marie-Ève Dubé. Bain St-Michel, Montreal. March 2008. Performance.

Szporer, Philip. "How Do You Critique a Dying Man's Art?" *The Dance Current*. Dance Media Group, 18 Feb. 2009. Web. 20 Dec. 2011.

Tastsoglou, Evangelia. "Race and the Politics of Personal Relationships: Focus on Black Canadian Women." *Affilia* 17.1 (2002): 93–111. Print.

Taylor, Drew Hayden. *400 Kilometres*. Vancouver: Talonbooks, 2005. Print.

---. *Only Drunks and Children Tell the Truth*. Vancouver: Talonbooks, 1998. Print.

---. *Someday*. Saskatoon: Fifth House, 1993. Print.

Taylor, Kate. "'*Da Kink's* Only a Start." *Globe and Mail* 30 March 2005: R1. Print.

---. "Fix the Colour Code in Canadian Theatre." *Diversity Watch*. Ryerson University School of Journalism, 6 Dec. 2003. Web. 17 Jan. 2012.

---. "Serious Street Theatre Offers Comic Relief." *Globe and Mail* 21 Apr. 2001: A3. Print.

Tembeck, Tamar. "Performer le réel: mise en scène et réception du corps souffrant." *Jeu* 135 (2010): 42–48. Print.

Thomas, Colin. "*Red Letters* is a Winningly Openhearted Musical." Rev. of *Red Letters*, dir. Andy Maton. Vancouver Asian Canadian Theatre, Roundhouse Performance Centre, Vancouver. *The Georgia Straight*. Vancouver Free Press, 29 Nov. 2010. Web. 8 Jan. 2011.

Tinic, Serra A. *On Location: Canada's Television Industry in a Global Market*. Toronto: U of Toronto P, 2005. Print.

Tompkins, Joanne. "Remember the Nation." *Canadian Theatre Review* 125 (2006): 56–61. Print.

Tremblay, Larry. "Résister à la littéréalité." *Liberté* 283 (2009): 7–20. Print.

Trey Anthony Studios. Home page. Trey Productions, 2010. Web. 31 Dec. 2011.

Triau, Christophe. "Choralités diffractées: la communauté en creux." *Alternatives théâtrales* 76–77 (2003): 5–11. Print.

Turan, Kenneth. "Movie Review: 'Morning Glory.'" *Los Angeles Times*. Tribune Co., 10 Nov. 2010. Web. 21 Jan. 2011.

Vanden Heuvel, Michael. "Complementary Spaces: Realism, Performance and a New Dialogics of Theatre." *Theatre Journal* 44.1 (1992): 47–58. Print.

Van Paassen, Kevin. Photograph of Police in Riot Gear at Queen and Spadina. "In Pictures: G20 Protests." Image 11 of 29. *Globe and Mail*. The Globe and Mail Inc., 27 June 2010. Web. 1 Sept. 2010.

Verdecchia, Guillermo. *Fronteras Americanas*. Vancouver: Talon, 1997. Print.

Vu, Liem. "Police Detail G20 Security Zone." *Globe and Mail.* The Globe and Mail Inc., 28 May 2010. Web. 1 Sept. 2010.

Wagner, Anton. Introduction. *Establishing our Boundaries: English-Canadian Theatre Criticism.* Ed. Wagner. Toronto: U of Toronto P, 1999. 3–60. Print.

Waldenfels, Bernhard. "In Place of the Other." *Continental Philosophy Review* 44.2 (2011): 151–64. Print.

Walker, Craig. "Colour-blind Casting and The Shaw." *Share the Stage.* Facebook, n.d. Web. 28 July 2010.

Walker, E.P. "The Dilemma of Multiculturalism in the Theatre." *TDR* 38.3 (1994): 7–10. Print.

Walker, Johnnie. "Lady in the Red Dress." Rev. of *lady in the red dress,* dir. Nina Lee Aquino. fu-GEN Asian Canadian Theatre Company, Young Centre, Toronto. *Torontoist.* St. Joseph Media, 4 Feb. 2009. Web. 8 Jan. 2011.

Watt, Ian. *The Rise of the Novel: Studies in Defoe, Richardson and Fielding.* London: Chatto and Windus, 1957. Print.

Webber, Evan, et al. "All Seams: Some Information from One Reed Theatre." *Canadian Theatre Review* 135 (2008): 28–30. Print.

Whittaker, Herbert. "Studio Must Grow Into Clinic." *Globe and Mail* 24 Oct. 1964: 15. Print.

Wiles, David. "Burdens of Representation: The Method and the Audience." Krasner, *Method* 169–78. Print.

Wiles, Timothy. *The Theater Event: Modern Theories of Performance.* Chicago: U of Chicago P, 1984. Print.

Williams, Kirk. "Anti-Theatricality and the Limits of Naturalism." *Against Theatre: Creative Destructions on the Modernist Stage.* Ed. Alan Ackerman and Martin Puchner. New York: Palgrave, 2007. 95–111. Print.

Wilson, August. "The Ground On Which I Stand." *American Theatre* 13.7 (1996): n. pag. *EBSCOhost.* Web. 30 Aug. 2011.

Wilson, Brian. "Gung Oh: *Grey's Anatomy's* Sandra Oh." *Mail Online.* Associated Newspapers Ltd., 2 Oct. 2010. Web. 4 Aug. 2011.

Wilson, Shawn. *Research is Ceremony: Indigenous Research Methods.* Winnipeg: Fernwood, 2009. Print.

The Wire. By David Simon. HBO. 2 June 2002–9 March 2008. Television.

Wood, James. "The Blue River of Truth." *The New Republic*. The New Republic, 1 Aug. 2005. Web. 2 Jan. 2012.

Worthen, W.B. *Modern Drama and the Rhetoric of Theater*. Berkeley: U of California P, 1992. Print.

Yee, David. *lady in the red dress*. Toronto: Playwrights Canada, 2010. Print.

---. Preface. Yee, *lady* vii–viii.

Yoon, Jean. "Great Show, Definitely Worth Seeing." Comment on Crew, "Play Has the Depth." *Toronto Star*. Torstar Corporation, 30 Jan. 2009. Web. 17 Jan. 2011.

---. "Reflections on the 'Roots' Panel and 'the Generational Divide.'" Aquino and Knowles 79–85.

York University Department of Theatre. Home page. York University, n.d. Web. 18 Jan. 2011.

Young, Harvey. *Embodying Black Experience: Stillness, Critical Memory, and the Black Body*. Ann Arbor: U of Michigan P, 2010. Print.

---. "The Influence of Lloyd Richards." *Public Theatres and Theatre Publics*. Ed. Robert Shimko and Sara Freeman. Cambridge: Cambridge Scholars P, 2012. N. pag. Print.

Zola, Émile. "Naturalism on the Stage." *The Experimental Novel and Other Essays*. Trans. Belle M. Sherman. New York: Cassell, 1893. 109–60. Print.

NOTES ON CONTRIBUTORS

Natalie Alvarez is Associate Professor at Brock University's Department of Dramatic Arts, where she teaches in the Theatre Praxis concentration. She has two edited books on Latina/o-Canadian theatre and performance for Playwrights Canada Press (2013). In 2010 she received a Social Sciences and Humanities Research Council of Canada Standard Research Grant for her book project, *Enactments of Difference: Simulation and Performance from Military Training to Dark Tourism*. Her work has appeared in *Theatre Journal*; *The Journal of Dramatic Theory and Criticism*; *Codifying the National Self: Spectators, Actors, and the American Dramatic Text*; *Canadian Theatre Review*; and *Janus Head: Journal of Interdisciplinary Studies in Literature, Continental Philosophy, and Phenomenological Psychology*. She also serves as co-editor of *Canadian Theatre Review*'s Views and Reviews.

Roberta Barker is Associate Professor of Theatre at Dalhousie University and the University of King's College. She is the author of *Early Modern Tragedy, Gender and Performance, 1984–2000: The Destined Livery* (2007). Her work on early modern and modern drama in performance has been published in *Shakespeare Survey*, *Shakespeare Quarterly*, *Modern Drama*, and *Early Theatre*, among other journals and essay collections, while her articles on contemporary Atlantic Canadian theatre have appeared in *Canadian Theatre Review* and *Theatre in Atlantic Canada* (2010).

Bruce Barton is a playwright, dramaturge, director, and scholar who teaches at the University of Toronto. His stage plays have been produced across

Canada, published, and nominated for multiple awards. He works extensively as a dramaturge with physically based and devising performance companies, including Artistic Fraud of Newfoundland, Zuppa Theatre, Theatre Gargantua, and bluemouth inc. He has also directed professionally for over two decades, most recently with his own company, Vertical City, *The Vertical City Project* (Harbourfront HATCH program, 2008–12) and *Swimmer (68)* (with Ker Wells, Hopscotch Collective, 2008–11). Bruce has published in numerous periodicals, including *TDR, Theatre Journal, Theatre Topics, Performance Research, Canadian Theatre Review, University of Toronto Quarterly,* and *Theatre Research in Canada,* as well as in several national and international essay collections. His books include *At the Intersection Between Art and Research* (2010), *Developing Nation: New Play Creation in English-Speaking Canada* (2009), *Collective Creation, Collaboration and Devising* (2008), and *Reluctant Texts from Exuberant Performance: Canadian Devised Theatre* (2008).

Susan Bennett is University Professor in the Department of English at the University of Calgary. She is the editor of *Feminist Theatre and Performance* (2006) and author of a wide range of publications about women's dramatic writing. Her current research project looks at the global circulation of performance culture.

Catherine Cyr completed a master's degree at École supérieure de théâtre de l'UQAM. Interested in interdiscursivity, performativity, and representation, she is currently pursuing a Ph.D. in Études et pratiques des arts (UQAM). She teaches modern and contemporary drama at the National Theatre School of Canada and at École supérieure de théâtre de l'UQAM. A member of the editorial board at *Jeu,* she has assumed the direction of four issues: *Paysages du corps* (2007), *Jouer autrement* (2008), *Subversion* (2010), and *Théâtres de la folie* (2011). She has also published papers in *L'Annuaire théâtral, esse arts + opinions, Recherches théâtrales au Canada,* and *Spirale.*

Catherine Cyr a complété une maîtrise à l'École supérieure de théâtre de l'UQAM. Intéressée par l'interdiscursivité, par la performativité, et par les discours de la représentation, elle termine présentement un doctorat en Études et pratiques des arts (UQAM). Elle enseigne la dramaturgie moderne et contemporaine à l'École Nationale de théâtre du Canada ainsi qu'à l'École supérieure de théâtre de l'UQAM. Membre de la rédaction de la revue *Jeu*, elle y a dirigé quatre dossiers: *Paysages du corps* (2007), *Jouer autrement* (2008), *Subversion* (2010), et *Théâtres de la folie* (2011). Elle a également publié des articles dans *L'Annuaire théâtral, esse arts + opinions, Recherches théâtrales au Canada*, et *Spirale*.

Jeremy Greenway is a Ph.D. candidate and a teaching and research assistant in the department of English at Western University. Exploring the aural spaces of music and modernism, his dissertation focuses primarily on cultural and musicological representations of gender and sexualities. Other projects include a manuscript on James Joyce and polyphonic prose, Oscar Wilde and the musicality of desire, and an article on the relationships between popular music and coming-of-age in contemporary French cinema. Holding a master's degree from Carleton University, he received a Graduate Student Teaching Award in 2010 and a SSHRC fellowship in 2011.

Elise Kruidenier is a French to English translator currently living in Montreal. She has a B.A. in French and Art from the University of Puget Sound, an M.A. in French Literature from the University of Wisconsin–Madison, and a graduate diploma in translation from Concordia University. Her literary studies focused on the intersection of art history and literature, and she is currently interested in applying her studies by translating literary and academic work.

Louis Patrick Leroux holds a joint appointment in English and Études françaises at Concordia University, where he teaches dramatic literature and creative writing. His research and graduate supervision areas include cultural discourse in Québec; self-translation; contemporary circus, theatre, and drama; and research-creation. He leads the Montreal Working Group on Circus, a collaboration between Concordia and the National Circus School. Patrick's academic articles have appeared in *L'Annuaire théâtral, Jeu, alt.theatre*,

Québec Studies, *Spirale*, and *Voix et images*. Recently published plays include *Ludwig & Mae* (2009), *Se taire* (2010), and *Dialogues fantasques pour causeurs éperdus* (2012). In 2010–11 he was named a Concordia University Research Fellow and was awarded the 2009 Prix Jean Cléo Godin, while in 2011–12 he held a research-creation lab at the Hexagram Institute for research/creation in media arts and technology. In 2012 he was a Visiting Scholar at Duke University's Centre for the Study of Canada.

Parie Leung is a Ph.D. student at the University of British Columbia, where she investigates the politics, dramaturgical practices, and ideologies of Asian Canadian and British East Asian theatre companies mandated to serve artists who identify with these identity groups. She has research interests in food and performance as well as in visual art and theatre, and has published articles on site-specific theatre and Vancouver's *The Lawyer Show* in *Canadian Theatre Review*. Recently, she began training with London's True Heart Theatre as a playback theatre performer.

Alex McLean is co-Artistic Director of Halifax's Zuppa Theatre Co., with which he has created and directed eleven original shows, including most recently *Five Easy Steps (to the end of the world)*, which won Theatre Nova Scotia's 2011 Robert Merritt Award for Outstanding Production. He was a founding member of Number Eleven Theatre, with which he co-created and performed *The Prague Visitor* and *Icaria* (1998–2006). Alex was a student of the University of King's College, Double Edge Theatre, Primus Theatre, and Philippe Gaulier. He has worked on projects with the Dalhousie University Theatre Department, Rising Tide Theatre, Two Planks and a Passion, and the International Theatre Institute in Copenhagen. He won the 2005 Robert Merritt Award for Emerging Artist and has received several other award nominations. He is currently a Ph.D. student at the University of Toronto's Graduate Centre for Study of Drama.

Anna Migliarisi holds a BFA in Dramatic Art from the University of Windsor, and an M.A. and Ph.D. from the Graduate Centre for Study of Drama, University of Toronto. She has taught at Ryerson Theatre School, the universities of Guelph, Toronto, and Waterloo, and most recently in the Department of English and Theatre at Acadia University. Her publications include numerous articles on directorial history and practice, and three books: *Renaissance and Baroque Directors* (2003), *Directing and Authorship in Western Drama* (2006), and *Stanislavsky and Directing* (2008). Anna is an established member of the professional theatre and film community in Canada.

Monique Mojica (Guna and Rappahannock) is an actor, playwright, and artist-scholar. Her first play, *Princess Pocahontas and the Blue Spots*, was produced in 1990 and published by Women's Press. She appeared as Grandma Builds-the-Fire in *Smoke Signals* and as Caesar in *Death of a Chief*, Native Earth's adaptation of Shakespeare's *Julius Caesar*, and was a co-founder of Turtle Gals Performance Ensemble, with whom she co-created *The Scrubbing Project* and the Dora-nominated *The Triple Truth*. She is co-editor, with Ric Knowles, of *Staging Coyote's Dream: An Anthology of First Nations Drama in English* (2 vols.), published by Playwrights Canada Press. Monique has taught at McMaster University and at the Institute of American Indian Arts in Santa Fe, New Mexico, and has been the artist-in-residence for American Indian Studies at the University of Illinois, teaching Indigenous theatre in theory, process, and practice. The Chocolate Woman Collective were artists-in-residence at the University of Toronto's Graduate Centre for Study of Drama, where Monique's collaborative, interdisciplinary play *Chocolate Woman Dreams the Milky Way* premiered in 2011. Monique is passionately dedicated to theatrical practice as healing, as an act of reclaiming historical/cultural memory, and as an act of resistance.

Kirsten Pullen is Associate Professor and Director of Graduate Studies in the Department of Performance Studies at Texas A&M University. She is also Director of the Academy for the Visual and Performing Arts. Her published work has focused on prostitution and performance, Internet fandom, theatre audiences, and actresses. She teaches courses in theatre history and intercultural performance at A&M, where she also directs departmental productions. Her first book, *Actresses and Whores: On Stage and in Society*, was published by Cambridge University Press in 2005; her most recent project, *Like a Natural Woman: Spectacular Female Performance in Classical Hollywood* (2012), explores how the embodied nature of performance undermines the assumed conservatism of naturalism.

Susanne Shawyer is a theatre historian and performance scholar who researches the history of applied theatre and the dramaturgy of protest. She holds a Ph.D. in Theatre from the University of Texas at Austin and received her B.A. from Dalhousie University. Her published work includes articles and reviews in *Canadian Theatre Review*, *Theatre Topics*, and *Theatre Journal*. She has taught at Dalhousie University, Mount Saint Vincent University, Texas State University, and the University of Ljubljana.

Kim Solga is Associate Professor of English at Western University and Senior Lecturer in Drama at Queen Mary, University of London. She is the author of *Violence Against Women in Early Modern Performance: Invisible Acts* (2009), and co-editor of *Performance and the City* (2009 and 2011) and *Performance and the Global City* (2009 and 2013), as well as guest editor of the summer 2011 issue of *Canadian Theatre Review*, "The Activist Classroom: Performance and Pedagogy." Her work on Canadian performance has appeared in *Theatre Research in Canada*, *Canadian Theatre Review*, *TDR*, and *Theatre Journal*, as well as in the essay collections *Judith Thompson* (2005) and *Performance in Toronto* (2011).

Jenn Stephenson is Associate Professor of Drama at Queen's University. Recent articles have appeared in *Theatre Journal*, *Theatre Research in Canada*, *New Theatre Quarterly*, and *English Studies in Canada*. She is the editor of *Solo Performance* (2011), and her monograph, *Performing Autobiography: Contemporary Canadian Drama*, was published by University of Toronto Press in 2012. With Natalie Alvarez, she co-edits the Views and Reviews section of *Canadian Theatre Review*. For more information, visit http://www.queensu.ca/drama/jstephenson.

Evan Webber is a writer and performer who works collaboratively in theatre. He was a founding member of One Reed, making collaborative works including *Nor The Cavaliers Who Come With Us*, *It's Hard to Count to a Million*, *Never Underestimate the Power*, and *2 Modern Feelings*. Evan also frequently contributes to performance works and projects with companies like Small Wooden Shoe (*Dedicated to the Revolutions* series, *Upper Toronto*, *Antigone*), Public Recordings (*Open Field Study*), and surPrise Performance (*Save Us!! [Hamletown]*). He has held writing and performance-making residencies at the Theatre Centre in Toronto; at the Tyrone Guthrie Centre in Annaghmakherrig, Ireland; and with Crow's Theatre and Small Wooden Shoe. His last play, *Little Iliad*, was presented by the Absolut Fringe, Dublin, Ireland, where it received a nomination for the festival's Best Production Award. Evan is also engaged in criticism and curation. He works as a programming consultant on special projects in performing arts at Harbourfront Centre, Toronto, and his writing about theatre, visual art, and performance practice has been published online and in print by *C Magazine*, *Alternatives*, and *Canadian Theatre Review*.

Harvey Young is Associate Professor at Northwestern University, where he holds appointments in African American Studies, Performance Studies, Radio/Television/Film, and Theatre. He is the author of *Embodying Black Experience: Stillness, Critical Memory, and the Black Body* (2010) and the co-editor of two books: *Performance in the Borderlands* (with Ramón Rivera-Servera, 2011) and *Reimagining A Raisin in the Sun* (with Rebecca Ann Rugg, 2012). He has published more than three-dozen articles and chapters on African American theatre and performance culture. His current book projects include editing *The Cambridge Companion to African American Theatre* and co-authoring an oral history of black theatre and dance in Chicago. Harvey has served as President of the Black Theatre Association and Vice President of the Association for Theatre in Higher Education.

INDEX

Gilbert, Helen 151, 157

The Glace Bay Miners' Museum 8

Globe and Mail 19–22, 29, 56, 192, 195, 203, 207, 209, 215

Great Hopewell Road 219, 238–39, 240

Great Serpent Mound 239

Greaves, William 15, 25–29

Grober, Chayele 24

Group Theatre 17, 24, 27, 38

Guilmaine, Anne-Marie 94–96, 98, 100–02

H

Habima 24–25

Herbert, John 7

Highway, Tomson 10–11

Hollywood 35, 36, 38, 40, 42, 44–48

  classic 37–38

Hornby, Richard 150, 166

I

Ibsen, Henrik 2, 5, 7, 134–35, 140, 176, 186, 187, 197

illusion 37, 69, 70–71, 75, 77–78, 89, 90–92, 109, 172, 181

  mimetic 90–91, 97–98, 102

  realistic 92, 109, 113

immigrants 52, 61–62, 64, 167, 170, 172, 176, 178

impersonnages 94, 103

Indian mounds 223, 224–25, 228

Indigenous peoples 9, 10, 15, 156, 191, 206, 219–21, 224, 237

J

Jafine, Hartley 12, 69, 76, 78–82, 84–85

Jeffers Mound 241

Jutras, Lisan 210–13, 215

K

kettling 15, 201, 210–11, 213–14

L

lady in the red dress 14, 164, 167–68, 173–74, 177–78, 180–81

Lainey Gossip 46

language 8, 26, 92, 106–10, 115, 123, 132, 164, 166, 189, 191, 194, 219

Latina/o-Canadian theatre culture 144, 146–47, 159, 161

Latinidad 144, 147, 159, 162

Lawrence Park, Toronto 12, 69, 76–81, 82, 84–85

Lepage, Robert 112n6, 113, 115

Leung, Kathy 14, 164, 166

Lill, Wendy 8

liveness 215–16

Lo, Jacqueline 151, 156

Loring, Kevin 10

Lui, Elaine 46

M

Mapuche 156–57

masks 94n, 114–15, 202, 210

mass protest 15, 201–02, 204, 210

Maxwell, Richard 138

McAdams, Rachel 12, 34–41, 44–49

media 114, 137, 166, 183, 198, 201–04, 207, 209–11, 213–15

  social 15, 201, 204, 215–16

melodrama 109–10, 123, 187

memories 8, 30n, 35, 60, 79, 93, 104–05, 111, 169, 208, 240

Poupart, Brigitte 117, 122n
Princess of Wales Theatre 51
protest 22, 200–04, 206–09, 211–14
    peaceful 206–07, 211, 217
    performance 204, 215–17
    performance, mass 201–02, 212, 216,
        217
protesters 200–01, 203, 207–08, 210, 214–15

Q

Québec 7, 13, 92, 106–11, 113–15, 118,
    120n, 122–23
    theatre 13, 107, 115
Québec City 203, 206, 208–09

R

race 39, 43, 49, 144, 150, 155–56, 161
the real 11, 13, 15, 39, 90–91, 97–98, 107n2,
    114, 116, 127–30, 133, 202
realism
    affective 57, 59
    conventional 164, 167, 171
    conventions of 51, 161
    critique of 1, 128, 144
    devising 124, 136, 143
    historical 128
    indexical 14, 161–62
    modern 171, 176
    new 15, 122
    nineteenth-century 9, 15, 74–75, 141
    operative 14, 165–69, 171, 173, 177,
        179
    post-lapsarian 13
    stage 1, 4, 6, 36, 108, 113, 154, 160,
        183–84, 190–91, 196

realism's paradoxes 145, 162
realist
    aesthetic 124, 147, 202
    approaches 14, 164, 174
    artists 205
    conventions 137
    dramaturgy 5, 9–10, 71, 190, 195
    form 6, 180, 189
    illusion 7, 38, 70, 72, 75, 77–78, 172
    paradigm 11–12, 33–34, 36–38, 47, 49
    performance 3, 69, 78, 155, 162, 194,
        204, 205, 216
    play 8, 71, 153, 177, 186–87
    strategy 81
Red Letters 14, 164, 167–74, 176, 179–81
The Refugee Hotel 13, 146, 152, 155–56,
    158
resistance 108, 120–24, 132, 139
The Rez Sisters 10–11
Richmond County, Virginia 233–35
Ringwood, Gwen Pharis 186–89
riot gear 201, 204, 207, 209, 212–13
Robillard, Claudine 92, 96, 100

S

Schechner, Richard 150, 152, 154
script 15, 139, 190, 192, 194–95, 201–02,
    204, 208–10, 213–14, 216, 219, 222
    protest 202, 206–07, 209–11, 213,
        216
    of violence 209–10
Sears, Djanet 66–67, 154
Soulpepper Theatre 193, 195–96
spectators 9, 47, 59, 83, 88, 90, 92–93, 95–
    105, 107–08, 117, 120–21, 139, 150, 155,
    160, 162, 166, 169
St-Pierre, Dave 108, 118–23